The Small Investor

The Small Investor

A Beginner's Guide to
Stocks, Bonds, and
Mutual Funds

REVISED

Jim Gard

Ten Speed Press
Berkeley • Toronto

Ten Speed Press
P.O. Box 7123
Berkeley, California 94707
www.tenspeed.com

Distributed in Australia by Simon and Schuster Australia, in Canada by Ten Speed Press Canada, in New Zealand by Southern Publishers Group, in South Africa by Real Books, in Southeast Asia by Berkeley Books, and in the United Kingdom and Europe by Airlift Book Company.

Cover design and interior illustrations by Gerry O'Neill
Text design by Larissa Pickens

Library of Congress Cataloging-in-Publication Data
Gard, Jim.
    The small investor : a beginners guide to stocks, bonds, and mutual funds / Jim Gard.—Rev.
    p. cm.
    Includes index.
    ISBN 1-58008-386-2 (pbk.)
    1. Portfolio management. 2. Investment analysis. 3. Stock exchanges. 4. Mutual funds.
    I. Title.
    HG4529.5 .G369 2002
    332.63'2—dc21   2002002294

First printing, 2002

Printed in Canada

1 2 3 4 5 6 7 8 9 10 — 06 05 04 03 02

Acknowledgments

When I was a freshman at Georgia Tech, we were all required to take a year of composition and rhetoric. That class probably contributed more to the success I have achieved than all of the math, physics, chemistry, and engineering that I studied over the subsequent ten years. The professors in the English department at Georgia Tech don't get a whole lot of recognition and applause. But they should, especially if they are still teaching the freshmen to write simple, direct sentences. I take this opportunity to acknowledge my debt to the Georgia Tech English department.

A number of people have provided more recent support. In writing this book, I have been fortunate to receive the advice and criticism of my sister, Susan Kolesar, and sister-in-law, Carol Sunderman. Jeff McGraw, owner of a bookstore in Roxboro, North Carolina, was a zealous champion of the readers' point of view. He repeatedly encouraged me to make the language simpler and more direct, and to remove the math lessons, which turned out to be good advice. And, finally, I would be nowhere without the support and confidence of my publishing house, Ten Speed Press, and editor, Meghan Keeffe. Meghan is a tiger of a project manager. Every author should be so fortunate to work with an editor who so tirelessly pushes to meet deadlines and make improvements. Meghan and her confederates contributed several ideas that have brought significant improvements to the second edition.

And, saving the best for last, I am indebted to my wife, Lynn, for taking care of everything else, so that I could do this. Yeah, right—everything. I could not go on without her.

Acknowledgments

Contents

Introduction

Well, why a second edition? Has the first edition gone sour? Were there so many errors that it became embarrassing? Thankfully, no, on both counts. But the world turns. Investing, in some ways, looks different today than it did in 1995. We all have better, easier access to immense amounts of useful information today. The lessons of the past few years are not much different from the lessons of the late 1920s or the early 1970s; however, they are fresher and more immediate for us and needed to be discussed.

Therefore, a second edition. There are a few things I wanted to accomplish with the second edition:

- update the examples and lessons to make them fresher and more immediate;
- bring in new ideas that would make it easier for you to manage your money;
- explain more about the power and pitfalls of the Internet; and
- sell some more books.

One stimulating aspect of the rewrite has been the opportunity to review the first edition to see what was good advice and what was weak. I was gratified to find that I didn't see any reason to retract any of the advice in the first edition. When I look at what has happened to many investors in the past five years, I feel confident that most of them would have done better if they had read the first edition of *The Small Investor*. When I look at my personal investment results for the same time frame, I know that following my own advice has made money for me and allowed me to avoid a lot of potential grief. In 1995, when I did most of the work on the first edition, my own personal investment results were better than those of 95 percent of publicly traded mutual funds. In 2001, when I was working on the rewrite, I again came close to that mark. So I know that the ideas in *The Small Investor* work. The lessons in this book will help you avoid trouble and losses. They will help you find good opportunities for buying and selling. They will help you choose the right mixture of investments to provide reasonable opportunities for protection, income, and growth. In the simplest view, if you just go to the end of chapter 1 and follow the eight rules printed there, that alone will go a long way toward keeping you out of trouble.

The question I hear most often is "Who is the small investor?" Well, I am, and if you have read this far, then you probably are, too.

Introducing the Small Investor

Whether or not you're a small investor is not determined by the size of your accounts. The small investor has a little money that can be spared and risked in financial markets. The definition of *a little* depends on each individual's point of view. It may be $1,000 or $1,000,000, but it is not just a question of being rich or not. About 2,000 years ago, the Roman senator Marcus Licinius Crassus explained to his friends what "rich" meant. According to Marcus Licinius, a man was rich if he could afford to recruit, equip, and maintain a private army. In 2002, we might estimate that that would require disposable income of $250 million a year for an army of, say, a thousand soldiers. So the definitions of rich or small investor can be hard to pin down.

It is not a question of size or wealth—it is a question of attitude. The small investor that I am writing for wants to make his or her money work and is willing to accept some risk, if that risk is measured and calculated to provide a margin of safety. The small investor has limited knowledge of finance and investing but is willing to work at improving that knowledge and using it. And, finally, the small investor has some suspicion and fear of the whole business of investing. If you don't share some of that fear and suspicion, then this book is not for you; go read a book with a title like *How to Turn $1,000 into a Fortune in the Coming Bull Market (or Bear Market)* or some such fairy tale.

The Small Investor Is Wary and Suspicious

The small investor would be worried about losing a fourth of the original investment, and seriously hurt by losing half. If you can't afford to lose any of it, then this business is not for you—go put your money in a bank savings account and add to it on a steady schedule. If you can afford to lose half of your investments without wincing, then this book may be too tame for you. Some of the lessons in this book are useful to the high rollers, or gamblers, but they are all intended and written for the small investors with the kinds of concerns I've described.

And I am one among you. I share the fear, suspicion, worries, and needs of many of my readers. But I have decided to press on and accept the risks that I can calculate and understand. The results have been satisfying. Sometimes better, sometimes worse. Some years of spectacular gains, some years of little or no gains, but no full calendar years showing a loss.

This book will help you reach for similar results. It is an introduction to a lot of work, some risk, and chances for reward. As with any subject, you may extend the study as far as you like. Once you finish the book, you will know if you want to extend your reach into financial markets. If you wish to continue, you will find recommendations of publications to read and things to do next. In the end, I hope you will create a plan with a mix of risk and reward opportunities that works for you. You will certainly understand that THERE IS ALWAYS A REAL AND PRESENT RISK OF LOSS, but an astute and industrious small investor can manage the risk so that it stays at an acceptable level.

How to Use This Book

I want to make useful information easily available to many readers, regardless of their prior experience or education in finance. You won't need any great experience or education to read this book and follow the ideas contained herein. The material has been organized in a straightforward manner so that each chapter supports the next, but readers who have a little prior knowledge should be able to select chapters in any order and follow the ideas.

One important idea of investing is that you should always consider your choices. We need to think about relationships between the different choices, such as stocks, bonds, and mutual funds, and doing so may lead us to connect them during the discussion. A consequence of this is that sometimes terms may be mentioned before we reach the main chapter for that topic. For example, chapter 1 has some examples about buying and selling stocks, but the main discussion of stocks doesn't come until chapter 7. Whenever that occurs, you will find that the early illustrations are simple enough to be easy to follow. Use them for vocabulary building and getting into the swim of ideas; don't let them stop you.

A new feature of this edition is the marginal illustrations. You'll find icons in the margins to draw your attention to specific lessons. The **warning sign** is meant to slow you down and warn you to pay particular attention to an idea that will help keep you out of trouble. The **key** is meant to highlight especially important lessons and to facilitate brush-up reviews of the text. The **mortarboard** is meant to point out topics that are a little more complex and so are just touched upon in this beginner's guide; you may wish to research these topics further. The **thumbtabs** will help you find the places where specific words are introduced or defined. (I get irritated with a book when I use the index to find the page where a specific word is used but then cannot find the word on that page. You will not have that problem with this book.)

Vocabulary

Another marginal icon is related to an important new idea in the second edition. In this book I introduce the friendly "PIG," which will help you keep track of what's important in your investment planning. PIG stands for Protection, Income, and Growth. Throughout this book you will be reminded that if you take care of protection, income, and growth—your PIG—then your PIG will take care of you. We use four icons to focus attention on the PIG theme. The **protection pig** wears a hard hat, the **income pig** wears a banker's hat, and the **growth pig** wears a gardener's hat. Finally, we use one **"general pig"** to focus attention on points that support more than one of the ideas of protection and income and growth.

To keep things simple, often I don't include mathematical calculations that might show how I got certain numbers. This is an investing guide, not a math text. Let's focus on main points and not get held up doing math lessons. Most of the calculations are of two types, simple percentages or basic arithmetic, but some involve more complex financial and statistical concepts. I assume you can do the basic arithmetic if you choose to, and you can certainly find plenty of other books that go into the financial and statistical calculations involved in investing, if you choose to pursue that.

So the point is to do something useful and not make it any more complicated than it has to be. We're not going to write any dissertations or win any Nobel prizes; we are going to do things to help you make decisions, make money, and stay out of trouble. And it can work out all right. I practice what I preach and not only make money at it, but keep the work and the worries within manageable bounds. You can, too.

Good hunting.

Good harvesting.

Chapter 1

The Small Investor

Small investors need to know:

- Is investing for me?
- How much risk am I inviting?
- How much time and work do I have to put into it?
- Do the big investors have all the advantages?
- Is there such a thing as safe investing?

Is This Book for You?

It is not too late to ask this question. Your time is important, and it's worthwhile to ask yourself if it's worth it to make the effort to really dig into the financial data for Ford Motor Company (symbol F), or do the research to select a mutual fund from among the thousands of funds available. By the time you finish this book, you will have answers to a lot of questions. There are no bad questions except those that we don't ask. For small investors like us, the consequences of not asking the right questions can be devastating. So this book will lead you to ask some of the questions that can help you avoid problems. I'll answer some of them and point you toward finding your own answers to others.

Neither this book nor any other will give you all of the answers. Many of the questions and answers depend on your experience, education, and lifestyle. For example, I can't tell you what stocks to buy; that depends on your personal financial situation and the level of risk you are willing to accept. Similarly, no book can tell you whether or not to buy

Should I Invest in My Library?

junk bonds; you have to decide for yourself. What this book will do is prepare you to make those decisions.

If you decide to do any kind of investing, it will affect other parts of your life. It will influence other financial decisions you might be considering, and it will affect your peace of mind when you are watching the evening news. You may choose to say, "No, thanks. I don't need the headaches." That is a reasonable decision for some people. If you stick with me to the end of the book, I think you will be able to make a comfortable and rational judgment. It is not my intent to persuade you to start investing or to quit or to change your current investing practices, if any. I just want to help you judge the consequences—in terms of work, risk, time, your comfort level about your finances, and other things you might be doing with your money.

Financial Markets Are Not Like Secure Savings

Investing means to give up some of your money for a time, in hopes that you will get it back with something extra. The extra return should compensate you for not having use of the money and for the effect of inflation. A bank savings account is one way to invest. You give up some money to the bank as a deposit, and expect that after a while you will get the money back plus some interest earned. All investing has this in common: we give up control of our money to another party and we expect to get it back later with a profit. But with stocks, bonds, and mutual funds, we are getting into a different league. A savings account requires little work and has strong assurance of return. The financial markets may offer greater returns, but they also involve much more time and work and risk of loss.

What Are the Risks and Rewards?

What if you buy the stock of a publicly traded corporation? For example, say some outfit called Mogul Corporation needed money to start operations. To raise money they could sell shares of ownership in Mogul. They might split the ownership into 1,000,000 shares (the *common stock*) and sell them for $20 apiece. If you buy 200 shares, then you own 0.02 percent of Mogul. You would expect to make money in two ways: first, if the company was profitable, they would pay you some part of their earnings, called a *dividend,* and, second, if other investors approved of Mogul's operations, they might want to buy your stock. If enough newcomers wanted Mogul stock, and not many of the owners cared to sell, then the newcomers would offer more than the $20 for each share of stock. You might have a chance to sell your stock for a profit, maybe at $27 per share. If you actually sold the stock and took the profit at this point, that would generate what's called a *capital gain.* If you kept the stock and merely acknowledged the potential profit, that would be called a *paper profit.* I suggest that you keep the view that you don't have a real profit until you sell, because paper profits have a way of disappearing. Likewise, if stock prices go down, you may have a *paper loss* in the value of your stock. If you choose to sell at that point, then the paper loss becomes a *realized loss.*

Along with the great expectations, there are two very real risks: first, Mogul might not be profitable in some years and might not pay a dividend; second, other investors might not like Mogul, so that, one day when you need your money back, no one wants to buy it (and you realize a capital loss). If you buy shares of well-established corporations, sold on a well-established stock exchange, there will usually be some-

Common Stock

Dividend

Capital Gain

Paper Profit

Paper Loss

Realized Loss

one around willing to buy the shares, but the price might be lower than what you paid.

An intelligent investor needs to consider different possibilities for what might happen after he or she buys a stock. The examples below are real-life cases.

The Standard Commercial Corporation—business is good and the investment is good: In late 1990, the Standard Commercial Corporation (STW), a worldwide tobacco- and wool-processing company, was earning about 62 cents per share of common stock for the calendar quarter. Their sales in 1990 had been 50 percent higher than the total market value of the company, which is good (market value means the amount it would take to buy all of the common stock). The stock price was then $10 per share, and for 1990 they had paid 52 cents in dividends for each share (a 5.2 percent yield). The prevailing market view was that this was the result of good business operations and was a good stock market opportunity. By the end of 1991 the stock price went up to $28 per share. Some lucky (smart) people bought Standard Commercial for $10 in late 1990 and sold it for $28 around the end of 1991. That's a good score in any league!

General Electric—business is good but the investment may fail: Even if business is good, stock prices can fall. This may seem strange—why should the stock value fall if the company is making good profits? Well, the stock market has a mind of its own and its logic is not always clear. Stock prices for any given firm are largely governed by the prevailing view of what profits will look like a year or two down the road, and by people's expectations about the economy in general. You see, everyone else is doing what we are doing: they are trying to evaluate current and future business prospects, but they are also trying to evaluate the broad market opinion of what's happening.

For many years, the General Electric Corporation (symbol GE) has been among the most successful companies in the world. In 1990, their revenues, profits, and dividends were all going up. GE was considered to be one of the safest stock investments available. In the middle of 1990, some conservative investors bought the stock for $75. Within three months, the price dropped as low as $50, even though sales, earnings, and dividend payout were still increasing. As I said, the stock market has a mind of its own. Those unfortunate investors were injured by the market psychology, which for some reason decided for a few months that GE was no longer attractive. Within another six months the values recovered, so the patient long-term investors were not hurt, but some people probably panicked and sold at $50. It is tough to make that judgment call when you watch your investment wasting away for a few months. But by 2001 those same shares were worth $500, after three *stock splits*. (A split occurs when a company issues additional new shares to replace the old and adjusts the price accordingly. So, after a two-for-one split each shareholder gets two new shares in place of one old. If the price of one share of the old stock was $10, the new will be issued at $5.)

Stock Split

Amazon.com—business is bad, but the investment is great: Sometimes stock prices may even go up when business operations are poor. Why should the stock value go up if the company is not profitable? The answer is in market expectations. Many investors plan to hold stock for a year or more. They expect that when they sell, circumstances will have changed. If they foresee that a company is conquering new worlds, they may bid up the price of the stock. Amazon.com (symbol AMZN) is a perfect example. An online (Internet-based) retailer of books, music, videos, and other small consumer goods, Amazon.com first sold stock to the public in 1997. Although they were consistently losing money on their operations, the price of the stock went through the roof. If you had bought 56 shares of their stock at the initial public offering in 1997, you would have paid $1,000. If you had held on until the end of 1999, you might have sold your shares (then 667 shares, due to stock splits) for over $66,000. There is no explanation for this to be found in their business operations, only in market psychology. Many people thought that they could foresee immense profits and future domination of retailing for Amazon. They bought the stock on leaps of faith that everything would work out profitably. Later, that turned out to be a mistake for many of the investors.

IBM—business was weak and the investment was terrible: Business is bad, stock price is down. This one makes sense, right? Well, maybe. It depends on the market view of the company's prospects for the next year or two. For instance, take IBM (symbol IBM). There has never been a more widely publicized stock decline than theirs. In mid-1989, the stock price bounced around $110 to $120 per share; in 1990 it was between $90 and $120; in 1991 it was between $85 and $140, and by late in 1993 it had fallen as low as $41. Some people bought stock in this profitable company, with an A+ rating in 1991, and lost 70 percent of their investment within two years. It goes to show that you never can tell. There were plenty of smart, experienced professional stock analysts who said the stock was a good buy at $100, and again at $85, and again at $60. Some people lost a lot of money.

The purpose here is neither to scare you nor to excite you about market investment opportunities. It is simply to inform you that if you decide to get into this business, then you or someone you hire must look at and evaluate a lot of different factors to make your investments successful. And it's tricky. I bought IBM at $85 and sold it three months later at $93. Pretty clever, right? Then I bought it again a few months later at $67 and sold a year later at a value of $54. Not so clever, right? In playing the financial markets, you have opportunities to win and opportunities to lose. The only guarantee I can give you is that if you are careless, you will lose.

Meet a Friendly PIG

Those four examples above may have scared you. You may be wondering, "Is there any sanity in the financial markets?" Well, maybe so, maybe no. The best chance to find some sanity in the markets is to bring your own. Don't try to make sense out of all the market forecasts. Half of them are ridiculous. Don't try to learn sanity from all the professional money managers and reporters. There is no way for you to discern whether they know what they are doing. You can start establishing the sanity and rationality of your investment plans by building on something solid.

Meet a Friendly PIG

Here is something solid to help you get started. You need to know what you are trying to do. Meet the PIG. Get to know the PIG. Cherish the PIG.

- **P is for protection:** You want safe investments . . . this pig looks for protection.
- **I is for income:** You want income from your investments . . . this pig seeks income.
- **G is for growth:** You want appreciation in your investments . . . this pig seeks growth.

The investments that serve one or more of those objectives may be good for you. Every investment should be evaluated on how well it serves the PIG.

This PIG will help you remember what you are doing with your money. Every investment you make should serve some or all of the PIG objectives. The best investments might serve all three objectives. It will be rare that you find an investment that seems to fit all three PIG objectives. It will be more common that you find that you are giving up some of the PIG in order to serve the other parts. For example, a high-quality municipal bond may very well offer income and protection, but almost no growth. At some point that may be the right investment for you. Buying stock of a new, small high-tech firm might offer a good chance of growth but no income and little protection. One day, that might be a good investment choice for you.

For every investment decision you make, consult the PIG.

- How much Protection do I expect with this investment?
- How much Income do I expect from this investment?
- How much Growth do I expect from this investment?

Make Money the Old-Fashioned Way— Earn It!

Time, energy, work, nerve, decisiveness. Different kinds of investing require various levels of those assets to reach success. One of the most famous and successful investors of the past thirty years is Peter Lynch. He was manager of the highly profitable Magellan Fund. Lynch is, indisputably, a market genius who says that the small investor can do all right in the stock market. He even implies that it's not terribly difficult, saying, "Everybody has the brains for investing in stocks; the question is whether you have the stomach." By "stomach" he means the will to put in the time and work, as well as the nerve and decisiveness to do something smart and take the risks.

Those four examples that we looked at earlier show that when you buy a stock you are really depending on two things. First is the fundamental business condition of the firm, or a judgment of what that may be in a year or two. That is something you can rationally analyze and try to predict. Second is market psychology. No one can consistently predict that. Market psychology can often be a ticking bomb. Listen to Tom Jackson, manager of the Prudential Equity Mutual Fund. He successfully manages a great deal of other people's money, and he has the experience and credentials you would expect in a market guru. Jackson says, "Nobody can forecast the stock market." We will not argue with that.

So before you put up your money, try to judge the amount and kind of work, try to judge the potential for profit or loss, try to judge how much professional help you want, try to judge where you can get information if you choose to go it alone. If you do choose to read this entire book, you will be ready to make those judgment calls.

Is There a Chance for Safety in the Stock Market?

Among some Midwestern agricultural circles you may hear a saying: "Even a blind pig will find the slop once in a while." Similarly, some people think that even a blind pig could have made money in the stock market during the great bull market of 1991–2000. That's true; however, the blind pig could have lost money, too. A case in point is Schering-Plough (stock symbol SGP on the New York Stock Exchange).

Plough is one of the larger and more successful drug companies. They had a great long-term record of steadily increasing sales, profits, dividends, and stock price. The company is financially secure, and many people have considered the drug industry one of the best areas for investment. It appeared to be a safe investment. If you had bought SGP in November 1999, you might have paid $46 per share. But surprise, surprise! Three months later it was selling for around $35. If you had bought 200 shares at $46 then got cold feet and sold at $35, after paying perhaps $20 to $40 for both the purchase and sale brokerage fees you would have about a $1,900 loss (as of late 2000, it rose above $60, and by early 2001 had dropped below $40 again). During all of that time, their revenues, their earnings, and their dividends continued to go up, so the company looked pretty solid. But the market has a mind of its own.

So where does that leave us in the search for safe and sound investing? In the financial markets, safety means a reasonable balance of chances for losses or profits. You don't get guarantees, and you don't get perfect information. Instead, you get a reasonable balance of risk and reward opportunities. One of the small investor's special advantages is the freedom to go for modest, safe gains. In another example, to make it more concrete, let's look at the Duke Energy Corporation (symbol DUK). This will illustrate what the small investor can do when safety (Protection) is a prime concern.

The Small Investor Goes Blind on Wall Street

Is DUK safe and predictable? Well, yeah, relatively safe and predictable. To learn what that means, we are going to look at three scenarios: a worst case (meaning a worst *realistic* situation—not nuclear war or the violent overthrow of the government), a kind of average conservative case, and a slightly more optimistic case. Remember there is always some risk, but DUK is about as conservative as it gets.

Let's analyze DUK a little. Is their market secure? DUK provides energy services to over 2 million customers in North and South Carolina. That is a secure market. Is their record secure? Their dividend rose each year from 1991 to 1998 and then held steady for the next three years. Are they strong? The company's finances have been evaluated by two prominent financial research organizations, Standard & Poor's and Value Line. Standard & Poor's rating of DUK's past performance and current position of their common stock is "A+" (highest out of eight possible grades). The Value Line rating of the company's financial strength is "A"; the Value Line rating of the common stock safety is "1," their highest grade.

The price per share and dividend for four years are given in the following table. "High" means the highest price during the year, and "Low" is the lowest price. "Div" is the total dividend amount paid during the year. (This table contains some rounding.)

	1996	1997	1998	1999
High	$25	$27	$34	$32
Low	$22	$21	$27	$24
Div	$1.04	$1.08	$1.10	$1.10

Now, let's look at our three scenarios. Suppose that you bought 100 shares for $32 per share at the beginning of 1999, and all dividends were used to buy new stock. Say the broker's fee to buy the 100 shares was $30, and the fee to sell at the end of 2003 was $35. The initial investment was $3,230 (that is 100 x $32 + $30). The final return would be the number of shares times the final price, minus the $35 broker's fee. I will do the math here, and let you just look at results.

For a worst-case scenario, suppose the dividend stays fixed at $1.10, but the stock price falls to its lowest level of the prior three years, $21. If you had to sell at the low in 2003, you would be selling 124 shares for $2,604. After the broker's fee that leaves $2,569, a loss of $661 over five years. That corresponds to a loss rate of about 4.5 percent each year. That certainly is not very good, but, if you think of it as the worst foreseeable outcome for this investment, then it does not look so terrible.

For a more normal result, assuming a more stable future for the stock, assume that the stock goes up to $38 over the five years, and the dividend stays fixed at $1.10. At the end, in late 2003, you could expect to have 117 shares, and sell them for $4,446. That leaves $4,411 after the broker's fee, a gain of $1,181 over the five years. That corresponds to a rate of return about 6.4 percent per year. Not so bad, for an investment with low risk.

Now, for a more optimistic view, let's suppose the stock price went up to $35, $37, $40, and $42 at the end of 2000, 2001, 2002, 2003, respectively, and the dividend was increased, too. Say the dividend went up to $1.12, $1.14, $1.16, and $1.16 at the end of those four years. Then at the end of 2003, you could expect to have 116 shares worth $4,872. After the fee, that leaves $4,837, for a profit of $1,607. That is equivalent to an 8.4 percent annual gain for five years.

Of course, there are no guarantees. The calculations depend on some rough assumptions, but this is one way you might analyze a conservative stock to estimate worst case and best case expectations.

It makes sense to compare this to some other investments that are known to be pretty safe, such as a bank CD paying 5 percent annually (compounded) and a savings account paying 2 percent (compounded).

Investment	5-year result	Annualized return
DUK: worst case	−$661 loss	−4.5 %
normal case	+$1,181	+6.4%
best case	+$1,607	+8.4%
Bank CD	+$892	+5%
Savings Account	+$336	+2%

So what "safe" means here is that we can find a stock investment that probably will not do terrible damage to your finances, even in the worst foreseeable situation, and has good chances to perform much better than other safe investments. Is DUK anything to get excited about? I think it is, for the small investor. This investment could give you low-risk, relatively predictable behavior, with expectations to do better than a bank account for a few years.

Were our assumptions realistic? Let's look at the worst events for DUK in the past thirty years. In the October 1987 brief market crash, the DUK stock price dropped from $13 to around $10, and quickly recovered to pass its previous high values. In 1994, the value went through a bad year, dropping from $22 to $17, but after another eighteen months, had climbed back past its old high values. In 1999, the value dropped from $32 to $24, and then within a few months roared back past its previous high values. If history means anything, and I think it does, then this is an example of a stock that is unlikely to hurt you.

It's Not a Contest

There is a competitive nature to many things we do in life, whether it's work, love, physical fitness, or investing. It is only natural for many small investors to worry that they can't win because they can't compete with the professionals and the big boys on Wall Street.

Keeping Up with Gabelli

Mario Gabelli is a famous and successful mutual fund manager. He and the people who invested in his Gabelli Equity Fund from 1987 to 1992 doubled their money—that's about 14 percent compound annual growth, which is great work. But who cares? Well, we care to the extent that we would like to find some such opportunities, but we don't need to worry about competing with them. Investing does not have to be a contest. Whenever I get too proud, or too discouraged, about my recent investment results, I just look in *Barron's* mutual fund reports. Every time, I can find hundreds of mutual funds that have done better than I have for the past quarter, or year, or five years, as well as hundreds that have done worse. In either case, that knowledge doesn't put any money in my pocket. Don't worry about what Gabelli is doing, just concentrate on how you are doing. That's enough to keep you occupied. Of course, if you really want to ride with Gabelli, then do it! Buy his mutual funds. Hire him to work for you.

Advantages of Professional Money Managers

A professional money manager may have $500 million to work with and may produce $10 million of revenue for an investment company. With this $10 million, the company can hire sharp folks, buy computers and research resources, and keep most of those resources busy 100 hours a week looking for opportunity or trouble on the horizon. Certainly in their business, just as in yours, experience counts. Money managers have quicker access to critical financial news because their people are paid a lot of money to look for it. The investment company analysts should be able to come up with some good ideas because they eat, breathe, and sleep investing every day.

The Small Investor Is Not in This Fight

You are not going to take money out of the professionals' hands just because you are a nice guy and need a comfortable retirement. But remember that all of that skill and experience is out there. It could be hired to manage your money for you, by investing in mutual funds. But you don't have to compete with these people; you don't have to beat them at their own game. They don't want to kill you, and in fact they don't even care whether you are in the market. If you don't have a noticeable success record with at least $10 million in the market, then none of the professional investors will ever know or care about what you are doing.

The Small Investor in the Market

But, in fact, we have some advantages over the big guys. For while they are not competing with you and me, they are competing with each other. And they are fighting every day to keep their jobs and professional reputations. A mutual fund manager who fails to lead the pack one quarter may lose a lot of customers and their money pretty fast. You and I don't have that handicap. If I fail to make a gain on my IRA one quarter, I might be annoyed, but I don't have to worry about getting fired. (If you find that your investment performance is consistently bad, you might want to fire yourself, as it were, and hire a professional.)

We can set our own standards of performance and risk tolerance, as part of setting our investment strategies. You have a real edge because no one else is evaluating you, and your decisions aren't made by a committee. Thus, you can set your own standards for the effort and scope of your research. If you decide to buy two stocks, you may choose to spend two months studying twenty companies, but you never need to be an expert on the entire market.

Finally, small investors get some advantages just because of the smaller amounts of money involved: flexibility and liquidity. On any given day, either you or Mario Gabelli may decide to buy or sell a position in stocks. You or I can complete the deal in five minutes and be very confident of the price we will get. Mario cannot. The person or investment company working on a $10 million stock position needs days or weeks to finish it, and prices can change over that period of time. An investment manager may see prices fall just because the word gets out that he is selling a lot of one particular stock. We don't have to worry about that.

Common Errors or Traps for Small Investors

If you do choose to get involved in investing, there are a few basic pitfalls to watch out for.

First, don't buy things you don't understand. Whether you're considering a stock or a bond or a mutual fund, it takes work to evaluate the risks and rewards. In some cases it will be too much work or too difficult for you to handle alone. While I was going through the process of evaluating brokers, I met a nice guy in Raleigh, North Carolina, who took me out to lunch and asked me about my objectives and interests. He seemed to be intelligent and well qualified to evaluate investments. A few days later, he called me with a hot item. It seemed some people were forming an investment trust to put money into a clever scheme, really clever. The plan was to take advantage of the depressed real estate markets in major cities by buying empty land and using it for parking lots. They could then realize the profits from the parking lots, or perhaps tax losses from the investment, and just sit back and wait for the inevitable recovery in real estate prices. Then it would be easy to convert the land to more profitable uses. Good idea, right? I passed. There was some logic in the scheme, and a chance that somebody would make money at it, but I felt that there was no way for me to evaluate the potential risks or rewards. Furthermore, I couldn't make any kind of judgment about what would happen if I needed to get my money back one day. One of the objectives of this book is to help you become confident in making that kind of decision.

Avoid buying or selling investments based on someone else's idea unless you have done your homework. This position can be modified after you have worked with an advisor or broker for a year or more and developed a trusting relationship, but it's your money and it should be your decision. Your investment results will depend on your decisions, and your decisions depend directly on your sources of information. (We'll talk a lot throughout this book about where to look for reliable information. There are countless investment publications. Part of your job is to review some of them and select two or three that you have time to read and that clearly address your needs.)

Some investors I know seem to think that when they buy something, they have a moral obligation to get all of their friends in, too. But what is good for someone else may not be good for you. If your coworker has a very conservative stock portfolio and has $10,000 available to take a high-risk plunge, then the investment she's looking at might be fine for her, but not for you. When someone comes to you pushing their latest hot investment, you don't have to present a counterargument to knock them down; it's good enough to tell them, "No, thanks. I wish you luck, but it's not for me."

Finally, if you do any investing at all, be aware that someday, when you least expect it, someone is going to call you to tell about a new or unknown stock that is certain to double in price over the next year. If an investment sounds too good to be true, that simply means that the true risks are not clear. No investment offers uncommonly high rewards without carrying commensurate risks. Or at least not to us; remember, there are 50,000 professional market analysts and money managers out there. Who do you think is going to hear about the real gold mines first? If the professionals passed on a great deal, they had their reasons. If the deal sounds too good to be true, that just means that we don't understand the risks and reasons why they passed on it. The risks are always there. Anytime you hand over your money to someone else, there is a chance you may never see it again.

Risk, Reward, and Work

Except for a few odd cases like me who find the whole process entertaining, what you are getting into is risk, reward, and work. And don't believe the old adage that says risk and reward always go hand in hand. It isn't so. Every time you buy a stock, bond, or fund, you get the risk. It is there right up front, immediately, as soon as you let go of your money. The reward, on the other hand, is not going to be apparent immediately. In fact, you may never see any reward.

However, you should be able to keep the distress accompanying such uncertainty at an acceptable level, if you are willing to do some work. Your first task is to get a handle on what kinds of risks you are willing to face. A seventy-year-old retired couple who rent a home and have a retirement income of $25,000 a year plus another $20,000 saved for emergencies would be devastated by losing half of their savings. They would only consider the very safest investments, perhaps tax-exempt municipal bonds for income purposes or very-low-risk mutual funds. On the other hand, a thirty-eight-year-old executive with excellent career prospects, her own home, and debts that can be managed out of current income might be willing to take half of her savings and put it into some more speculative action, such as growth stocks or growth stock funds (or parking lots!). Whatever money went into those investments, she'd better be able to face the prospect of losing half of it in one year without going out of her mind.

We never think that we are going to lose when we make an investment. We would rather talk about a 50 percent gain. But we need to be aware of the possibilities. A lot of people had a major portion of their retirement funds in Nortel stock (symbol NT) in 2000 and may have been hurt beyond all expectations as the stock fell from over $80 in mid-2000 to under $6 in early 2002. You don't have to look very far to find mutual funds that have lost 20 percent of their value in a given year. The Franklin Natural Resources Fund lost almost 50 percent in twelve months spanning 1997 to 1998. The AXP Precious Metals Fund fell from $13 to $6 over the two-year span covering 1997 and 1998 and stayed near $6 for the next four years. The First American Technology Fund lost 85 percent of its value between March 2000 and August 2001. If you had been buying individual stocks, you could have bought Midway Airlines (symbol MDWY) for about $20 in early 1998 and sold it for $13 at the end of 1998; or sold for $7 at the end of 1999; or sold for $4 at the end of 2000; or used it for kindling in August 2001 when the company went bankrupt. And even the biggest and best of the "blue chips" sometimes bring trouble, too. Mighty AT&T (symbol T) went from $55 in early 2000 to $20 at the end of the year. Goodyear Tire and Rubber (symbol GT) lost 65 percent of its value from early 1999 to the end of 2000.

Your job, if you want it, is to decide what parameters of risk and reward you want to work with, and then find the mixture of investments that fit. For example, when I was looking for something safe to start with, I did my analysis of GTE (which has since become Verizon—symbol VZ) and decided that I had a very good shot at 10 percent annual return, with very low chances of losing any more than 10 percent over a couple of years. However, as a sobering note, when I bought IBM, the second time, at $67, I thought that the dividend was secure at about 7 percent (wrong!) and that the lower limit on the stock was maybe $60 (wrong!). The point being, as I will keep repeating, that the risk is always there.

After you decide on some kind of risk-and-reward guidelines that you can live with, you can be almost assured that there are some investment opportunities out there that fit your needs. You just have to go find them. That can be quite a job, however. Which leads us to our other major concern: time. Your investment research and analysis should not come to dominate your life. So how much work should you plan to do? Good question. If you are going to buy individual stocks, then you may end up seriously studying ten or twenty for every one that you buy. You need to read this book and some others. You need to read some of the financial magazines regularly, and the

Wall Street Journal (WSJ) or the *New York Times* business section twice a week. Plan to spend some time in the library with *The Value Line Investment Survey (TVL)* and other relevant periodicals. A continuing theme of this book will be how much work you have to do to be fairly safe.

The trading floor at the stock exchange is not open to the public. You have to, at some point, get a connection with a brokerage firm or investment company. That search for the right professional contact is perhaps the most critical thing you will do. You should only have to do it once, if you get it right, but plan on spending a month studying the choices and visiting people. I did it wrong the first time. I just walked into a convenient local brokerage office and took the first broker who was available to talk to me. More fool I! We will get into this in more detail in later chapters, but the point for now is that investing requires work, and time, and planning. Figure out how that is going to fit into your life, and how much time you want to devote to it.

Reading this book is your starting point. Next, sit down—perhaps with your significant other or a friend—and make some notes. You need a good picture of your current and future financial prospects. Make sure you know what your assets and current risks are. Then you can reasonably decide how much of your money, your time, and your energy you want to put into risk-oriented investing. And keep in mind that one of your options is to "just say no." Many readers may quite validly end up deciding that they just don't want to step into these waters.

Some Rules to Remember

In hopes of bringing some discipline to my own investments management, I have been developing a list of helpful rules as I go along. If you don't want to read the book, that's all right—I don't mind. However, buy the book anyway, tear out this page, and carry it in your wallet all the time. If that's too much dead weight to carry around, just snip out Rule #1, and carry it with you.

Rule #1:
If you don't understand it, don't buy it.

Rule #2:
Don't expect to find perfect information (this is a counterpoint to Rule #1).

Rule #3:
Risk and reward do not always go hand in hand.

Rule #4:
Investing is not a contest. Don't worry about how someone else is doing—just pay attention to how you are doing.

Rule #5:
You can't convince the market that you are right and it is wrong (the market is always right).

Rule #6:
You never have a real profit until you sell.

Rule #7:
Buying is easy. Selling takes character and discipline.

Rule #8:
Respect the PIG.

Recommended Further Reading

Throughout this book, at the end of each chapter, I'll be recommending books that elaborate on or help out with ideas raised in the chapter. Some of these books are out of print but can be found in used bookstores and libraries—and reading them is worth the effort of finding them. One such out-of-print book is *Once in Golconda,* a wonderful account of the 1929 crash, its causes and consequences.

Brooks, John. *Once in Golconda.* New York: Harper & Row, 1969 (out of print).

Chilton, David. *The Wealthy Barber: Everyone's Commonsense Guide to Becoming Financially Independent.* 3rd ed. Roseville, Calif.: Prima Publishing, 1998.

Lerner, Joel. *Financial Planning for the Utterly Confused.* New York: McGraw-Hill, 1994.

Chapter 2

It's Not a Game

Small investors need to know:

- Do people sometimes get hurt in this business?

- Can I count on my broker for protection?

- Who are the bulls and the bears?

- Does good information guarantee safety?

- Can a market crash happen again?

Happy Talk

Too many people see Wall Street as a street paved with gold. I don't know how skeptical you are by nature, but when you're thinking about buying stocks, bonds, or mutual funds, be very skeptical. Your stockbroker, the mutual fund industry, and your friends are usually all too eager to bring you the good news. Your broker wants to talk about how much money you would have if you had invested $100 a month in stocks for the past ten years. The mutual fund companies want to advertise how well they have done for the past year or five years, whichever is more advantageous to their cause. And your friends who bought Internet stocks in the fall of 1998 want to brag about how much they made in the subsequent eighteen months (if they had the good sense to sell in the spring of 2000).

Sure, a lot of smart, happy people bought into the Magellan Fund in 1982 and have profited greatly thereby. And some brave pioneers bought stock in Microsoft (symbol MSFT) in 1982, and now they pave their driveways with gold. But we are not going to look at the markets through rose-colored glasses.

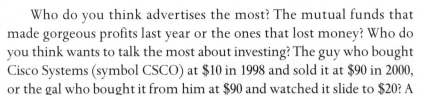

Who do you think advertises the most? The mutual funds that made gorgeous profits last year or the ones that lost money? Who do you think wants to talk the most about investing? The guy who bought Cisco Systems (symbol CSCO) at $10 in 1998 and sold it at $90 in 2000, or the gal who bought it from him at $90 and watched it slide to $20? A lot of people want to bring out the good news, but the sadder stories get buried and forgotten.

Even the Mighty Can Fall

Have you heard about Richard Whitney? He was a man who had it all. Born to one of the most famous and respected old Boston families, he eventually became the president of the New York Stock Exchange. His brother was a partner in J. P. Morgan & Co., the leading investment banking firm of the day. In 1912, the young Richard bought a seat on the New York Stock Exchange and later founded his own brokerage firm. This guy started out with good money, good family ties, all the professional and "old school" connections, and all the training and experience that Wall Street could provide. A lot of people in the business wanted him to succeed. But where was he in 1938? Playing first base for the Sing-Sing Prison baseball team and bankrupt.

It is not for us to judge Richard Whitney, but there ought to be a lesson in his story somewhere. He wanted to succeed, perhaps more so than you and I. He thought he had good information. He should have had the experience and good judgment to buy and sell at the right times, probably more so than we do. But Whitney wasted a fortune. He bought things he didn't understand, and he failed to take profits when he might have. Finally, driven to desperate measures by the pressures of his failures, he embezzled money from his customers and lost that, too.

In fairness, we should note that Whitney was caught up in a maelstrom of markets gone mad, but he above all should have recognized the risks and known how to work around them. If the president of the New York Stock Exchange, with all his connections, experience, and resources, can find his way to ruin, then it could happen to any of us. Don't ever think that you or your broker or your friends are too clever to get hurt—really and truly hurt.

The Small Investor Can Get Hurt, Too

Games People Play

In 1992 Cigna Corporation, a financial services company, was ordered to pay $5.3 million to a retired investor for selling him unsuitable limited partnerships. Cigna was found to have sold twelve risky limited partnerships to a retired GTE executive who had $2 million to fund his retirement. Those investments lost 90 percent of their value, leaving him with less than $200,000. Cigna was also found to have misrepresented the progress of those investments and to have charged their client $22,000 in fees for handling the investments.

In 2001, an administrative judge ordered the brokerage firm Josephal & Company and two of its officers to pay over $3 million in restitution to clients, and more in penalties for improper stock trading. The firm had identified a stock it wanted to dump and decided to dump it on its own customers. The company offered their brokers exorbitant fees to sell the stock to the clients. It may be assumed that the customers trusted the brokers and the firm, and that they believed the advice and explanations they were offered. The stock ended up being peddled to the unfortunate clients at ridiculous prices, and eventually it crashed, a worthless investment.

Who is going to protect you? An arbitration panel ruled that the Advest Group, Inc., was not required to refuse to execute clients' orders that would implement a foolish strategy. Other findings on securities disputes have ruled differently on the broker's responsibility to save a client from his own errors. If you do have an account with a broker, and you lose a lot of money through carelessness or poor decisions, you can take a complaint into the courts or to arbitration, but it is never clear which way the decision might fall.

Raymond James and Associates is a successful and respected brokerage firm in St. Petersburg, Florida. They make a lot of money for themselves, and they make a lot of customers happy. They also make the occasional mistake. In September 1991, a panel of arbitrators ruled that Raymond James should pay over $400,000 to one of their clients who had lost nearly $100,000 in an account with them due to a broker "churning" her account. *Churning* is the industry term for when a broker uses a client's account to make a large number of trades and produce large amounts of commissions for himself. Raymond James claims that the broker was a bad apple among a bunch of conscientious professionals—probably true—but this knowledge provides little relief to the customer. We can only speculate that the problem may have been due to carelessness, poor training, inadequate supervision, a foolish client, or some other factor. Name your own poison. The point is that the poor lady lost a lot of money, and the same thing could happen to us.

Churning

Inside Information

In 1983, I was working for Florida Federal Savings and Loan in St. Petersburg, Florida, when they offered some twelve-year, 12 percent bonds. I was pretty sure the company was financially sound and growing (it was, then). I thought I knew the management and the business, so I felt very confident enough to buy a bunch of those bonds and let them sit around and roughly quadruple my money in twelve years. I walked into the nearest brokerage store, opened an IRA account, and put up my hard-earned money to buy some. And I essentially forgot about them. Every once in a while, the broker would send me a statement, which I didn't study very closely, showing the values rolling right along.

One sunny day in 1991, I wanted to get that money back and put it into a new IRA, so I called my broker and said, "Sell 'em!" The good news was that they still had some records of the account. The bad news was that the little devils had not been just growing right along at 12 percent but were worth far less than I had expected. After I left Florida Federal, around 1989, the place went belly-up and the feds took over. The Resolution Trust Corporation seized all the assets and took over the liabilities, including my bonds. But the taxpayers didn't want to pay me 12 percent. They offered to pay somewhat less until such a time as a solvent bank might be found to manage that money. So here is how I stood on my bonds:

- There was no market for the bonds, which I could not cash in.
- Their current value could only be guessed at.
- Their value was certainly far less than I had previously expected.

In brief, I had purchased an investment that I had good reason to be confident in. I knew the company was sound. I had access to all of their financial information. But I failed to keep close watch on the bonds, and my broker never offered any advice on the situation. Eventually, another bank took over those bonds and paid enough to make the nine-year compound rate work out to a little over 8 percent, so I wasn't hurt too badly. The point is that even the cautious small investor, who is pretty confident of having good information up front, can get tripped.

Markets

There are several kinds of financial markets that we will look at throughout the book, but in this chapter, focusing on risk, it is

Stock Market

enough to just talk about stock markets. A *stock market* (or stock exchange) is set up to provide several services: it provides the location and mechanisms for people to buy and sell stocks, and it collects and reports information about price changes and sales amounts for every individual stock that is traded each day. The most famous of these is

NYSE

the *New York Stock Exchange (NYSE)*, with its headquarters on Wall Street. At the end of 2001, the New York Stock Exchange provided those services for the stocks of more than 3,000 companies, traded through the brokerage services of over 250 member firms. The combined market value of all the companies listed on the NYSE was approximately $16 trillion.

The NYSE is a business, not a charity. Trading at the exchange is limited to member firms, who pay a high price to hold a seat on the exchange. You and I can place orders through one of these member firms, paying them a brokerage fee each time we buy or sell stocks. (We will talk about finding a broker to work with in a later chapter.)

There are other stock exchanges around the world. Some other American exchanges include the American Stock Exchange (AMEX), the Pacific Stock Exchange, and the Philadelphia Stock Exchange. Every economically important nation has its own exchange, or *bourse,* as they are often called. There are bourses in Brussels, Paris, London, Tokyo, and Stockholm, to name just a few. An American small investor will usually stick with the American markets. A small investor who wants to get into foreign markets should do it by buying a mutual fund that buys foreign stocks, since it is difficult for small investors to get reliable information about foreign business activity.

Bourse

Market Averages

The mechanism for tracking sales and prices on a minute-to-minute basis is essential to an orderly market. The results are available to the public in the widely reported market averages. No one person can keep track of every daily price on every stock available. Instead, we often use broad indicators, called *market averages,* that tell us something about the trends of a group of stocks. Such an indicator will not show the price of any one stock. These indicators of stock prices include the Standard & Poor's 500 Stock Average, the Value Line Arithmetic Average, and several others. Each is computed differently, using different groups of stocks and different calculations. The most famous and most watched of them all is the Dow Jones Industrial Average (or the *Dow*). The Dow is widely reported every day to indicate the changes in stock prices of large industrial firms. It is not a true average of stock prices but is computed by applying a special formula to the prices of thirty individual stocks.

Market Averages

Dow

The Dow does not show exact price changes for any one of the group, nor does it show the mathematical average of the group. It is, however, a rough indicator of general price trends for those thirty and other similar companies that include the largest American industrial firms. Those firms constitute a large part of the total value of major American businesses. Most of them are registered and traded in the New York Stock Exchange. Investors look at the Dow as a general indication of trends in stock prices for major corporations. If the Dow goes up 1 percent one day, you might take that as indicating an approximate average 1-percent gain for investors in large, well-established American businesses. If you mainly buy stocks of large American firms, then the Dow is a barometer of your portfolio value. Since it is the most widely known and most widely reported of all the stock averages, the Dow also has great influence on market psychology.

Bulls, Bears, and Greater Fools

If stock prices stay flat, or nearly constant, for a long time, then investors only make money from dividend payments. Most investors and market analysts devote more attention to price variations than to dividends. For example, I once held Bank of America stock (symbol BAC) —back when it was NationsBank—over a fifteen-month period. The dividends paid $188, but the capital gain was $1,600. On the other hand, I once held IBM for three months and earned $121 in dividends, but the falling stock price produced a loss of about $1,700. You can see why many people devote more attention to prices than to dividends.

Bull Market

During a time of generally rising prices, the market is called a *bull market*. For example, the New York Stock Exchange was a bull market for most of the years from 1982 to 2000, notwithstanding temporary setbacks in 1987, 1994, and 1998. Investors who predict rising prices and invest accordingly are called *bulls,* and they generally want to buy more than they sell.

Bulls

The major industrial stocks were in a pretty strong bull market from 1942 until 1973. Anyone who had followed a plan of investing $1,000 each year, buying the Dow stocks at their average values, would have realized tremendous gains. For those thirty-two years, one could have seen results about like these:

Invest $1,000 per year	→	$32,000 total investment
If she had spent the dividends	→	Final account value of $92,000 left, after she already received and spent $54,000
If she had reinvested all of the dividends	→	Final stock holdings worth $227,000

That is the kind of growth and profit that characterizes a powerful bull market.

A declining market is called a *bear market*. People who predict declining prices and act accordingly are called *bears*. They generally want to sell more than they buy. The greatest (worst) of all the bear markets was the stock market of 1929 to 1933.

Bear
Market

Bears

Sometimes We Ride with the Bulls and Sometimes with the Bears

Market
Sector

A *market sector* is a group of related companies such as drug companies or automobile manufacturers. You will also hear about bulls or bears for individual market sectors, and advisors who change from bullish to bearish sentiment at different times. For example, a money manager could easily be bullish on automobile stocks, bearish on oil companies, and neutral on banks—all at the same time. He might be buying General Motors (symbol GM) or Ford, but selling Exxon (symbol XOM) or Chevron (symbol CVX).

The bulls and the bears also have a couple of friends, who don't get as much publicity. We'll refer to them as "Someone" and the "Greater Fool." "Someone" is the unknown investor who takes the opposite side on your purchase or sale of a stock. If you plan to either buy or sell stocks or bonds, then you need to deal with Someone on the other side of the transaction. That Someone probably has a different opinion of the current market and price levels than you do.

I bought stock in National Presto Corporation (symbol NPK) after the stock price had been running up for a while. Whoever was on the other side of that deal probably was taking a good profit and didn't see much room for more advancement. I bought the stock at $61.50 from Someone who wanted to sell (she may have thought I was the Greater Fool). People kept on buying at successively higher prices, assuming that more Someones would keep buying. Over the next few months it got as high as $83—a level that was probably not justified by the company's business earnings. At that point, if the price had kept on going up, it would have been because some buyers thought there was a Greater Fool around who would pay higher yet. I sold as the price fell through $76, for a good profit.

Greater
Fool

The *Greater Fool* is the buyer who comes in at the end of the price run-up and doesn't do his homework on the underlying value of the firm. That process can go on for a while, as long as more Someones and more Greater Fools keep on putting in their buy orders. But eventually a day comes, or a price is reached, when no one, not even the Greater Fool, is willing to buy more. When buyers disappear, there will always be people who want to sell and start offering their shares at lower prices. Then the bullish Someones, and the Greater Fools who bought near the top, are stuck. They can sell immediately and take their losses, or hold the stock and watch the value of their investment fall every day as prices go lower and lower. Then one stock or the entire stock market may become a bear market with prices falling ever lower, until a point is reached where all of the bears have sold and a few people start looking at the stock as a bargain. A few bold new bulls start to pick up the stock again and the whole cycle repeats.

A trend of falling prices can be established on any kind of evidence, and it will continue until the sellers are worn out. Sometimes these turning points are precipitated by news about the company or its industry. For example, in late 1992, with the presidential election nearing, there was a lot of talk that a Democrat would win and that he would roll back prices on drugs. That was enough to stop a bull market in major drug companies. The threat scared away the prospective new bulls and Greater Fools from buying at the current prices, and the bull market in drug companies was stopped.

Liquidity

On any given day, some of us may see a sudden and unforeseen need for cash. How much cash could you raise in 72 hours if you needed it? Suppose you have a home worth $190,000 with $85,000 left on the mortgage, bank accounts holding $18,000, cars worth $30,000, plus some stocks and bonds with a current market value of $62,000. How much cash can you raise in a short period of time? To make it easy, say this is Monday morning. I'll guess that in 72 hours you might raise $40,000 on the house (depending on your relationship with your bank), $18,000 from the bank accounts, $20,000 from the cars, and $55,000 on the investments (depending on your broker). That is assuming that you can swallow those heavy losses on assets.

One of the primary components of safety in anything you own is liquidity. *Liquidity* means the ability to quickly use assets to cover your current needs. Different kinds of assets carry different measures of liquidity. Cash is perfectly liquid, because Uncle Sam says it is "legal tender for all debts." (Someday in the future, if U.S. currency fails to be an acceptable medium of exchange, we'll have to find another measure of liquidity; but if that ever happens, we'll all have worse problems than paying our bills.) Other assets have different measures of liquidity. For example, the gold in your dental crowns may be valuable, but it's not a very liquid asset.

Liquidity

Let's look at a few types of assets and their varying levels of liquidity:

Asset type	Liquidity
Cash	Perfectly liquid
Savings account	Almost perfectly liquid, except on holidays and provided you don't want to withdraw a large sum on short notice
Stocks on NYSE	Usually highly liquid; may fail in times of market panics; you may have to wait five to seven days for cash
Mutual fund shares	Usually highly liquid; same warning as stocks
Your home	Not very liquid; varies with the local real estate market
Jewelry	Liquidity depends on how much you're willing to cut the price

One of the important characteristics of any investment or financial market is the liquidity it presents. Liquidity helps all investors feel confident of what they have from day to day. How does that work? Suppose you own eighty shares of General Motors and, for whatever reason, decide to sell them. In an active, liquid market, such as the New York Stock Exchange, it's easy. Maybe this morning you checked in the paper and found that GM closed at 54.50 the night before. You can be fairly certain of a gross sale amount very close to $4,360 (80 x $54.50). So maybe at about 10:00 A.M. you call your broker and ask for a current price. She tells you, "The price is 54.88 bid, 55.00 asked." You say, "Sell eighty at the market," and probably within thirty seconds she will tell you they can confirm the sale of eighty GM at a price of 54.88 for a total value of $4,390. The brokerage fee is $110, and they will transfer $4,280 into your cash account (in five days). Nice day's work, since you bought it at $30 three years ago.

But what if the market wasn't liquid? Suppose you put in your call to the broker at 10:00 A.M. and asked for a price on GM. How would you feel if she said, "We don't have a price, there have been no sales since yesterday"? If you go ahead and tell her to sell the eighty shares at whatever price she can get, she might say, "OK, I'll get back to you later." Then about the middle of the afternoon she calls back and tells you, "We can confirm the sale of your eighty shares of GM. We sold sixty shares at 54, and the last twenty at 52. That's a gross sale of $4,280, with a brokerage fee of $350." (The brokerage fee had to go up, because their job became much more difficult, and their volume went way down.) You get $3,930.

So in a less liquid market, you might lose in several ways: possibly lower prices when you need to sell, uncertainty about how or when the deal might go through, and much higher fees paid to the salesperson. My Florida Federal bonds deal was a liquidity disaster.

Any investment gains in value if it has better liquidity, and it loses value conversely. Liquidity of anything you own will vary with the price. You may own 100 shares of stock that can be sold quickly at $48 but has no buyers at $50. If you hold a stock or a bond, you always hope and assume that Someone is there to provide liquidity.

You won't know on any given day if Someone is going to be a bull or a bear. If he is a bull, he may offer a higher price just as you offer to sell. If he is a bear, he may wait and not offer to buy until you have lowered your price enough to satisfy his bearish tendencies. Another Someone may even be selling the same stock or bond at lower prices than you want to accept. When IBM fell from 100 to 46 in a few months, the drop was likely not based solely on a rational reevaluation of the company's finances. It was also a reflection of the fact that Someone was not there to buy; in fact, she was an active seller. The stock lost value because shareholders could sense that the buyers were running for the exits. When the price was 70, the company didn't suddenly lose its assets or accounts receivable, but the stock lost its liquidity in the market at that value. The fundamental conditions of IBM's business had not changed very much, but the market perception of the stock investment, hence the liquidity, changed dramatically.

On different days, the market may swing through bull or bear moods. In 1997, 1998, and 1999, investors were excited about companies that were working on new Internet commerce development. Many of those companies had never sold a product nor made a profit nor paid any dividends to stockholders. But their prices went up. Amazon.com (symbol AMZN) went from a price of $6 in early 1998 to $100 a year later (prices adjusted for splits along the way). DoubleClick, Inc. (symbol DCLK) went from $5 in 1998 to $125 in 1999 (adjusted for stock splits). The story on Wall Street was that they had great expectations, and the Greater Fool was coming in. The buyer was going to make a profit too because the new bulls had brought their foolish friends. That process can go on for an indefinite period, until the Greater Fool fails to show up for work one day. And woe to the market if word gets out that he is taking a vacation.

Bear Markets, Panics, and Crashes

Through most of the years from 1983 through 1987, the stock market was enjoying a spectacular run, going from a Dow Jones Industiral Average of 1,000 to one of over 2,700. Now, if market prices nearly triple in five years, that's a good deal for most investors, but it should not be expected that it can continue forever. One day in October 1987 (as he had done before a few times), the Greater Fool failed to show up for work. Taking notice of that (and the related fact that bond yields were getting a bit high), the stock market promptly took a dive. Stock prices, as indicated by the Dow Jones Industrial Average, lost 20 percent of their value in one day. You could have seen your savings, invested in stocks, fall from $50,000 to $40,000 in one day.

Wall Street was seized by a panic on October 19, 1987. There were probably any number of good reasons to think that prices were too high, but the reaction was out of proportion to existing business conditions.

The Small Investor as the Greater Fool

The Dow was on a roller coaster as different market forces came into dominance, but in the end, pandemonium reigned. Even seasoned investors started selling everything at whatever price they could get because the market ran away from any rational analysis. Within a few days, after people had had time to digest what had happened, buyers were back in picking up loose bargains in everything from H&R Block (symbol HRB) to Honda Motors (symbol HMC), both of which very quickly recovered the lost ground and went on to higher values.

In 1987, the pain was over pretty fast. Within a few weeks the market was advancing again. In 1929 something worse happened: The Mother of All Bear Markets. When the bear seizes investors' minds, they become willing to sacrifice more and more of their value for liquidity. They may watch helplessly as their investment values fall lower and lower day after day with no end in sight. In October 1929, after two years of strong price increases on the New York Stock Exchange, the Greater Fool failed to report for work. Well, prices fell a good bit, and, in fact, by the end of the year, they were down roughly 50 percent, but it didn't end there. In 1930, prices fell another 20 percent, and in 1931, another 50 percent. A retired couple who had their entire savings of $5,000 in the market in 1929 would have been down to about $1,000 by the end of 1931 (if they had held onto their stocks). It got worse in 1932 and only slightly recovered in 1933 and 1934. From the market crash in 1929, it took almost twenty-five years for the Dow to recover its previous value. (That's right, *twenty-five years!*) And, of course, almost all of the people who had been buying stocks in the years leading up to the crash were dead or otherwise out of the market long before that full recovery. There have been other significant bear markets in 1940–42, 1969–70, and 2000–2001. Each time, stockholders were faced with the difficult choice of whether to sell at a loss and just get out of the market, or hold on and wait to see how long it would take for recovery. Each time, they were in the position of not knowing if the bear market was to run for six months or six years. However, the brave individuals who started buying a few stocks every month, beginning in 1942, rode a thirty-two-year bull market to a comfortable retirement.

What about the bear market in 1969 and 1970, you ask? Well, most people who were holding stocks or trading them did show a loss in those years. But the long-term trend between 1942 and 1973 was up.

The Dow went from an average value of about 107 in 1942 to an average of 920 in 1973. Every bull market and every bear market has days, weeks, or even months of corrections, or reversing action. So, for example, at the beginning of 1942, the end of 1957, and the first half of 1962, prices generally fell. But for someone who had been consistently putting money into stocks every year from 1942 to 1973, there would have been a large profit for the entire period.

On February 3, 1993, the Dow went up about forty-five points. That was approximately a 1½ percent gain in one day with an unusually large number of trades. Pretty hot stuff. Some commentators spoke of it as a buying panic. Apparently a lot of people, predominantly professional money managers, got scared. They weren't scared of a crash; they were scared of missing the boat. Remember, those guys' jobs and customer loyalty depend on what they have done lately. A lot of people must have feared that the market was running away from them, and they felt that they just had to spend that money. Does that sound like a healthy investing environment to you? In a market where prices suddenly run away, with little apparent relationship to the underlying business realities, that action is called a *mania* or a *bubble*. In 1928 and 1929 the mania lasted for most of two years and led to a crash. The process repeated in 1995–2001. It will repeat again.

Mania, Bubble

History indicates that prices will eventually return to a level that is supported by business conditions. If that happens over a decent time period and prices fall into a reasonable value level, it is called a *correction*. Late in 1998, during a long-running bull market, the Dow lost about 20 percent of its value over a couple of months. That was uncomfortable for most investors, but it probably qualifies as a respectable correction. It then recorrected over the next month and got back to the previous high. If that first correction had occurred in a week, it would have been called a *panic,* or a *crash*, depending on your point of view. (Probably a panic in this case because market values stayed in the ballpark range of reasonable value.) The really wild times come when a panic becomes excessive. Fear, of course, breeds more fear and confusion. That applies to professional money managers, just as it does to us.

Correction

Panic, Crash

The nightmare of all investors is a genuine crash. It can begin whenever a bull market becomes ridiculous and prices reach their tops.

The early stages of the dying bull can be unpredictable, because, as an old Wall Street saying goes, "Every bull market climbs a wall of worry." That means that the experienced investors are aware of risks and uncertainty all along the way. How nervous is the mob at the top? Several things can happen. Maybe nothing happens for a while. Prices may stay in a trading range, perhaps moving up and down 5 percent for a few months, or longer, as in early 2000. The important question is whether one day a crowd of sellers will show up with no new bulls in sight. How many sellers will cut their asking prices, and how far, in order to unload stocks?

The delicate balancing point hangs on the market's consensus perception of selling pressures. As long as most investors feel that the selling is orderly and that the market is just a little overvalued, then there can be a managed retreat to a reasonable level of prices. But if the balance of investor confidence tips to the side of fear of big losses, then a panic may start. If the panic runs its course in a day or two, then many cool-headed professional investors will come back in to pick up some bargains. This is called *bottom fishing*. But if the panic really picks up a head of steam, it can turn into a horrible crash, such as the one that occurred in 1929–1931.

Bottom Fishing

In 2000–01, there was a bear market of technology and telecommunications stocks. They steadily lost values from early 2000 to the middle of 2001. Some of them lost 70 percent, 80 percent, or even 90 percent of their values. Some of them were still falling at the end of 2001, and others had started to recover. The stock market reaction to the events of September 11, 2001, was a panic rather than a crash. The market was closed for four days, and it dropped severely the first few weeks after it reopened, but it began a new growth trend soon and recovered most of the lost values within a few months.

Tell Me It Can't Happen Again

But, you may say, this is the twenty-first century, and we are all much smarter than folks were back in the 1920s. That kind of insanity couldn't get hold of us, or our fellow investors, could it? Well, folks, you place your money, and you make your bets. You can read any kinds of opinions you want, from knowledgeable, experienced investors. My own personal investment philosophy says that a global market crash that makes the financial world sick for years is unlikely but still possible. On the one hand, investors today have far better, easier access to good information about individual stocks and the entire economy. Everyone has access to a television and a public library. That means that every small investor today can be better informed than the wizards of Wall Street were in 1929. That should help to maintain a rational and balanced market. However, on the other hand, much more money is in the hands of professional money managers. Along with their superior analysis and information, they have superior discipline. The result is they don't sit around and watch values erode. The professional money manager is quicker to cut his losses by quick selling, which can contribute to panic in the markets. You will have to figure out your own approach to the questions about possible crashes; don't just put your head in the sand. Too many nice people have gotten hurt that way. As we read along, there will be a few suggestions about how to deal with mania, panic, and crash scenarios. But just remember, when/if it happens, I'll be taking care of my own money, not yours. And so will your broker.

Compound Growth

I have to introduce a little math lesson here. You don't have to read it, but if you do, it will help you understand some other financial information you may see. Everybody talks about or writes about compound growth, so we should, too. All investors describe and compare investment results by giving the change per year, called the *rate of return*.

Rate of Return

The rate of return of an investment *for one year* is the change in the investment divided by the original value.

Investment	Final value	Change	Rate of return
$100	$120	$20	20 ÷ 100 = 20%
$100	$85	−$15	−15 ÷ 100 = −15%
$8,000	$12,500	$4,500	4,500 ÷ 8,000 = 56.25%

But when you see a series of annual gains or losses for an investment, it is usually not helpful to simply average the yearly rates of return to get an overall figure for the duration of the investment.

The *compound rate of return* (or equivalent annual rate), for a period of more than one year, is the one annual rate that would have produced the same final value, if applied each year throughout the period, with all gains reinvested.

Here's the deal: you invest $1,000 for five years in something that gains 8 percent per year. That's fine work. If you took the profit ($80) each year and spent it on caviar, then the value of your account would look like this at the end of each year: $1,000 . . . $1,000 . . . 1,000 . . . $1,000 . . . $1,000. That is not compound growth.

If, instead of buying caviar, you reinvest the profit each year, that is compound growth. The value of your investment would grow like this: $1,080 . . . $1,166.40 . . . $1,259.71 . . . $1,360.49 . . . $1,469.32; after five years that is a $469.32 profit, which is 47 percent on your investment. That looks better than five times 8 percent, doesn't it? That is the benefit of compounding the earnings.

If you took out the earnings, then after five years you profited by $400. If you left the profits in to earn more, than after five years you got $469.

When you talk about investing, or read other books or magazines about investing, you must deal with profits in terms of compound earnings. You do not have to do the math, but you do have to deal with the idea. Here are some examples to illustrate compound growth without the complicated calculations:

Example: The Elrods invested $25,000 and left it for six years. They told their broker to reinvest all of the dividends or capital gains. After six years they had an account value of $52,000. Their profit was $27,000, which is 108 percent of the original $25,000. That looks like an average annual gain of $27,000 ÷ 6 = $4,500, or 18 percent per year. In fact, though, the important value to consider here is the equivalent compound rate of return. For a return of 108 percent in six years, the equivalent compound rate is 12.98 percent. If the Elrods had invested their $25,000 for six years and reinvested the dividends at a fixed rate of return of 12.98 percent, then after six years they would have made the same profit.

In investing, *compounding* means to reinvest all dividends, yield, capital gains, or whatever cash flows from the investment. If an investment returns a profit each year, and you compound the investment every year, then the compound rate of return will not be the same as the average of the six years' returns. The compound rate will be smaller than the average.

Example: Major Jones had an investment that returned profits of 2 percent, 8 percent, 9 percent, and, finally, 6 percent over four years. The average rate for those four years was 6.25 percent. If he did not reinvest the earnings, then the total return over the four years would be 25 percent. If he did reinvest, the total return would be 27.3 percent, the same as a compound annual rate of return of 5.74 percent.

Example: Eleanor Marbake had some money in the stock market for three years. Her stocks did not pay any dividend, so there was nothing to compound. In 1994, her stocks were down 25 percent, in 1995 up 50 percent, and in 1996 down 25 percent again. The average of the yearly rates of profit was zero (the average of –25, +50, and –25). But the average compound rate of return was –6.5 percent. How so? Well, if she had started with $1,000 she would have seen the following:
- First year: lose 25 percent of $1,000, to leave $750;
- Second year: gain 50 percent of $750, to reach $1,125;
- Third year, lose 25 percent of $1,125, down to $844.

If she had simply invested $1,000 at a fixed yearly rate of –6.5 percent (a loss) per year, that would have produced the same result after three years. So the compound rate of return was –6.5 percent.

You do not have to do the math, and I don't want to spend a whole chapter on it, so let's just let it go. But the critical points to understand are these:

1. The average of the yearly returns is not the same as the compound rate of return.
2. The average is generally more than the compound rate.
3. Most people who analyze or write about investments prefer to use the compound rate of return, so we should, too.

Recommended Further Reading

John Rothchild's book *A Fool and His Money: The Odyssey of an Average Investor* is a little autobiographical sketch of his own investing adventures over a couple of years. It is particularly worthwhile as instruction for us. He was a small investor who tried everything to turn a fast profit. The book describes how he jumped from stocks to options to futures to commodity trading with his eyes always on the prize, ignoring the risk as he went along. It is well written and entertaining, and it has some serious lessons between the lines. The other books listed here are worth checking out, too.

Chase, David. *Mugged on Wall Street.* New York: Simon & Schuster, 1987 (out of print).

Elias, Christopher. *Fleecing the Lambs.* Washington, D.C.: Henry Regnery Co., 1971 (out of print).

Niederman, Derrick. *The Inner Game of Investing.* New York: Wiley, 1999.

Rothchild, John. *A Fool and His Money: The Odyssey of an Average Investor.* New York: Viking Penguin, 1989.

Chapter 3

A Personal Investment Strategy

Small investors need to know:

- Is there an easy way to achieve success?
- What kind of planning do I have to do?
- What is asset allocation?
- Where is the risk?
- Where is the work?

Talk Is Cheap—Get to Work

Talk, talk, talk. Enough talk already. Talk is cheap. It is time we get down to work. The preceding chapters were filled with ideas about the nature of investing, but they didn't say much about making any specific decisions. In this chapter we will get into a plan to do something—actually not a single plan, but more like many possible plans, with as many variations as you could ever want.

There is an old saw about explaining things: First, describe what you are going to do; then do it; and, finally, explain what you have done. Well, that's useful, even though it requires repetition. Similarly, this chapter may require more than one reading. You may want to reread several sections to get a grip on how the ideas interrelate. And you need to understand those interrelations, because they will help you start making some real decisions about how, or if, you will begin investing. This is not a simple process. Some other investment books represent aspects of investing as simple ideas, when in fact they require a lot of work or expertise to put them into practice. For example, some authors recommend that investors evaluate the strength and experience of a company's management. That's a fine idea, but it would be difficult for a part-time investor who has no experience in that industry. We need to be realistic and practical about what we can do. I won't present the ideas as if there were one simple process to guarantee success. If you are going to be investing, then you will have too much at stake to treat it as a simple process.

Your Personal Investment Strategy

If you planned to drive from Kansas City to New York and visit the New York Stock Exchange, you would plan ahead, right? You would need a map, hotel reservations, some idea of how you could get into the stock exchange, and some estimate of the costs and time required for the trip. Well, if you are not going in person but just sending your money, you had better have a plan, too. I call that plan a personal investment strategy.

Remember the PIG: Protection – Income – Growth. If your plan serves the PIG, then it will serve you well.

The plan can be as detailed and complicated as you like, or it can be much looser and general, but one way or another, you need to have some kind of a plan. Here are a few of the questions that the plan should address:

- How much money do I want to put into risk-oriented investing?
- How should I divide that money between stocks, bonds, and mutual funds?
- How much work and research will I do myself?
- How much could I lose, without destroying the fabric of my life?
- Do I want to find a full-service broker to advise me, and how much will I rely on him or her?
- What types of diversification methods will I use?
- What is my target for annual gain?
- What discipline will I use to control losses?

You will certainly think of more questions as we go along. Remember, the aim of this book is not to answer all your questions, but to help you have the confidence to find good information and determine your own answers.

Now, the best-laid plans may go astray. You know that. You know that every major corporation, every military leader, and every lover has seen his or her plans disintegrate in the face of changing events. You know that we are not likely to think of everything, and that even if we did think of everything, circumstances would change by the end of next week. The planning process may be difficult and possibly discouraging because you see the complexity ahead of time. But don't give up. Get a plan. What would you think about a captain who led his battalion into battle without a plan?

The military analogy is appropriate here. A smart and responsible military leader has to be both organized and flexible, as does the small investor. An officer leading a unit has to have a clear objective that he understands. We do, too. He has to have an idea about the cost and risks of going after that objective. He has to have the discipline to stick to the plan in the face of difficulty and resistance, but he also must keep his eyes open and his head clear. A battlefield leader should be constantly collecting and analyzing new information about his situation, and he should be prepared to make changes in the plan when necessary. We should, too. We and the battlefield leader should both respect our plans and stick to them with discipline, but we should not stick to them with blind obsession. In other words, a plan is better than no plan, but you can't expect the plan to be perfect.

You start out with a plan, because that provides a better start. You stick with the plan because that will make you more effective in achieving your goals. You can change your plans when it is necessary to change, but only you can make that choice for your personal investment strategy. To begin your trip to the financial markets, you are going to need these things:

- A plan: Develop a personal strategy for protection, income, and growth.
- Discipline: Stick to your plan and work at it.

- Effort: Analyze the opportunities, and keep collecting new information.
- Flexibility: Keep your eyes open; don't be afraid to modify the plan or too proud to admit your mistakes.

The Small Investor Has a Smorgasbord of Investment Options

A Smorgasbord of Investment Options

At first glance, the choices seem simple enough. As the introduction explained, this book is concerned only with stocks, bonds, and mutual funds. That looks like three choices, right? Not exactly. That looks like thousands of choices, possibly more.

Now we are getting into the process of establishing a personal investment strategy. Part of the plan is to make this a realistic and workable process for you. Even though there are many ways to set up your investments, we don't have to study them all. You don't have to be knowledgeable about every one of 10,000 mutual funds, or every one of 10,000 publicly traded stocks. You just have to find a plan and a mixture of investments that work for you. So let's explore this gray area between the many, many choices available, and begin the practical matter of selecting something that works for you.

Many Investment Mixtures

Following are some of the available options. Pretty soon you will see the ideas developing, and you will think of many more options for your money. Then you will be able to focus on the areas that seem appealing to you and explore in depth perhaps a few different possibilities that seem to fit your investment strategy.

Four Ways to Allocate Your Money

A simple view of your asset allocation can be described in four choices: buy individual stocks, buy bonds, buy mutual funds (which may be funds that invest in stocks or bonds), or don't buy any of those. The last option we will call the cash option. The cash option assumes you don't keep your money at home, but rather in a savings account or money market account. The cash option should fit into your personal investment strategy, because it takes care of your reserve funds. When you sell an investment or collect interest and dividends, you might not want to reinvest that money immediately, and so it could go into your cash funds. There may also be times during which you feel the markets are too risky, and you decide to keep most of your investment money in cash. If you use a broker to hold your account, then the cash will probably be held in a money market account. A *money market account* is a very-low-risk mutual fund investing in bonds. It would be quite rare for a money market account to lose money. Before you make decisions about stocks, bonds, funds, or keeping cash, you should read the chapters dedicated to each of the investment choices. They will help you understand the trade-offs between risk, reward, time, and work for each choice.

Money Market Account

Many Ways to Allocate Your Money

To reiterate, you might decide to divide your money among stocks, bonds, mutual funds, and cash, or some combination of these. Here are a few of those combinations:

1. Buy stocks and bonds.
2. Buy stocks and bonds and mutual funds.
3. Buy mutual funds and keep cash.
4. Buy bonds and keep cash.

Well, you get the idea. Let's look more closely at a few possible choices. Let's say you have $20,000 to invest. Here are some possible ways to divide the money among the investment choices that match the combinations above:

	Stocks	Bonds	Mutual funds	Cash
1	$4,000	$16,000	0	0
2	$7,000	$10,000	$3,000	0
3	0	0	$10,000	$10,000
4	0	$15,000	0	$5,000

Of course, there are many more ways to divide the money. And, in addition to choosing how you're going to allocate the money, you also have to make choices within each option. If you wanted to put $4,000 into individual stocks, for instance, you would need to choose some stocks to buy from among the thousands available. If you wanted to put $10,000 into mutual funds, you might want to pick two to five from among the thousands of funds. We can imagine a vast number of possibilities for how you might invest your money.

One of the most challenging tasks that you have is to figure some allocation that works for you. That will be affected by the variations in risk and work for each option. We will get into this in a lot more detail later, but, for starters, look at the risk, work, and reward estimates for the first four.

	Risk	Work
Buying individual stocks	highest	highest
Buying individual bonds	variable	medium
Buying mutual funds	low to high	medium
Holding cash	low	none

The possible reward levels of the above options are roughly commensurate with the risks. Note that there is no guaranteed reward level, only a possible reward level. And in the final analysis, you always have the choice to simply walk away from it all. I hope that your final decision on that will be an intelligent and informed one.

More about Risks

Risk again! The guy never gets off of it! Will he never relax on the subject of risk? Not in this lifetime. And not in these markets that we are studying. If you ever, for one little second, lose sight of the risks in investing, please don't tell anyone that you read my book.

We need to make rational judgment calls on how to minimize the risks. In order to figure things out, we need to look at different kinds of risks that occur in different markets or at different times. My philosophy says that we have three good ways to avoid or minimize risk. We can work hard at research, diversify investments, and keep money in cash. Practicing each of those ideas will help, some more and some less in different situations. There is no single magic key to the kingdom of low risk, but we can try several strategies.

On every investment, the small investor should try to do three things: Protect the principal, earn some Income, and Grow the principal. With different investments, you emphasize one or another of those. The cash option is almost entirely focused on protecting the principal, while some high-risk stock investments are almost entirely focused on increasing the principal. All three concerns should be important. You will balance them out in deciding which mixture of investments to use.

This leads us to three kinds of risk:

- the risk of loss of principal (which may, for example, occur if you buy junk bonds),
- the risk of low income (as with a stock that pays no dividend),
- the risk of no (or low) growth in principal (if you keep all of your money in the bank).

If you think that the last is a red herring, that it's not really a risk, then you haven't heard about inflation. The family that put $10,000 in a shoe box in 1953 could have bought a new home with the money. If they opened the shoe box today, they could not buy so much. The original economics lesson is this: Wealth is not measured by dollars, but by the amount of goods and services you can purchase. For a fifty-year-old couple who are planning their retirement today, the risk of no growth in principal is a very serious risk.

Different Kinds of Risk

To explore all the risks would require the life's work of ten thousand economics professors. Our eyes glaze over. In addition, the very term *risk* has extremely technical and specific meanings to economists, and they might well quibble over how I use the word. Well, that's fine for them, but I when I say "risk," I mean it in the common English sense of the word: a danger, a potential hazard, the possibility of a loss. I want to widen your vision to see risk all around. To see risk all around, no matter when or how silently it approaches, we should become familiar with some of its usual faces. We know and accept the fact that every purchase of a stock, bond, or mutual fund involves some risk. Those risks show up in different forms. The likelihood of each type showing up may change from day to day, and our ability to predict and manage each kind is different. Let's look at some of the ways that risk creeps in.

Risk

The Risk from Dishonesty

In late 1992, a broker in Knoxville, Tennessee, was fined $200,000 and barred by the National Association of Securities Dealers for converting customers' accounts to his own use. The most obvious, but probably least common, risk is simply that a broker is either crooked or stupid. You give him $20,000 to buy General Motors stock and he uses the money to buy his girlfriend a new Mazda—that's misappropriation of funds. The initial buy or sell order is the first or last step in the sequence of events that take the money out of your hands, around the market, and back to you eventually. But if the buy or sell order is never followed, or if someone else grabs your money, then it doesn't matter how sharp your planning and analysis were. We should not blindly trust just anyone who calls him- or herself a securities dealer. There are a lot of things you can do to get a relationship with one who is smart, honest, and productive. So the very first risk is that the person or firm with whom you do business is not good enough. The next chapter focuses on this problem.

The Risk from Poor Decision Making

There is a risk of poor decision making. This is probably the most common risk of all. Furthermore, it is a risk that you will have to learn to live with. If you do any investing of any type, you will have to make some decisions, and sometimes your decisions will not work out for the best. No matter how hard you work or how smart you are or how cautious you are, some of your investment decisions will go wrong. It may be because you didn't see all the available information. It may be because you could not foresee the future. It may be because your advisor had those same shortcomings. Live with it, get used to it! If you are an investor, then occasionally some of your decisions will lose money. If you cannot live with that risk, then do not put your money into the financial markets.

The Risk That You're Not As Smart As You Think You Are

In the case of my Florida Federal bonds, I was confident that I knew the business, the competitive environment, and the management. I knew for sure that the company was financially healthy and making good profits. But I made two misjudgments: first, I was wrong about the management (I didn't dream that they would find a way to ruin the company within the few years after I left), and, second, I thought that I didn't have to keep a close eye on that investment. There is a lesson, or two or three, in this: even the wise guys with inside information, guys who are trying to be careful, will make some mistakes. It has happened before, and it will happen again. Do your research. Try to manage your money carefully. But don't give up the first time you make a mistake. Mistakes are good teachers.

The Risk That Good Judgment Can Still Fail

A good decision to buy a stock can be turned sour by a poor decision about when to sell. Let's look at the case of Barnes and Noble (symbol BKS). Their revenues and earnings had climbed steadily for most of the 1990s. Their stock had been up and down for several years during the late 1990s. The company was steadily expanding, and they experimented with the Internet, which didn't do too much damage. I had bought and sold some at a profit several times, and in August 1999 I decided it was time to buy again. That was not necessarily a bad decision, but it turned bad because of what I did later. I bought at $24 a share and watched it bounce around between $17 and $25 for a while. I was very uncertain about what to do. I thought the company was pretty sound, but I could not figure out the stock price gyrations. In late 2000 and early 2001, the stock market in general was pretty shaky. There were signs of deterioration of the economy, and some segments of the market were crashing. I watched and waited and finally decided to put in a *stop loss order* on my BKS at $22 per share. The stop loss order told the broker to sell, at market level, if the price ever dropped as low as $22. Pretty quickly, the price fell to $22, and I was out with a small loss. Very shortly thereafter, the price started running up and soon went above $40 per share. Where I had an opportunity to make a gain of about $16 a share, I turned it into a loss of $2 because I was nervous.

Stop Loss Order

Obviously I remember that mistake. I am writing about it today. But I have never regretted it. I had made a plan to protect my capital and was following through on it. I didn't want to sit idly by and watch the stock fall to who-knows-where. Even though everything about the business looked solid, it was necessary to remember that the market has a mind of its own. It will go where it will go, and we must either follow or get out of the way (we don't have the option to lead—you have to have $10 billion to do that). Sometimes it will work out that you do the smart thing, and the market makes it into a mistake.

The Risk That Good Research Isn't Good Enough

I was looking for a safe dividend-paying stock. I went through a risk analysis on Potomac Electric Company (symbol POM) much like the analysis of Duke Energy described in chapter 1. I also talked to several experienced professional money managers and looked at the current portfolios of some good, conservative mutual funds. Many of them held Potomac Electric. I knew something about how POM did business, as well as about the Washington area economy in general, because I had had personal experience living in their service area. I studied their annual report and their report to the Securities Exchange Commission (called the 10 K report), and I bought some shares at 23⅜. It was a good, safe investment for me. But no matter how carefully you research your investments, bad things can always happen, in any market. Later, the share price of POM rose as high as $28, and I was feeling pretty good about it. Suddenly and unexpectedly, over a few weeks, the price dropped to about $23. I lost about 18 percent of the share value for no reason that I could understand. Well, I learned later that Potomac Electric had a little side business going, which I had never heard of (I didn't read the reports closely enough). They owned and leased out some airplanes. The lessors' business went sour and the planes were returned. So POM had a few hundred million dollars' worth of assets sitting around with no income being produced. They also sold another 6 million shares of the common stock, which diluted the value of other holdings. That apparently spooked the analysts and their 1993 profit projections went down the drain. Since then, the stock price climbed back to near $40 in 1999, and is currently bouncing around between $20 and $25. Even your best-reasoned, most conservative investments will hiccup once in a while. Can you sit calmly and wait for the market to correct itself?

In the summer of 2001, everyone knew that the economy was somewhat shaky, but we all tried to analyze the chances for recovery and decide where there might be decent investment opportunities with moderate risk. Many investors, including yours truly, put a lot of work, research, and thinking into deciding where to put our money. A few weeks later, terrorist attacks on September 11 overwhelmed all of our logic and thought. We all had to learn the frailty and limitations of our attempts to prepare for the future.

The Risk That There Ain't No Justice

Sometimes you just can't make a buck. Hewlett-Packard (symbol HWP) fell to a bargain price level, and I bought some. It kept on falling and I sold. Wrong! IBM fell to a bargain price level, and I bought some. It kept on falling and I held it. Wrong again! Can you stand the aggravation? Remember what Peter Lynch said about having the stomach for investing.

The Risks in Forecasting Business Conditions

If you buy stock in Ford Motor Company, it stands to reason that you want Ford to build good cars and sell a bunch of them. The stock price and the dividends will not give you much reward unless Ford's autoworkers and dealers are doing their jobs. There are two parts to this picture: first, you have to do good analysis to predict the success of the company and, second, their management has to make the profits come through. You can't control their management or the actions of their competitors, so you are left with trying to predict their chances of success. That is an extremely tricky business. The people who successfully predicted the 1991 turnarounds of Chrysler Corporation and Unisys were greatly rewarded. Investors who predicted a resurrection of computer maker Wang Labs might have bought the stock at a "bargain price" of $4 to $5 a share in 1991. Wang closed 1992 in bankruptcy with the stock worth less than 50 cents per share.

So it is difficult. In later chapters we will get into more ideas about finding good information and trying to forecast things. But for now let's look at the most immediate and obvious problem: Can you forecast future earnings? No. Among the very best sources of data, opinions, and analysis for stock research by individual investors are *The Value Line Investment Survey* and *Zacks Investment Research*. Let's watch them forecast earnings for some of the companies in the Dow. It should be easier to forecast business for these very large, long-established companies, rather than for newer companies. After all, it's easier to predict where a fifty-year-old oak tree will be next year than to make the same prediction for a potted plant. Here are some examples of published estimates and subsequent results.

Company	Date of forecast	For year ending	Forecast earnings ($ per share)*	Actual earnings ($ per share)*
AT&T	10/18/91	12/31/92	3.00	2.59
Citigroup	6/19/98	12/31/99	1.91	2.15
Disney	9/03/99	9/30/00	0.78	0.90
Eastman Kodak	9/20/91	12/31/92	4.10	0.91
General Motors	9/20/91	12/31/92	2.75	– 6.26
General Motors	6/19/98	12/31/99	7.81	8.53
Home Depot	9/03/99	1/31/01	1.18	2.42
J. P. Morgan	6/19/98	12/31/98	3.21	2.82
Philip Morris	9/27/91	12/31/92	5.85	4.95
Philip Morris	6/18/99	12/31/99	3.31	3.19
SBC Communications	6/18/99	12/31/00	2.69	2.26

Earnings
per Share

*Earnings per share equals total company earnings divided by the number of shares of stock.

This is not a terrible record (*Value Line* and *Zacks* are among the best sources for any investor)—note that some of the estimates were fairly close. But several of them were so far off as to seem ridiculous. It is backup for my contention that forecasting earnings is really tough. The more dramatic discrepancies between forecast and actual earnings can be explained away because this happened or that happened, but so what? That's life. Stuff happens. The point here is that there are always surprises, and it is extremely difficult to forecast business conditions. If you intend to invest in individual stocks, then you must try to estimate future company earnings, but you must realize the uncertainties of such forecasts.

The Risks of Being in the Market

Some folks argue that you don't have any choice in whether you take risks. They say that whether you invest or not, inflation, the economy, and taxation will affect you one way or the other. They argue that not investing is simply a bet that the pieces of paper called cash are better than the pieces of paper called stocks and bonds. We cannot resolve those arguments, but there are risks associated with having money tied up in investments.

The Risks from Outside Forces

In the week of September 17 to September 21, 2001, the American stock markets all took a dive. All of the major averages used to report stock prices showed large losses. All of the markets were closed from September 11 to September 14 due to the terrorist attacks in New York and Washington D.C. At the market close on September 21, the Dow was 15 percent below its value of the day before the attacks. No one could have predicted that two weeks in advance. Many people had more important things to do than manage money that week. Many were too confused and shocked to make decisions. Some could not get through to their brokers, and some just decided to wait it out, come hell or high water. If you are going to have your money in the markets, then you have to recognize that sometimes the market may take you for a ride where you have little control.

Outside forces also control bond prices. We will get into this in greater detail in chapter 6, which is devoted to investing in bonds, but for now it is enough to note that when overall interest rates go up, the resale value of a bond goes down, and vice versa. If you buy a high-grade $1,000 bond and hold it to maturity, you can expect to get the $1,000 back. If, however, you want to sell it before it matures, the value will be affected by interest rate changes that have occurred since you bought it. Interest rates vary because of changes in economic conditions around the world. Unemployment in Germany will affect the value of a bond you bought three years ago in New York. Even though some types of bonds are among the safest investments, it is still worthwhile to balance them with other investments that may behave differently relative to interest rates.

At one time, part of my strategy was to invest in companies that had strong marketing and sales outlets in Europe. European economies were not healthy, but I expected to see improvement in the near future, figuring that the companies with good markets over there would be strong. Some of the candidates that I liked were Ford, General Motors, IBM,

General Electric (symbol GE), and Wolverine World Wide (symbol WWW—maker of shoes).

Well, that ship has not come in. I made good profits on Ford and GM because they were way down when I bought, and I am looking at some profit on GE, although I expect to hold it a long time. The European countries generally went from bad to worse, and there didn't seem to be a whole lot I could do about it. Then, after I sold Wolverine, it tripled! In short, then, my European strategy has never paid off. I'm still not sure that I exercised bad judgment—but this does illustrate the problem of investing in the face of economic forces that dwarf one's power to predict.

We can't really run away from that. Even if you confine your investments to Georgia chicken ranches, there will be outside factors that you cannot always predict or control. The smart small investor buys a mixture of investments that should behave differently as market and economic conditions change. We hope for the best and plan an investment strategy to avoid the worst. Work hard and diversify!

Risk and Volatility

Volatility is an indicator of how much a security's value fluctuates. Highly volatile securities are assumed to be more risky because you might have to sell when they are down. Volatility should be understood relative to what is expected, or normal, for the markets at that time. Higher volatility means that a stock price fluctuates up and down more than the broad market averages do. There is no single agreed-upon best formula or method for judging risk, so many people substitute their view of volatility for risk. I think that is a mistake. It is not necessarily true that a stock is risky just because it is volatile, but it is worthwhile for us to be in tune with the normal language and usage of the markets, so we will look at volatility.

In the first graph below, ABC and XYZ are two stocks that both start at $20 and, after nine months, end at $23. XYZ is more volatile and presumably would be regarded by many investors as more risky.

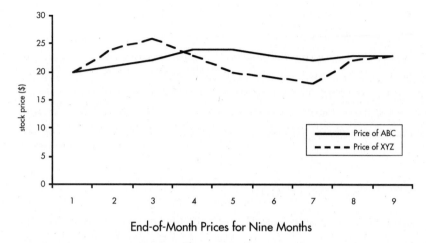

End-of-Month Prices for Nine Months

In the second graph, RST and PDQ are two stocks that have good growth during the nine-month period. RST climbs steadily from $18 to $23, while PDQ climbs, not so steadily, from $15 to $27. PDQ is more volatile and, by a certain point of view, more risky, but it is a superior investment over that time frame.

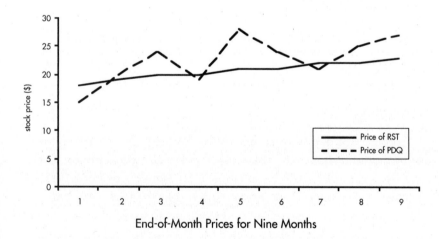

End-of-Month Prices for Nine Months

If you had held PDQ, you would have had more headaches and nervousness over it than you would have had over RST. You might have been scared into selling during one of the dips. There were also some opportunities for people to buy PDQ and sell it at a loss, whereas RST was profitable no matter when you bought and sold within this period.

Volatility should be interpreted as indicating chances for loss, and more chances for worrying, but it does not necessarily indicate a bad investment. There is no exact, clear way to measure risk—but we can measure the volatility relative to some agreed-upon standard. For instance, we might show that stock XYZ was 30 percent more volatile than the Dow Jones Industrial Average over some set time period. This is done by calculating a value called beta, which we will discuss further later on.

What Is Diversification?

Diversification is a tool to help you with Protection. Diversification is one way to ensure that your investments won't all go sour at the same time. There are a million flavors of diversification. There are many ways to do it right, and a few ways to do it wrong.

Let's start by looking at some examples of how it works. Suppose you and I and Jack have a chance to invest in three ways: bond A, stock WXZ, or stock OUC. We each put up $1,000. Jack buys the bond, I buy WXZ, and you buy OUC. In five years we each evaluate our holdings and find the following returns:

	Cost	Return in 5 years
Jack bought Bond A	$1,000	$1,400
I bought stock WXZ	$1,000	$2,200
You bought stock OUC	$1,000	$600

You are not happy with the results. But suppose we had pooled our money and shared the risk and reward of all three options. Then, after five years we would be splitting $4,200 among us, for a total of $1,400 each. Having each bought an interest in the three investments, and thereby passing up the best and worst results, we achieved a good average result. We have all diversified our risk and reward expectations. (We actually formed a tiny investment club.)

But you wish we had all bought stock WXZ and made a killing. A delightful wish, but not practical, for we could not have predicted the outcome of each investment with any certainty. The good news and bad news of diversification are that we avoid both the best and the worst, in search of an agreeable middle ground.

Diversification is an investment practice of combining investments to try to reduce risk without sacrificing too much potential gain. Diversification does not guarantee safety—it seeks safety and improves your chances for safety.

Diversification

The real value and science of diversification come into play when you foresee some risk and reward possibilities for each investment, and you try to balance them for protection. To illustrate what an individual investor can do, and how to do it, let's look at another, slightly more complicated example.

Let's imagine three $1,000 investments. Call them Mighty Motors (MM), Good Food (GF), and U.S. bonds. Let us also imagine only three possible future economic scenes for the next three years: recession, slow growth, and strong growth. Suppose we can make some decent guesses at the value of each investment, in each possible economic situation, three years down the road.

	Recession	Slow growth	Strong growth
U.S. bonds	$1,225	$1,225	$1,225
Mighty Motors	$700	$1,300	$2,200
Good Food	$1,100	$1,400	$1,700

So, in a recession we might expect the bonds to grow in value to $1,225; in a case of slow growth, we guess the MM stock would grow in value to $1,300; and so on.

Suppose you have $6,000 to invest. Obviously, if you care to gamble on the strong-growth result, then you'll put all your money into MM, hoping to turn $6,000 into $13,200. But you face the prospects of losing in a recessionary economy, and then only having $4,200 to support your retirement.

The conservative investor will avoid the worst risk by diversifying the money among two or three investment choices. Here are three such diversification plans:

Plan 1: Broad, even diversification. Put $2,000 into each investment.

Plan 2: Buy $3,000 of MM, $1,000 of GF, and $2,000 of U.S. bonds.

Plan 3: Buy $3,000 of GF and $3,000 of U.S. bonds.

After three years, here's what you might see, given each of our three economic situations:

	Recession	Slow growth	Strong growth
Plan 1	$6,050	$7,850	$10,250
Plan 2	$5,650	$7,750	$10,750
Plan 3	$6,975	$7,875	$8,775

Plan 1 offers low risk and possible high gain. Plan 2 offers more risk and possible higher gain. Plan 3 offers the lowest risk and possible lower gain. All three plans reduce the worst-case risk and seek a happy middle ground.

Is plan 3 a risk-free investment? No—there are no risk-free investments. These calculations are subject to the estimates we started with, which are no better than our sources of information and our analysis. And sometimes unexpected events affect the value of our investments. For example, MM might have a strike, or the stock markets might crash.

The scenarios in the table above depend on how much money you started with. If you wonder about the results in terms of percentage growth of investments, look at the table below, which shows the annualized compound rate of return on each investment.

	Recession	Slow growth	Strong growth
Plan 1	+0.3%	+9.4%	+19.5%
Plan 2	−2.0%	+8.9%	+21.4%
Plan 3	+5.1%	+9.5%	+13.5%

You pay your money, and you take your choice. Different people will have all kinds of different feelings about which of those choices is more or less attractive. The choice of how to diversify requires a personal investment strategy. No one method can suit everyone. And you could choose from a lot of other ways to invest your money, or even bank part of it, if you wanted other options.

Diversification in Practice

Now how do we put this theory to use? We just looked at three choices: an automobile company, a grocery store chain, and a very-high-grade bond. You would normally expect that each of the three would react differently to different conditions in the economy. That is what you want. When looking at the many investment options available, you want to choose a range of investments so that they won't all go bad together. If interest rates go down, you would like to have at least one investment that does well. If the government imposes higher taxes, you would like to have at least one investment that does well (good luck on that). If the price of oil falls to its lowest level in twenty years, you would like to have an investment that does well, perhaps a trucking company. If your judgment just turns out to be bad, you would like to have an investment that does well, maybe Treasury bonds.

Many Different Ways to Diversify

In the rest of this chapter, we will explore some of the different ways that you might diversify your investments. As we saw at the beginning of the chapter, there are unlimited ways to diversify. I am going to present some of the ideas that I have used, and I expect that you will think up a hundred others. As a general rule, try to identify any factors that you think might affect your results, and then buy investments that will react differently to those factors.

DIVERSIFY ACROSS MARKETS

First, don't put all your money into individual stocks that you pick or into individual bonds. The stock market is mean country. It is tough on everyone who comes in, and it requires constant monitoring. It is certainly the highest-risk choice that we are considering, although it might offer a high reward. In chapters 7 and 8 we will explore what you can try in the stock market, and we will offer some support to ease the risk and the work, but it is at all times the high-risk option.

Furthermore, depending on your background and education, it is entirely possible that you might start picking stocks and do everything wrong. If you want to work that side of the street, then ease over to it. Test yourself and see how you are doing before you make any huge commitment. What I have done is buy both mutual funds and individual stocks. I slowly worked up to a position with eleven individual company's stocks. That number has varied from one to fifteen at a time, and I took a long time to get more than four. Early in my investment work, I owned five to ten different mutual funds, and my plan was to watch things for two or three years. If I found that my own stock picks were doing either much better or much worse than the mutual funds, I would make some adjustments. It is even possible that I might have quit buying individual stocks. As it turned out, my stock picks did better than the mutual funds, but I still include four or five mutual funds in my portfolio for better diversification.

Some of the same ideas apply to the bond market, although it might not be quite so dangerous. Of special concern is the so-called junk-bond market. Those are bonds that offer unusually high yields. Remember that higher return implies there probably are higher risks.

DON'T PUT ALL YOUR EGGS IN ONE BASKET

Diversify by choosing more than one investment. The people who had most or all of their retirement funds invested in Nortel (symbol NT) stock in 2000 and 2001 were hurt badly as the stock price fell from $80 to $5. Some others who balanced those investments among five or six others were not hurt as badly. If you have discretionary, risk-oriented capital of perhaps $10,000 or more, then you, or a good advisor, should be able to identify four or five decent investments you can use. That could provide a reasonable balance of risk and return in different situations. If you have no more than $4,000 or $5,000, use a diversified mutual fund, so that its managers will plan and provide the diversification for you. Or use two or three mutual funds with different investment strategies. If you buy a mutual fund that specializes in small companies, you might balance that with another fund that specializes in the Standard & Poor's 500 companies. If you choose to buy stock in several oil companies, you might balance those with a trucking company stock, on the theory that they will do better when gasoline prices are down. This kind of diversification is complex, and it may be the area where you have to do the most homework or seek some outside help (perhaps from an investment club).

Practice Time, Game Time

DIVERSIFY YOUR 401(K) PLAN

Late in 2001, the Enron Corporation, a very large dealer in gas, oil, and energy trading, went bankrupt. For years before that, many of their employees had been investing large chunks of their retirement money in their 401(k) plans in the company's stock. Many of those employees lost their jobs and most of their retirement funds at the same time. The same thing has happened to employees of other companies. Even if a company does not go bankrupt, loss of stock values can devastate the retirement plans of employees. If you work for a company that allows you to buy the company's stock in your 401(k) account, be very careful.

It is not good diversification of your total financial position to make both your job and your retirement funds dependent on one company. It happened to IBM employees in 1994. It happened to Nortel employees in 2001. Don't let it happen to you.

Neither would it be a good diversification strategy to put all of your money into five different savings and loan companies or to buy four automobile companies or five gold-mining outfits. The reason is that if you own stocks or bonds of companies that all share the same markets and products, they might all go bad at once. There is usually a presumption that when you buy a mutual fund, you get automatic diversification, but that can fail in some ways. If the fund buys only oil-company stocks or biotechnology companies or candy companies, then there is not much diversification in that. The advantage of using Mighty Motors, Good Foods, and U.S. bonds in our earlier example was that each could be expected to behave differently in different economic conditions.

DIVERSIFY OVER TIME

When you first start out, you should plan on keeping a lot of money in cash or money market funds. No matter what your investment plan is, it would probably be a mistake to invest all of your money at once. There is no great hurry, and haste can cost more than it rewards. Take time to buy one stock or one mutual fund. Then take time to think about how you are doing before you pick something else—perhaps a bond or a fund of bond investments. For most small investors who might end up buying five to ten investments, it would be reasonable to take six months to get 75 percent of your money invested. I took over a year, of which the first six months was dedicated to research. But you should make the initial investments keeping in mind a view of what your final mixture of stocks, bonds, and funds could be. That means you should be following a plan.

One popular plan for diversification over time is called dollar-cost averaging—investing a fixed amount of money into the stock market on a regular basis (monthly, quarterly, etc.) We will discuss more at the end of chapter 7, but one factor is worth looking at now. Market values fluctuate. Prices run through peaks and valleys. You don't want to put all of your money in at the market's peak, but you can't tell when the peak has been reached. Dollar-cost averaging helps you avoid investing everything at the peak.

It is easy to use examples that make it look like dollar-cost averaging guarantees safety. Many people believe that it does. That is a great error. Dollar-cost averaging is one method of diversification that is often useful, but it does not guarantee safety. It merely seeks safety.

If you have found a very reliable broker or financial advisor, it might seem reasonable to throw in all the money at once. She could probably make up a good plan in a few days. There's a catch, however: how will you know she is smart and experienced and reliable until you see how she works for you? Remember that any recommendations or results you hear initially are part of a biased sample. Your friends' recommendations may be valuable, but their financial plans are different from yours. When will you know how this broker will work for you? Only after you have tested her.

DIVERSIFY ACROSS COMPANY SIZE

As of this writing, small company stocks have, on balance, done better than big company stocks for much of the past year. That may continue; it may not. The small company stocks are interesting because they offer the greatest chances for strong growth. It is easy to see that if a huge company, like GE, does great work, revenues might increase by 10 percent next year, but if tiny Fred's Fertilizer in Nashville does great work, they could have a 1,000 percent increase, with profits going through the roof. Of course, Fred also has a greater risk of going bankrupt than does GE.

Another fact of life for the small companies is that it may be more difficult to get good, up-to-date news. Every day, *WSJ* is going to tell me all the news on GE, but they may never report about Fred's new fleet of trucks. Or his high debt from buying them.

With a multibillion-dollar corporation there is a legitimate presumption that they know something and have well-established markets for their products. With the small and new companies, we might have to search for months to find two of them that look promising. If you decide to try the small-company stock market, it might be best to buy a mutual fund that has a good record on specializing in that group. Another way is to study small publicly traded companies in your own town or state. You should have a better chance of getting good information about them. The two greatest stock investments I ever made were in small companies located within fifty miles of my home.

Diversify Your Sources of Information

Remember that we shouldn't be too confident in our own judgment. Pretty soon, we will explore the ways to find good information, but whichever sources you decide to use, be receptive to different ones. I read some local papers for local and North Carolina business information. That's part of my investment strategy. I study the *WSJ* and *Barron's* for the national business scene and hard data on my investments. I have selected some sources of published investment advice that seem to make sense for me (*The Value Line, Zacks,* Martin Zweig). All that research takes a good bit of time and energy, but I still keep an eye open and an ear alert for ideas or news or recommendations from other directions. Most of what I read and hear will be rejected as excess noise, but I don't totally ignore it. You never can tell. My best investment moves have been with companies that do not get a lot of news coverage.

The Expenses That Attend Diversification

If the small investor does her own stock picking, then typically she might own five to ten stocks. That number is restricted by the amount of money available, the amount of time for research, and the investor's knowledge. If the fees for each purchase and sale average out to 1 to 3 percent of the amount invested, then that is a lot of money going into the broker's hands. The total fees can be reduced by buying bigger blocks of stock. You can buy 200 shares of one stock a lot cheaper than you can 50 shares each of four stocks. For example, if you had $6,500 to put into stocks, with one well-known broker, you might make four purchases of different stocks and pay $100 to $200 in brokerage fees, but if you bought just one stock, the fee might be just $30 to $50. That is a significant difference for a small investor. One of the difficult problems for the small investor is to manage the balance of diversification against brokers' fees. There is no simple way to work around that problem. That is one of the reasons we lean so much on mutual funds.

Tax Considerations

I am not a tax specialist, and I don't wish to advise anyone on tax matters. However, a few things are fairly straightforward. If you can invest in a tax-sheltered plan, such as an IRA or a 401(k) plan, that is better than paying taxes on all of your dividends and capital gains each year. There are two possible reservations: First, the money in tax-sheltered plans is generally not readily available whenever you want to use it. Second, some employer-sponsored 401(k) plans don't offer a lot of investment options or much diversification (although some of them do offer good choices). If you have a chance to invest through an IRA or 401(k) plan, then certainly look at it very closely. You might even want to place some money in tax-sheltered plans and keep another side account for ready access to other money. One important advantage of an employer-sponsored 401(k) plan is that you can probably put more money into it than into an IRA, and your employer may contribute to it, too.

If you have money in a tax-sheltered account, it may be one where you can choose any investments you want, for example, a self-directed IRA. In that case, do not use tax-exempt investments within a tax-sheltered account. The tax-exempt bonds, for example, municipal bonds, pay less than other bonds. A municipal bond paying 6 percent is better than a corporate bond paying 8 percent if you are paying taxes of 30 percent on the dividends, but if the income is already tax sheltered, then the higher yield is better. (Even that idea depends on some assumptions about your tax rates after retirement.) Also, don't buy zero-coupon bonds (see chapter 6) until you understand the tax requirements. There are a lot of different angles to figuring tax advantages. The planning has to be tailored to the needs of each individual or family.

If you are in a high-income situation where the tax costs become serious, then by all means include tax planning in your personal investment strategy. Talk to a professional who can help you see the costs and benefits of different options.

A Review of Personal Investment Strategic Planning

Let's review and summarize some key ideas.

1. What is your plan? Without a plan, you're just playing games with your money.
2. Remember the PIG. Every investment decision should consider the potential for:
    P: Protection of your capital,
    I: Income from the investment, and
    G: Growth of the investment.
2. How much money can you risk? Your entire personal financial situation and expectations should be reviewed.
3. Are you ready to face up to the risks? The stock market, bond market, and mutual funds involve more risk and more work than just keeping your money in the bank.
4. How much work and research can you do? If you fake the work, you'll fake the profits, too.
5. How much experience in business and finance do you have? Picking stocks requires some knowledge and experience, bonds perhaps less, and mutual funds still less.
6. How much do you want to rely on a paid professional? You can pay higher fees for a full-service brokerage firm, or rely completely on one or more mutual funds.
7. How do you want to diversify? Again, there is the question of whether you want to manage it yourself or pay someone else to plan it.
8. What kinds of risk and reward guidelines will you try to meet? If your investments do very well or very poorly, how will you decide when to sell?
9. Do you have the stomach for investing? Can you keep at it, make the decisions, put your money at risk, and accept occasional losses?
10. How will this affect the rest of your life, and is it worthwhile? There will be some sacrifice of time and attention that might serve other needs.

The Small Investor Looks for a Safe Path

I strongly urge you not to do any investing at all until you, and perhaps your spouse, have worked through and answered all of the questions above.

Recommended Further Reading

Of the books listed below, I particularly recommend *The Money Game*. Never mind that it's over twenty-five years old—some of the basic facts of life just don't change that much. These are books that will help you to know yourself as an investor. That is a good way to avoid a lot of grief.

Bernstein, Jacob. *Investor's Quotient: The Psychology of Successfully Investing in Commodities and Stocks.* New York: John Wiley & Sons, 1993.

Pring, Martin. *Investment Psychology Explained.* New York: John Wiley & Sons, 1993.

Smith, Adam. *The Money Game.* New York: Random House, 1976.

Smith, Adam. *Supermoney.* New York: Random House, 1972 (out of print).

Chapter 4

Professional Help

Small investors need to know:

- What kind of help is available?

- What does the help cost?

- How does professional help fit into my personal investment strategy?

- How can I choose a good broker or other professional?

- Where should I look for more information?

An investment strategy has to be built to recognize and manage risks. That's kind of tough if you haven't seen enough of the investing history or learned enough about other people's losses. It might be wise to ask someone who has been around longer or who has an education in finance or who has access to a lot of research material. You might think, for instance, that there is no risk in buying long-term U.S. Treasury bonds—guess again! Ask a pro, and he or she will tell you about the very real risks. Your investment strategy should guide your money into places where the balance of risk and reward fits your personal situation. An important part of that strategy might be finding professional help.

You understand about dentists, plumbers, and lawyers. There are some things in life that we just don't tackle alone. That also applies to getting in and out of financial markets. The starting point is this: No matter how smart and independent you may be, if you decide to invest in the financial markets, at some time you will have to actually buy a security or a fund. Later on, you may want to sell it. When you buy, you will need the services of some sort of investment professional and again when you sell. There are many different types of investment services available, and this chapter is going to help you decide which and how many of

76

The Small Investor Hires a Gun

those professional services you want to hire. You don't need to become an expert in all of the varieties and flavors; you just need to decide on one or two that will help you be a successful investor.

Insurance Companies and Annuities

There is an investment vehicle called an annuity, which is different from the stocks, bonds, and funds that we are concerned with but is frequently peddled by various financial advisors or salespeople. Annuities are frequently offered as alternatives to stocks, bonds, and mutual funds. Annuities are established and guaranteed by insurance companies.

In economics, an *annuity* means a string of payments over some period of time. For small investors, an annuity is an investment account with some kind of insurance attached that may produce a string of payments at some later time. I have not studied every annuity ever offered to the investing public, but I have studied enough of them and talked to people who owned them.

In each case that I have closely examined, the annuity was a bad investment for two reasons. First, the annuity came with complex

Annuity

contracts and conditions (in very small print) that very few investors were likely to understand. In fact, in *every case that I have reviewed,* the person who bought the annuity did not have any idea what they had purchased and did not read the contract. That violates rule #1: If you don't understand it, don't buy it. Second, each carried conditions that if the investor needed to get the money back within a few years, substantial penalties would be extracted.

Every annuity offer that I have seen turned out to be bad practice as an investment, and the annuitant (the buyer) had unsatisfactory choices as how to modify the investments. If you want insurance, buy insurance. If you want investments, buy investments. There is precious little reason to mix them. The only time you should consider an annuity is if you have a very trusted financial advisor who has thoroughly reviewed the terms and conditions and investment choices and says they are appropriate for you. Just remember that the advisor will probably collect a large fee for selling you the annuity.

It is possible that someone may offer an annuity product that is a good deal. I have never seen one that came within a hundred miles of being a good deal. The biggest single objection is that they are too difficult to understand because of the way the contracts are written.

Investment Companies and Mutual Funds

In chapters 9 and 10, we will take a long look at the opportunities and risks in mutual funds. Mutual funds offer an excellent way for the small investor to have a chance at reasonable returns with controlled risk. For many individual investors, mutual funds offer the only reasonable avenue for getting into the markets. For example, if you absolutely detest reading financial statements or working any calculations with percentages, or if you don't want to do any more than the minimum amount of work, then mutual funds may be right for you. Or you may be better off simply staying away from financial markets.

The full discussion of mutual funds starts in chapter 9, but, briefly, a mutual fund is a business managed by an investment company that will sell you shares and promises to buy them back from you at the current fair price on any given day. They will use your money to invest in stocks and bonds and share the profits or losses with you.

There are many potential advantages to using mutual funds. For the small investor who might want to risk $100 each month, it would be impractical to buy individual stocks or bonds. The transaction fees from a broker would be greater than the profits. Some mutual funds will let you buy in at that rate, or perhaps $300 each quarter, an appropriate strategy if you are working on a retirement account. Some mutual funds require an initial investment of $3,000 or more but will waive the minimum, or greatly reduce it, for an IRA. Even if you have built up a pile of savings to start with, if it is less than $20,000, you should use mutual funds. You probably could not get decent diversification investing on your own in individual securities.

The three main promises of mutual funds are *less work, better diversification,* and *better management* than most of us could provide on our own. In fact those three promises make sense even for those of us who might use a broker or a professional money manager.

Not Enough Good Professionals to Go Around

The paragraph above described the benefits of mutual funds. In reality the situation is not so simple. There are more than 10,000 mutual funds holding perhaps 6 to 8 trillion dollars in stocks and a few trillion more in bonds. Suppose that each fund has at least one manager, and an employee for every 100 million dollars of assets. This adds up to maybe 80,000 people (a very rough estimate) who share the responsibility of managing the funds. Do you believe that those 80,000 people are all experienced, intelligent, well trained, and ethical? Do you believe that most of them are more capable than most of us? I do not. The results achieved by mutual funds over the past quarter or year or ten years show that there are always some losers. In the year ending October 1, 2001, the Merrill Lynch Premier Growth Fund lost 76 percent of its value. At the same time, the Fidelity Japan Fund lost 47 percent, and the Invesco European Investor lost 55 percent. Every week, *Barron's* runs a full section of mutual-fund results. They show recent dividend yields and total return over the preceding year or three years, compiled by Lipper Analytical Service. That is one of the places to look for help when you start studying mutual funds. That list will always include a bunch of funds that you will be glad not to have owned.

Choosing an Investment Company

Chapter 10 is devoted to the question of picking a mutual fund, or two or three, that might be good for you. That is a critical decision that deserves your time and attention. After all, you understand there is no free lunch. If the only work and the only decision that you will handle on your own are to pick mutual funds, you had better get it right.

Mutual funds are managed by investment companies. If you are planning to buy mutual funds, you may buy only from one company that has several funds or from several companies. If you choose to use several companies, you will obviously have more choices of funds to buy, but staying with one company would be simpler. Of course, simplicity and convenience are among the main reasons for choosing mutual funds for investments.

How should you go about selecting a company? Some of them offer dozens or even hundreds of funds. If an investment company has a local office close to your home, that might be of value to you. Some folks just feel better if they have the chance to sit down face-to-face and get to know a real, live person who represents the firm. All of your mutual-fund business could be handled over the telephone and the Internet, but it might be easier or more satisfactory to get questions answered by a nearby representative. What are you going to do if they send you a monthly statement that you can't understand? It is easier to arrive at a clear understanding if you can sit down next to a representative who will go over the statement with you.

What about your bank? They probably advertise their investment services, and you may well feel that it would be nice to keep your financial business with the bank you know and have been dealing with for years. However, I'm afraid the news is not very comforting on that. I contacted four large banks in my area that currently advertise investment services, including my own bank, with whom I had been doing business for fifteen years. Those banks did not have much to offer. I have never yet, after repeated tries, been able to find a service representative on duty in any office who had any knowledge of the investment services other than the number of another office that I could call. Usually, banks do not offer investment services through their branches. Instead, they purchase or set up subsidiary businesses for brokerage service. They want you to contact and deal with a brokerage firm with whom the bank has an arrangement to share fees or profits.

Your bank may have 10 to 100 offices in your area. Ask them if their brokerage affiliate has any. Ask them if they can consolidate your financial statements to show your loans, savings accounts, checking accounts, credit cards, and investments on one useful monthly statement. Ask them if they can arrange to have funds automatically transferred in or out of your money-market account when you buy or sell mutual funds or stocks. Find out if your personal bank service representative has any knowledge of investing or is willing to counsel you. Find out if the bank has anything to offer besides giving you a name and telephone number of a broker. If they do, that may be of value to you. My experience has been that they generally do not.

On the other hand, the larger investment companies do offer many services similar or identical to those found in banks, and they will offer to integrate those services with your investment needs. It might make more sense to take your banking business to an investment company rather than vice versa. You should carefully evaluate both convenience and breadth of services before deciding whether to consolidate the two areas.

If you do decide to handle your investments through your bank, it is essential for you to learn the number of mutual funds they can sell and the fee structure they offer. Do not let your bank push you into the arms of a broker that only sells funds with sales commissions attached (front-end loads; see chapter 9).

Stockbrokers

The following is a critical exercise. Keep your money carefully locked away until you are confident that you can pass this test. Repeat in a firm, loud, and clear voice:

No, thank you.
No! I am not interested in that investment.
No, I do not want to hear any more about it!
No. Thank you, and good-bye.

Repeat that out loud, several times, until you feel comfortable and confident saying it. If you cannot get comfortable saying it, then do not contact any stockbrokers—leave your money in a bank or in a mutual fund.

If you cannot do this and you nevertheless persist in talking to stockbrokers, then you are (pardon the expression) dead meat.

Practice Saying No!

One of the large national brokerage firms ran a series of ads on TV in which they showed people at work being annoyed by their stockbrokers. They then interrupted the scene to describe how their brokers are so much nicer, how they don't harass clients, how their attitude is a more refined and professional approach of waiting on your pleasure and convenience. Their point was that you should find a sweet broker. The ad missed the mark. The fault is not with the aggressive brokers, but with the passive clients. The clients depicted are apparently unable or unwilling to tell their brokers, "Buzz off, Charlie, I'm at work and have business to attend to. Don't call me, I'll call you."

A relationship with a stockbroker is a business relationship, not a social one. Woe to you if you can't remember that! You may find a broker who is competent, friendly, sociable, honest, and successful. But he or she is also a shark. It's a business for sharks. They live on commissions and competition with all of the other brokers. The industry is cutthroat and aggressive. For a stockbroker, no sales mean no income.

The *WSJ* regularly runs full-column stories in small print about disciplinary or legal action taken against brokers or firms in the business. Do you know why they run them in small print? Because there are too many cases to run all of them in standard-size type. I think I know some honest, reliable, professional brokers. But there are as many types of broker as there are of doctor, lawyer, or writer. Be prepared to deal with the dishonest as well as the honest types.

If you do begin talking to brokers, investment companies, or financial advisors, or if you subscribe to certain publications, there is a good chance that your name and telephone number will get spread around. Be prepared to say no. Be ready to call your state securities registration office if anyone harasses you about investing.

But now, even with all that negativism, maybe you can find a good broker, with good references and experience. By all means, try. It can be a rewarding experience if you succeed. Here are a few ideas that should help.

Try the following approach and talk to four or five brokers if you are going to talk to one. Ask your friends. If any of them have a broker they have been happy with for several years, talk to him or her.

Seek a broker with several years' experience. I would insist on at least five years. If you merely call or walk into a brokerage office, you may be assigned to the newest greenhorn in the office who doesn't have much to do. If you haven't been referred to a specific broker, ask for their most experienced broker or one with at least several years at the firm. I know from personal consultation that one of the large and highly regarded brokerage firms with an office nearby has both one of the best brokers I have ever spoken to and one of the dumbest. You don't want to call that office and just settle for anybody who is available.

Be thoroughly honest and direct with the broker, and expect the same in return. If at any point you feel as though she is pressuring you, then say so or leave. If she says things you just don't understand, then tell her so. If she cannot or will not simplify the discussion to your comfort level, then leave or cross her off the candidates list. Do not try to pretend to have any greater knowledge than you have—the broker will be able to tell, and she may use it to your disadvantage.

Ask the broker about her career, training, and experience. Ask for references. Ask how she would evaluate your investment needs and risk tolerance. Judge whether she is listening to your interests and needs or trying to fit you into her plans. Take notes so you will be able to compare several brokers after you have completed all of your interviews.

Full-Service, Discount Broker, or Internet Broker?

The brokerage business is highly competitive. As you might expect, people invent many clever ways to discriminate their services and price structure. One of the most popular methods is the "discount brokerage service." Their fees for handling each individual transaction may commonly be one-third to one-half of a full-service brokerage firm's fees. Firms that offer discounted service include Olde Discount Brokers (now a division of H&R Block), Fidelity, Charles Schwab, and TD Waterhouse, among many others. But not all "discounts" are created equal. Some discount fees may be five to ten times higher than others. The full-service firms include most of the biggest names in the business: Merrill Lynch, Prudential, Morgan Stanley Dean Witter, PaineWebber. There are also Internet brokers who offer you the chance to do all of your transactions online, through the Internet. Some people think that is neat, but some people think it is terrifying.

Every broker has some special services or convenience that might be attractive to you, but the primary differences between the discounters and the full-service firms are in research and price. A full-service broker probably has the benefits of a large research department offering steady new evaluations of the economy, the markets, and individual stocks or bonds. You pay for that. The discount broker will usually just take your order and send a monthly activity statement for your account. The Internet broker will typically just allow you access to a website where you can look at your account and put in orders for changes.

How should you decide which type to use? There is no universal answer, but here are a few guidelines. The discount broker is cheaper. If you feel that you need the advice of professional analysts before buying or selling, the full-service broker may be right for you. If you consider yourself knowledgeable and confident in making investment decisions, a discount broker will be easy to work with. If you are willing to spend some time doing research and you feel that you can understand the financial news, a discount broker may be good for you. Certainly if you are in an investment club and have six or eight friends sharing the thinking and research, a discount broker or Internet service can handle all your needs. However, the full-service brokers at PaineWebber, American Express, and Merrill Lynch might disagree with me on that.

The full-service brokerage firm may only handle their own mutual funds, or those that charge a load (to pay a sales commission). The discounter may not be any better, or it may handle hundreds of different mutual funds. The full-service broker may be part of a larger financial empire that offers other financial services. Do you need those services?

Just as with any other business decision, the bottom line is, do they offer the services that you need, and is the cost reasonable? Brokerage fees vary widely, and they change whenever the brokers feel the heat of competition, but here are some representative numbers that were effective in 2001. The table below shows a range of fees that you might expect to see for various stock transactions.

# of shares bought	Share price	Lowest likely fee for Internet account	Likely fee to deal with a person	Highest likely fee for advice & service
1,000	$25	$7	$50	$400
100	$25	$7	$50	$80
50	$30	$7	$50	$80

The lowest likely fee is always from an Internet broker. If you see an ad for free stock transactions, read the fine print. Something is up.

Most brokerage firms will also offer to simply take your money, manage it for you, and make all the decisions. You never see a bill or make a decision after you sign on with them. The fees vary widely for that service but are never really cheap. Most of the firms have a minimum acceptable amount for a new account of $50,000 or higher. If you had a $75,000 account, your annual fees would be $1,000 to $2,000, depending on which firm you chose. Here are some examples (some fees have been rounded):

Firm	Minimum account size	Annual fee for $75,000 balance
American Express	$25,000	$1,500
Merrill Lynch	$50,000	$1,500
Morgan Stanley	$50,000	$1,690
Prudential	$50,000	$1,875 plus other fees
Salomon, Smith Barney	$50,000	$1,125
PaineWebber	$50,000	$1,875

Most brokerage firms have figured out that they need to offer you a variety of service choices. Many of them will allow you Internet trading at a very low price, trading through a telephone representative for a higher price, or trading with research and advice service for a much higher price.

When dealing with the Internet firms, be particularly wary of how you will deal with a problem. If your account statement shows a trade that you don't think is accurate, what are you going to do? About all you can hope for is to call some unknown, minimally trained person in who-knows-what remote location and complain. You probably won't have any records if they say the mistake was yours. If you accidentally do something that is very dumb (it might happen), who is going to say, "Wait a minute, did you mean that?" With an Internet account, no one will. With a discount broker, there is a possibility that the telephone representative might. With a full-service broker, the representative certainly should be reviewing every trade to see if it makes sense for your account.

Why do I keep saying representative instead of broker? Because the person you deal with is almost certainly not a broker. He or she is an subform who is technically designated a broker's representative. Theoretically, the representative is well trained and properly supervised. Sometimes it works out that way . . . but often not. It is not always perfectly clear what they are getting paid for. It may be for generating business, it may be for customer service, or it may be to keep the broker's time free to deal with wealthier clients. Some, perhaps many, of the representatives are intelligent and conscientious professionals. Some are not.

The Problems with Getting Mutual Funds Service through Your Broker

If you want to buy stocks and bonds, most brokers can probably handle your purchase or sale. This, however, is not the case with mutual funds. If you select any group of five mutual funds, you will probably have to use several different sources to trade them.

For example, I selected these five mutual funds, more or less at random:

Name of fund	Type	Sales commission
The Berger Mid-Cap Value Fund	stocks	none
The Eaton-Vance Growth Fund	stocks	5.75%
Harbor Funds Short Duration Fund	bonds	none
MFS Funds High Yield Opportunity	junk bonds	4.75%
Target International Equity Portfolio	foreign stocks	none

I called some brokers to see if they could buy and sell those funds in their customers' accounts. The brokerages I spoke with were Brown & Co, BBT Investor Services, Fahnestock, H&R Block Financial Services, Scott & Stringfellow, Merrill Lynch, and PaineWebber. Here are their answers:

	Brown	BBT	Fahnestock	H&R Block	Scott & Stringfellow	Merrill Lynch
Berger	yes	yes	yes	no	no	yes
Eaton-Vance	yes	yes	yes	yes	yes	yes
Harbor	yes	yes	no	no	no	no
MSF Funds	no	yes	yes	yes	yes	yes
Target	no	no	no	no	no	no

The Eaton-Vance and MFS funds were the two with sales commission attached. One local bank's brokerage service and the PaineWebber office I called did not provide answers to the questions.

Some of the larger brokerage firms, especially the so-called "full-service" firms, don't want to handle funds that do not have a sales commission attached. That may be fair, since they have to make a living too, but it may also restrict your choice of funds available. The same bias may influence them to steer you toward funds that are sponsored by their own firm. In that way the firm will have the advantage of collecting the operating expenses of the fund. It is not uncommon to find a full-service broker that will offer you a few hundred funds to choose from, for each of which the firm would collect fees and sales commissions. Guess who pays those fees. That's right—you. It is also fairly common for discount brokers to offer a selection of thousands of funds, with or without sales commissions.

Does this all sound like too much trouble? It is! The only way to make it easier is to find out which funds a broker will handle before you commit to working with that broker. If a broker says, "All of them," she is almost certainly lying to you—ask about those five listed above or five funds that are interesting to you. If the broker doesn't know, why would you want to do business there? Ask for a list of all the funds that the broker can sell.

Several brokers or funds managers have suggested to me that I could simply establish another account to accommodate buying a different fund. Then what? Open another account for the next one? And if you want to sell Fund X and buy Fund Z, do you have to go through the exercise of withdrawing money at one brokerage account and taking it to another?

What if you want the money in your IRA? Will you establish multiple IRAs and transfer money between them? Do you think that sounds extreme? It is not uncommon—several brokers suggested to me that I should do just that, although it is a practice the IRS frowns upon. The only time it gets fairly simple is if you decide to use only mutual funds that are managed by a single investment company. For example, Fidelity Investments, Merrill Lynch, and some other financial services firms offer diverse groups of funds that would appear to satisfy many investment needs. Of course, there is no guarantee that all of their funds will have relatively high performance or low costs.

Build this factor into your advance planning. Decide ahead of time how important mutual funds will be in your investment strategy. Ask every broker or investment company to give you a list of all the mutual funds they work with. If they don't have such a list, they don't need your business.

Ask them to give you a written guide to procedures and expenses for redeeming one fund and using that money to buy into another fund from a different investment company. If you don't get a clear response, then the broker doesn't want your business.

Investment Advisors and Money Managers

As an investment advisor, I have to admit I am prejudiced. I will, however, do my best to be fair and evenhanded. Brokers are mainly salespeople (sniff). What can one expect? On the other hand, there are several types of financial professionals who sell advice and service for a fee, rather than selling the goods for a commission. They go by the title of registered investment advisor, financial manager, or investment counselor, among others. Some of them specialize in working with retirement planning, overall financial planning, business employee benefit plans, or almost any subset of financial planning.

There are certain financial services that are available for free. Some companies, including many insurance companies, will offer free financial planning and advice. Truly free! No obligation. Possibly good advice. I would be reluctant to make any generalized evaluation of these folks, though. I have talked to some who are knowledgeable and helpful. However, be advised: these people do not work for fun only. Someone is paying their salaries while they are helping you. If Prudential is going to pay someone to offer you free financial counseling, then is it not possible that they expect some return for their largesse? Is it possible that the advisor might feel a bias toward insurance or annuities? Maybe. It might still be good advice; you will have to decide for yourself. But whenever you find yourself talking to someone who offers free financial counseling, keep in mind that their employer expects to somehow make a profit on the situation.

The Small Investor Gets Free Advice

Investment Advisors

You gotta love us! For a fee, we will spend some time with you and tell you how to invest. Or, for a fee, we will take your money and invest it for you and keep the records.

The fees may typically run $60 to $120 per hour for advice, or 1 to 2 percent of the total amount under management. There can of course be extremes of very low or very high fees in some cases. An advisor with an office in Manhattan will probably be more expensive than one with an office in Paris, Kentucky.

There is no way to judge the quality and value of the advice unless you know the person's track record or spend some time talking to him. Do not be deceived by his title. In order to be a registered investment advisor, one must pass an exam on investment law, but nobody ever checks up on actual investment skill or judgment. Be just as cautious when selecting an investment advisor as you would be when choosing a broker. Also, check with your state securities registration office, which keeps records on all the advisors registered in your state. They can tell you whether any advisor or broker has been the subject of complaints.

You might choose to hire an investment advisor who offers only advice, not brokerage or money management service. That may be worthwhile, but keep in mind that you still have to go to a broker somewhere along the line to actually buy and sell stuff, and that will require another fee.

Money Managers

People who label themselves money managers typically don't offer much advice. They basically just take the money and manage it. Such managers will usually offer their services for some set annual fee, which may be 1 or 2 percent of the amount you have invested through them. Most money managers will have some minimum amount that they are willing to handle. The minimum will commonly be perhaps $1 million or more. Some small investors may be shut out of this service due to the costs.

Michael Stolper is the president of a company that, among other things, evaluates money managers. He has written a nice guide to selecting a money manager (available by writing to the following address: Stolper and Company, 600 West Broadway, Suite 1010, San Diego, CA 92101). Generally, we will not be using the same managers that he rates, because they have minimum investment limits that shut us out. However, the book is still very instructive and useful for all investors. My favorite line is his description of computer methods: "Computer prowess is a myth—intellectual and judgmental skills are the only sustainable edge in this, or any other, business."

Stolper also observes that people have been known to manipulate statistics in order to make their own results look good. Of course, every financial services firm does that to some extent (it's called advertising). As Stolper wryly suggests, "Methods of manipulation are only limited by the imaginations of those looking to mislead you." Accuracy in advertising has improved some recently. The Securities Exchange Commission has made new rules to limit some of the more outrageous abuses of statistics.

Is there a lesson here for us? Indeed there is. Be suspicious of all of the statistics and claims you see. Think about whether you actually understand what the numbers are supposed to represent. If you do not

understand, it is not your fault. It is the fault of the person who prepared the advertising claims.

Special Attention for the Elderly

Any financial services professional should be able to help any client. Do
the elderly have special needs, and can they get specialized help? They
may or may not. It depends on the individual. Certainly their money is
just as good as anyone else's, and they want to be careful with it.

There are a few financial managers or investment counselors who
give more of their time and attention to older people. They might well
have greater knowledge of conservative investments, tax advantages, or
estate planning. They might be more patient and skillful at simplifying
the choices to be made. They might offer help with managing insurance claims or paying routine bills. Some advisors might even help you
find other services such as cleaning or transportation. If you or a loved
one needs this sort of financial help, ask around among friends or
senior citizens' organizations. There may be an advisor like these in
your city. Such an advisor will probably not come any cheaper than
others, but might be easier to talk to.

Grading the Service You Buy

Any financial professional you deal with needs your fees and commissions. He or she will try to hold on to you and your business. He or she
may even act like you have a lifetime service contract and have no business thinking about other options. But don't be fooled! It's your money
and your future, and you bear sole responsibility.

I am reluctant to tell you that you absolutely must do anything,
but just this one time: You must evaluate the results on a regular basis.
If the results are not satisfactory, consider making a change. You may
or may not want to discuss it with your current broker/advisor/manager,
but you have to make up your mind about what to do. Nobody else can
make that decision for you. If you don't make the decision, that is
equivalent to simply putting your future in that person's hands.

How to evaluate? Here are some guidelines.

First of all, be reasonable. If you required your broker to sell you stocks that always increase 50 percent each year, then no broker would ever be good enough. If you required your mutual fund to be in the top 10 percent for gains every week, you would always be changing funds and always losing money on commissions.

So what is reasonable? That is up to you—it's a judgment call. For me, reasonable means that the investment results consistently avoid major losses and usually do better than some other safe choices. For example, I know I could make around 3 to 5 percent on U.S. savings bonds, so I want my investments to do better than that.

For instance, I went into one recent year thinking that the major stock averages might appreciate 8 to 10 percent. I set a goal of doing at least that well. You might reasonably decide to require that your investments meet the following target goals:

1. Each mutual fund should stay in the top half of its peer class each year. *Barron's*, and the *WSJ*, and *Business Week* and numerous other publications will give you the data to check on this.
2. No investment should ever lose more than 10 percent in a given quarter, but the results should be compared to overall market performance and otherwise tempered with reasonableness.
3. No individual stock should fall more than 20 percent (or maybe 25 percent) below the purchase price.
4. The yearly results should always produce profits at least 3 percent above what you could have had on a five-year CD from your bank. You should get a risk premium (the 3 percent) for accepting the risk of investing in financial markets.
5. The investments that you regard as being high risk should usually return greater profits, as a group, or else you should stop using them. Those same investments will probably contain occasional losers—that's what risk means. Get used to it.

There are other ways to do this, but the point is that you should set some goals or standards. Evaluate your results once every six months or so. If the results are repeatedly not satisfactory, then make a change. That change might mean selling a stock, or changing mutual funds, or changing your broker or advisor.

Bad News! Changing Brokers

Sometimes, for any one of a variety of reasons, you may want to change brokers. The change process can be quite simple, but might be a nuisance or a disaster.

> **WARNING**
>
> Before you sign a contract with any broker, find out what you would have to do if you wanted to leave their firm and take your assets elsewhere. If you don't get a simple and clear response, then do not walk, but run like mad for the nearest exit.

If, at any time, for any reason, you lose confidence in a broker, then drop him or her. Never stay with a financial advisor who is causing you anger or frustration. Don't stay with a financial advisor who has consistently failed to achieve the goals you have set for yourself. Any investor may take the occasional loss, but you must be willing to weed out a regular loser.

One problem commonly arises when moving your assets. Let's assume you have made a decision to move the account, and you have successfully completed the process of finding a new broker. If the old

The Small Investor Fires His Gun

account held a mutual fund that was sold only by that brokerage fund, then you would have to sell that fund before transferring the assets. Some financial services firms might allow you to transfer their funds across brokerage accounts, but there is no uniform practice on that yet.

Before moving anything, ask your new broker to review everything in the old account. She should tell you just what part she recommends you should keep or sell, and what can be directly transferred to the new account without going through a sale. The new broker should also be able to take care of the details and paperwork of the asset transfer. Be prepared for this process to take a few days. The brokerage firms haven't learned much about data communications yet. If you considered the possibility of a move before you invested at the first broker, then this should be painless. If you did not, then it could get complicated and unpleasant. For example, if you held a mutual fund with a deferred sales charge (back-end commission) and wanted to move on after just one year with the old broker, that charge might eat up 3 or 4 percent of the value in the fund.

If you hold stocks that are traded on a major stock exchange, a direct transfer of the stocks will be done through the Automated Customer Account Transfer System. Don't let the old broker persuade you that you have to sell them and transfer the cash; this would just generate unnecessary extra commissions and extra costs for you. If the investments are part of an IRA, you do not want to take any money in hand during the transfer, since that might generate some surprise extra taxes.

If at any time, for any reason, you feel as though the broker whom you are dismissing is not helping you make a smooth and orderly transfer, call your state securities registration office. I guarantee you that this will produce immediate full cooperation from all concerned. The brokers are not going to risk their state registration because of your little account. It might also be helpful to contact the stock exchanges or the NASD (National Association of Securities Dealers), but I would start with the state office.

Guidelines for Finding Help

In summary, here are a few things that you might think about when hiring a broker or any kind of professional financial help:

1. **Professionalism:** Advisors should have their skin in the game, too. Be very cautious about accepting advice from people who are not actively working as both investors and advisors.

2. **Compensation:** What are the fees? How do they get paid? What are they selling?

3. **Experience:** There is very high turnover and lots of shoddy training going on. Experience and recommendations should be counted heavily.

4. **Convenience:** Even if you do 95 percent of the business by telephone, it might be worthwhile to sit down face-to-face with the broker sometime.

5. **Sincerity:** This is a very tough call—the field is wide open to phonies and sharks. Find a person who is a good listener and has time to talk about your personal situation. Ask several candidates to make up a short list of what might be good investments for you, and use the lists to try to evaluate whether the broker was really listening to you and understood your needs.

6. **References:** Advisors and brokers should be willing to provide names of a few of their current clients—or you might ask some friends whose judgment you respect for recommendations.

7. **Reputation:** Again, a tough call; you have to look at both the individual broker and the firm and then sort through the tons of good and bad things that people might say about them.

8. **Price:** Costs vary dramatically. Insist on getting straight answers on fees. You might not want to go with the firm that promises the lowest costs, but you certainly want to know what the fees will be.

9. **Service:** Will this particular professional person provide all of the services that you want from them? Buying and selling stocks, bonds, funds, annuities; advice and research; checking accounts; credit cards?

Recommended Further Reading and Internet Resources

There are no credible, unbiased reference sources on the Internet that provide thorough evaluations of brokers or financial advisors. However, there are many websites that offer useful information; those are mainly the websites of the brokerage firms. Those websites will help you collect information about the firm's range of services. They quite often do not include information about their fees. You would have to make some telephone calls and ask some very direct and pointed questions to get the fee information, but that might still be more convenient and comfortable than going to a broker's office.

Smart Money magazine regularly publishes ratings and opinions of brokerage firms. This is particularly helpful in showing some of the trade-offs of price against range of services. It will also help you to pick a firm that offers the specific services you want.

Brimelow, Peter. *The Wall Street Gurus: How You Can Profit from Investment Newsletters.* Alexandria, Va.: Minerva Books, 1988.

Marcial, Gene. *Secrets of the Street: The Dark Side of Making Money.* New York: McGraw-Hill, 1995.

Mayer, Martin. *Markets.* New York: W. W. Norton, 1990.

Smith, Charles W. *The Mind of the Market: A Study of Stock Market Philosophies, Their Uses, and Their Implications.* Lanham, Md.: Rowman & Littlefield, 1981.

Chapter 5

If You Snooze, You Lose

Small Investors need to know:

- What am I going to put at risk?
- Can I control the risks?
- How do I plan my personal investment strategy?
- How much work will I have to do?
- What are my resources?

Do It the Old-Fashioned Way

I do not personally know anyone who has gotten rich quickly or easily, and this book is not about the easy way. I don't know about the easy way. Although I once held a stock that went up tenfold in a year, I don't believe that will ever happen again. Charles Dow, who had a lot more experience than we do, said that the folks who try to get rich quickly usually end up losing, and those who try to gain steady, consistent, reasonable profits sometimes end up getting rich. This chapter is about finding and using information to help you do the essential work and make you a better investor.

Don't Kid Yourself—Face the Facts

One of the best sources of information is at once the easiest and the most difficult: it is your own knowledge about your situation. It is the easiest because it is always right at hand and you are the expert, but it is difficult because it requires you to take a hard and honest look at your lifestyle and finances. That can be a challenge, but you have to do it. By doing this, you can begin to do some of your own investment planning.

Take out a piece of paper. Right! Take out a piece of paper! If you are not going to do a little bit of work, then this business is not for you. The numbers and examples that follow are just fictional samples of what someone might do; they are not recommendations for you, just examples.

1. List things of value that you own that might be converted to cash for investing. Presumably, that would not include your wedding ring or family heirloom furniture. It might include the vacation home or the boat or part of the equity in the house.

Make some notes as you work on the list. Making notes will help you keep things in perspective. Consider your age, health, and prospective continuing income. How will these factors affect your ability to accept risk and loss? Spend a little time with your spouse, a friend, or somebody else who cares enough to share their thoughts. Talk about your housing assets, mortgage, and vacation or education plans, and how much of your income those will require. Look at your legal commitments such as taxes, loans, or child support. If there is something in there that you might put at risk in financial markets, and you can accept the possible loss of part of it, then write that something on your list. List 1 might look like this:

Asset	Value if converted to cash
Boat	$3,000
Rental property	$52,000
Home equity	$70,000

2. List ongoing, steady sources of income that you think will continue for the foreseeable future.

List 2 might look like this:

Asset	Value
Salary	take home $2,900 per month
Alimony	$870 per month

The Small Investors Talk It Over

3. List cash stashes that you have now. This includes the savings
   account, bank certificates of deposit, current mutual funds, and
   so on.

Consider your savings, retirement accounts, or tax-deferred investment accounts. What assets do you already have that are exposed to
market risks or other financial risks? Look at your insurance. Do you
need insurance? Do you know what you are insuring? Can you estimate
the value of your insurance in future payments or current cash values?
Is this a source that you would want to use to provide funds for investing? For many folks, the answer is probably no; they would prefer to
keep their insurance separate from their investments. But the choice is
worth considering.

No one else can tell you exactly how to balance the assets that go
into investing and the other financial or real assets that you keep secure
from financial markets. What every financial advisor will tell you is that
it would be unwise to even look at financial markets unless you have
thought about those other factors. This book will help you organize
your thoughts about how the markets fit into your overall financial
plans. If you have great difficulty with or concerns over this part of the

planning, that might indicate a good reason for you to talk to a professional financial planner or investment advisor.

By now you should have considered most of your assets, current
income, projected future income, home, paid-up insurance, and annuities. Current investments, such as the 401(k), are also assets. The current
investments should be included to remind you of the full extent of your
diversification and your possible losses. List 3 might look like this:

Asset	Cash value
401(k) plan	$61,000
savings account	$11,000
inheritance	$22,000

4. For each of the above lists indicate how much of the money you
   might put into risk-oriented investing.

Part 4 is the hard part. What are you willing to put into risk-oriented
investing? Write down the amount of each current asset you are willing
to put at risk: how much of current income you are willing to put at risk,
and how much do you need for current living expenses or for current
savings? (Current savings includes the money you set aside for unexpected needs such as car repairs. You need to have several months' worth
of take-home pay set aside for emergencies.) List 4 might look like this:

Asset	Value to use for investments
401(k)	$61,000
Boat	$3,000
Home equity	$15,000
Inheritance	$15,000
Salary	$200 per month

5. Now suppose that all of that money in list 4 went up in smoke.
   What would you do now? Could you face your family, neighbors,
   and creditors, and get on with your life? How would your spouse
   feel about that situation?

6. Go back and adjust the numbers in list 4 to more comfortable amounts. Then go back to item 5, and suppose you don't lose all of it but just 50 percent, or 30 percent, or whatever. Find some numbers that work for you. Review and repeat the allocation of numbers until you find some mix of things that gives a sane answer for item 5.

Adjust the numbers in list 6 until you can answer the questions with reasonable confidence that you are not kidding yourself. It may require that some of the at-risk numbers go to zero. If that's the case, you've learned something important about your willingness to take risks. Also, in the exercise above, you have to think about what kind of investor you are going to be. How much is really at risk? If you only buy short-term and intermediate-term government bonds, or the Pimco Low Duration Bonds Mutual Fund, the greatest risk of loss might be just 10 percent. On the other hand, if you expect to plunge into buying stock in new, small companies with little or no current profits, then your risk might be 100 percent of the amount invested. You should think about what kind of investor you want to be, plan your dollar value of at-risk capital so you can live with the risk of loss, and then manage your investments to maintain that risk level. It would be equally false and self-defeating to plan for low-risk and then buy high-risk investments, or to plan for high-risk and then buy only low-risk investments such as U.S. savings bonds. Figuring out your plan is a matter of personal choice and personal analysis. You have to do the hard part yourself.

Now you have an indication of how much money you might put into risk-oriented investing, and how much risk you might accept when choosing your investments. If you ended up saying your acceptable level of risk of loss was 10 percent, then you should not be putting much money into the stock market. If you said that your acceptable level of risk was 50 percent, then you would have a lot more leeway in choosing investments.

Now, are you still with me? You may continue reading, but do not invest any money until you have dealt with the preceding difficult questions. You, or you and your family, must accept the personal responsibility for coming up with the answers to these questions.

The Small Investor and Family Face Loss

Your Investments Are Only As Good As Your Information

Your personal investment strategy is going to be strongly influenced by how much work you leave to a professional and how much you do yourself. Most of this chapter will focus on finding information to make your own investment decisions, but even if you choose to use a hired investment advisor, money manager, or broker, you still have some work to do.

What kinds of decisions? Certainly to buy, or sell, or hold any particular investment. But there are many others, such as whether to use a certain mutual fund company or change brokers, or simply whether you are satisfied with the results you have had in the past year. The rest of this chapter will help you find and use information to make these decisions.

What Kinds of Investment Tools to Use

This section introduces some tools for different jobs. These are only some of the tools of the professional money managers. They have more experience, more resources, and more money to manage than we do, so they use more and fancier tools. These are the tools and sources that we can use. They are effective, generally cheap, and readily available. They can work well if you are willing to apply your own time and decision-making skills.

Newspapers

Look in your own locality for good investments. Some of the best opportunities may be close at hand and not yet discovered by many professionals. Your local newspaper probably carries news of local business interest. Read it—someday it will tell you about a small local business that is growing rapidly. See whether it is a publicly traded company; if so, you can buy stock in it. If you can get a local business newspaper, that's even better because it can provide more information that is focused on your investment needs. My greatest investment success came after I read in my local business newspaper about an initial public stock offering for a new research-and-development firm in the area.

You should also try to keep current on national and international business activity. That doesn't mean learning everything; remember rule #2—don't try to obtain perfect information—but do try to maintain general knowledge of the major stories and trends in business. The best way to do that is to read the major national newspapers. Make a habit of reading the business sections of newspapers such as the *Washington Post, New York Times, Miami Herald, Los Angeles Times, USA Today,* or comparable major papers that devote significant resources to business coverage every day.

And, first and foremost, read the *Wall Street Journal (WSJ)*. The single most valuable thing that you can do to improve your knowledge, power, and effectiveness as an investor is to read the *WSJ*, preferably every day, or at least a few times a week. It offers the best combination of business and general news with analysis of the links between different trends, and it is written in such a way that everyone can follow most of the stories.

Another excellent and widely circulated investment newspaper is the *Investor's Business Daily (IBD)*. It may be a good choice for you, but I don't read it more than a few times a month. Why not, you ask? Well, basically, no one can read everything. We can't even read all of the very good stuff. There is just too much of it. *IBD* is certainly a fine paper, and it may turn out to be your favorite, but it's not for me. The distinction is that *IBD* focuses on markets and market action and stock prices, whereas the *WSJ* offers a broader perspective of business activity and trends. For me, the view and the perspective of the *WSJ* are more useful. By all means, try both and see which works best for you.

For another view that is focused on markets and finance and investing opportunities, try *Barron's,* a weekly newspaper published by Dow Jones. It usually hits the local newsstand on Saturdays, or you can subscribe for home delivery. It requires a little more background to read, and it may be only for investors who are fairly serious about doing their own analysis, but for filling that need it is excellent.

IBD will give you a free ten-day subscription. Take them up on it; it's a real bargain. See their website at *www.investors.com* or their ads in *Barron's* and the *WSJ* or on CNBC.

Magazines

Almost every general circulation magazine will carry the occasional article on investing: *Time, Ladies Home Journal*—any of them. I can't judge their value; I don't read them. But you should look at the magazines that are focused on business, money, finance, or investing. There are a lot of them, and everyone has their favorites. Among the excellent choices are *Forbes, Fortune, Smart Money, Business Week,* and many more. How shall you sort through them to find something worthwhile? Aha! Again that demon, personal choice. Go to the library or bookstore and sample some of them a few times. After a while you will find one or two of which the writing and logic seem to suit your needs and interests. Then think about how much time and energy you will put into financial reading and research. Do you want to give the time, energy, and money to subscribe to a weekly or monthly business magazine? How many magazines do you have coming in now that go largely unread?

There is a distinction between the value of general reading and in-depth research. If you decide to learn about a certain area of business in greater detail, then you can consult the many specialized magazines that focus on almost any business you can imagine. I used to subscribe to the *Oil and Gas Journal* because I was making an effort to be informed about those kinds of investments, although many people would find it a bit tedious. There are special journals about the business of tires and rubber, restaurants, food processing, hog raising, whatever you want. If you have good experience in a particular business and consider making investments in that area, it might be worthwhile to subscribe to that trade journal. Your library or a local business could help you identify it.

Suppose, for example, that you have some knowledge about the automobile business. You might decide to make that an area of invest-ing specialization where you choose and buy individual stocks. It might then be worthwhile for you to read the *NADA AutoExec* magazine (online at *www.aemag.com*).

Investment Newsletters

Investment newsletters are usually small monthly publications that focus on news and opinions of current financial markets. They present the authors' opinions and analysis and perhaps some specific buy or sell recommendations. A small sample of these might include *The Blue Chip Investor, Dow Theory Forecasts, The Cabot Market Letter, The California Technology Stock Letter,* and *Grant's Interest Rate Observer.* There are a lot of others. The cost of a year's subscription may be $100 to $500. So what do you do? These folks offer a lot of advice. Some of them offer good writing and interesting market analysis. It may or may not be worth the cost and your time.

How to decide? Well, your library probably carries a few, and per-haps some of your friends subscribe to one or two. Sometimes the larger financial newspapers or magazines will carry advertisements offering a free sample of one issue of an investment newsletter. Even if they don't advertise the free sample, many of them will give you a free sample if you call and ask. Figure out for yourself whether you under-stand what the author is saying. Does it appear to be logical and clear?

You can get help with this from a specialized publication called *The Hulbert Guide to Financial Newsletters.* The *Hulbert Guide* rates the value and quality of a lot of investment newsletters. It is excellent, and your library may have a copy. If they don't, then check the nearest university library or their website at *www.hulbertdigest.com.* They will offer one thing free—a list of investment newsletters along with telephone numbers and websites for many of them. You can go to the individual newsletters' websites, where many of them will offer a free issue or two for you to review.

No one can forecast what value you should get from one of these newsletters. They offer a lot of advice ranging from the very specific, "buy Coca-Cola, sell Ford," to the very vague, "be cautious."

Some of the investment newsletters are particularly offensive, presenting opinions that are simpleminded. For example, many of them rely on such "advice" as "The technology area may be putting in a significant near-term top," or "The Dow Jones Industrial Average could pull back to the 4,500 area if it fails to finish at a new high next week." Well, what does that mean? "May be putting in a near-term top"? "Could pull back to 4,500 if . . ."? Those kinds of statements are so vague that they are of no value to anyone. Nonetheless, some of those newsletters make interesting reading; just approach them with a critical eye. None of them come with any guarantee. I rarely study investment newsletters, because their sources and analysis are usually too vague, and also because there are numerous other publications that give a better payback for my time and attention, such as *Barron's.* But some of the newsletters may have value for general market education, and some may offer a path to profit if you follow their specific recommendations. They're a mixed bag.

As a special case, *Grant's Interest Rate Observer* is certainly of value for general education. It is expensive and not elementary. But if you want some serious facts and opinions about the economy and the market, *Grant's* is one place to get them. Check your library for *Grant's.*

There is another class of periodicals that serve the investment community and include the most famous publications in the field. These are larger and more comprehensive than the investment newsletters mentioned above. In this class you should consider, among others:

The Value Line Investment Survey
The Value Line Mutual Funds Survey
Morningstar Mutual Fund Reports
Standard and Poor's Outlook
Standard and Poor's Bond Guide
Standard and Poor's Stock Guide

These publications offer in-depth research, analysis, and historical data on many companies or mutual funds. They typically cost $300 to $600 per year. If you decide to use those publications, and if you are influenced by their recommendations, remember that the writers do not know you, your current financial situation, or how much risk you're willing to accept. You have to weigh all of your personal factors against the recommendations in the survey. We will come back to these sources again when we deal with buying and selling stocks or mutual funds.

The analysts and editors at Value Line, Morningstar, and Standard & Poor's do not know you or your current investments or your risk tolerance. They are not telling you what to buy and sell. They only present useful data and opinions, to help you make your own decisions.

Computers and Online Services

In this section, I'll give you some ideas about the possible uses and limitations of computer methods of investing. Keep in mind that software and online providers change pretty fast.

No computer system has ever been built that is good enough to do your thinking for you. No software program has ever been developed that is good enough to take responsibility for your money. The essential skills are analysis, judgment, decisiveness, and nerve. The computer doesn't do those things.

But computers are good for what they can do. The areas where they might help the small investor include the following:

1. Collecting information about a company or the entire market,
2. Seeing other people's opinions about specific investments,
3. Doing analysis that requires a lot of calculations or graphing,

The Tool Doesn't Do Your Thinking for You

4. Tracking and analyzing your investments.
5. Keeping up on recent news on your investments.

The first question is what kind of computer, Macintosh or Windows-compatible PC. If your main need for the computer is something other than investing, then let that guide your purchase decision. For the investor, the most important aspect of computer performance is Internet access. If your computer purchase is primarily driven by investment needs, simply make sure the seller knows that and helps you maximize that access.

There are several useful software applications available that help with investing (in reading any of the financial newspapers or magazines mentioned in this book, you cannot avoid the advertisements for such software). However, almost everything that is available in the software is also available on the Internet, without the extra software. For instance, a news retrieval service provides up-to-the-minute news on companies (or markets) that you want to follow. By dialing into the news agency's computers you can search for stories on particular firms and make copies of any that interest you.

Most brokerage firms give their clients Internet access to track their investments, make trades, and do research. They may also provide some sort of a window into a major news retrieval service such as the Dow Jones Service. The ease of use and depth of information of those Internet services vary widely among various brokers.

Value Line and Morningstar have websites that give access to their systems and reports. They also include specific screens and controls to help you through searches and analysis of large amounts of data. Some of their web services are free and some require that you pay a fee.

The Internet has great potential to help you or to waste your time. It is easy to find all manner of information, opinions, data, reports, misinformation, and anything else you might imagine. It is somewhat more difficult to separate the wheat from the chaff. General services sites, such as Yahoo!, Quicken, or America Online, provide financial-interest group bulletin boards where you can eavesdrop on discussions or present your own questions and thoughts. You will see all kinds of replies from people who may or may not know anything. My experience has been that maybe once in a long while you might see something that looks worthwhile. There are many self-proclaimed "experts" out there in cyberspace who will offer advice and try to sell their services. Just give them as much credence and caution as you would anybody else who was trying to influence your spending. Just because someone can set up a nice-looking web page doesn't mean they ever made a nickel in the markets.

Try the Internet. You'll learn something. There are many valuable websites that can help you with your education and decisions. There are also many that are a complete waste of time. And the mix is changing every day. You have to keep busy and keep looking if you want to get the best online sources. At the end of this chapter, you'll find a list of recommended sites that are very useful and well established.

We are accustomed to accepting information that comes through a computer as reliable. It is obvious that the Internet carries the promise of giving us up-to-date information to support sound decision making. However, I check several Internet sites every day for new financial information, and every time I find examples of old data that is no longer accurate and is potentially damaging to an investor.

The curse and the shame of the Internet are that so much information out there is incorrect and out of date.

It is often impossible to tell when information was first published. It is also often impossible to tell when information was last checked or updated.

Even some of the best sites listed at the chapter's end may show old and wildly incorrect financial data days, weeks, and even months after new reporting was available.

So what? Does that mean do not use the Internet? No. It means be aware of the problem. Use the Internet as much as you have time for, but whenever you get ready to put your money on the line with a buy or sell decision, check on whether your information is accurate and up to date. If you read a company's earnings report online, then you could call them to see if they have published a new quarterly report recently. Try to see if the website shows when the information was current. You could check two different sites to see if they are all reporting the same price, earnings, sales, and yield data for the company. Be skeptical, and be careful.

The computer is a tool. It will not do your thinking for you. The Internet is a resource. No one out there cares whether you succeed or fail.

Brokers

The full-service brokerage firms can be excellent sources of research information. Major financial services firms like Merrill Lynch or Fahnestock keep large research staffs and produce research on individual companies, bonds, segments of industry, and general business trends. These reports are generally available free to their customers, one reason why it may be reasonable to pay their fees. You cannot assume that their research is always right, and no one guarantees a profit, but at least you can read the opinions of professionals who have done their best to evaluate the chances. In addition to their research reports, or as part of them, they also give buy, sell, or hold recommendations for individual stocks or mutual funds. For each company that they follow closely, they will have an opinion on the attractiveness of the stock. It is also helpful to keep in mind that some of the new opinions published by the brokerage research departments will influence stock prices. The research doesn't have to be right—just the fact that Merrill Lynch publishes an opinion may be enough to have an effect on prices.

Books

Most bookstores have a section containing books on investing or personal money management, and your library should have a wide selection of these books as well. It is certainly a matter of choice just how much time you will spend reading books. Also, some of them contain inaccurate or less-than-useful information, and some others are out of date. That said, do not reject a book just because it was published a few years ago—or more. Some older titles may still be valuable or interesting, and there's absolutely nothing wrong with having a lot of background information. Just be a critical reader and select for yourself what is helpful to you. Start with the recommended further reading in this book to ensure that you don't waste your time initially. Then you can branch out to try the rest of the offerings on your library or bookstore shelves.

Television

There is something of value for the small investor on television. The leading financial news network, CNBC (available in most areas as a cable offering), offers full-time, all-day tracking and reporting of markets and major business stories, while the markets are open. In the evenings and weekends it offers various business commentary or roundtable discussions. Public television also offers several shows such as the *Nightly Business Report* and *Wall Street Week*. CNN and C-Span carry regular or irregular business news and analysis programs that may offer valuable commentary or education. All of those have something of value at different times. If you sample them a few times, you will probably find one or two shows that suit your areas of interest and experience.

If you do watch financial news programs on TV, then sooner or later you will run into the Buy-Sell-or-Hold quacks. These quacks are people with some kind of credentials in the business who recommend specific stocks to buy, sell, or hold. The trouble is they offer blanket recommendations without consideration of your specific needs. A stock that looks like a buy for them might be too risky for you. A stock that looks like a sell to them might enrich your portfolio diversification. Do your best to ignore them. These people know nothing about you or your financial needs. They make as much sense as doctors who recommend drugs on the air to millions of unknown, gullible patients. Whatever the person advises may be based on good analysis, but for every one who says, "Buy now," there are other, equally credible analysts who say, "Don't buy now." In fact, virtually every stock is a buy for some investors who understand its prospects of risk and potential reward, and every stock is a sell for some investors who have good reason to want the cash back more than they need to hold that stock.

Brokerage Seminars

Pretty soon, if you haven't already, you will be invited by some financial firm to a free dinner and seminar. Before you attend one, refer to the "No, thank you" exercise at the beginning of chapter 4. Most brokerage firms offer occasional free seminars on different investment topics. These can be interesting and worthwhile. They will probably be advertised in the local paper from time to time if you have a brokerage office in your town. Just be forewarned that the brokerage has its own reason for offering the seminar, and they will get your name and telephone number if you attend. Be prepared for the ensuing sales pitch. That said, however, I have found some of them to be interesting and educational.

Other Sources

In chapter 6, we will discuss in greater detail the sources of information that are available for bond investors; in chapters 7 and 8, we'll look at information sources for stock pickers; and in chapters 9 and 10, we'll look at information sources for mutual fund investors.

The Bottom Line on Individual Work and Commitment

1. You have to make some decisions for yourself.
2. You have to face the real risk of losing 30 to 50 percent of the money you invest, but you can manage the risk if you work at it.
3. Your decisions cannot be any better than your sources of information and your judgment.
4. There are a great many good sources of information available, and you should take a look at a wide range of them before making any important decisions.

There are many more complex and sophisticated sources of investment information out there that we have not mentioned. You will start to bump into them if you begin with the ones we have mentioned. Then you'll discover what works for you. The great, rich, free sources of information are your best friends: the Internet and your local library.

Recommended Further Reading and Internet Resources

Wall Street Journal

New York Times business section

Barron's

Investor's Business Daily

Financial News Network, CNBC

Morningstar Mutual Funds Reports

The Value Line Investment Survey

Kiplinger's Financial Digest

2002 Mutual Funds Fact Book, published by the Investment Company Institute, available online at *www.ici.org*

The following Internet resources are all excellent and educational . . . *and* they all occasionally show old, misleading, or incorrect information. This list is just to get you started:

www.bondresources.com

www.bondsonline.com

www.savingsbonds.com

www.smartmoney.com

www400.fidelity.com

www.quicken.com/investments

moneycentral.msn.com/investor

cbs.marketwatch.com

biz.yahoo.com

Chapter 6

Bonds and Bond Markets:

The Standards of Comparison and Value

Small investors need to know:

- What is a bond?

- Can I make money in bonds? Can I lose money in bonds?

- How do bond markets affect stock markets?

- What are Treasury bonds, state bonds, corporate bonds, municipal bonds?

- What is "fixed income" investing?

Do Me a Favor—Read This Chapter, Please

Even if you don't care about bonds and expect to never buy a bond, read this chapter anyway. Any time that you consider spending or investing money, think about the other choices you have. Think about other things that you might do with that money. Most other smart investors will be examining their choices. To protect yourself and make sure you understand what is going on, you should, too. It is important to remember, when you are considering investing in the stock markets or mutual funds, that bonds offer additional reasonable choices.

If the bond market becomes very appealing, other investors may sell stocks and move the money into bonds. That event would cause a loss of value in stocks and might have a great effect on your investments—one reason for not ignoring bond markets, even if you don't want to buy bonds.

Here is another reason. To evaluate the quality and appeal of whatever you might consider buying, you should compare it against some standard. Bonds generally offer a good standard for comparison. Their values and fluctuations are published in newspapers every day. Many of them are relatively stable and predictable. Therefore, the bond markets offer important information, even if you don't deal in bonds. One thing you will soon learn is that the fair market value of stocks is forever debated. Reasonable, intelligent analysts may have widely differing opinions on the fair price of one stock or another. However, because of the pricing and market mechanisms, people seldom have much dispute about the fair value of a Treasury bond or a high-quality corporate bond.

What Is a Bond?

A bond is a security that conveys a promise of two things:

1. that the bond holder will receive a regular schedule of interest payments, and
2. that the bond holder will receive the face value at the maturity date.

Bond

A bond represents a loan. More specifically, it is the promise to repay the loan on a given schedule, with a specified interest rate. If you lend $1,000 to Uncle Jack, and he gives you a signed note promising to repay $10 on the first of each month for five years and then repay the original $1,000, his promissory note is a bond of sorts (except it is not registered with the SEC).

In the financial markets, a bond usually represents a loan to the United States, or to a state or county, a government agency, or a corporation. The promise to repay becomes a financial instrument (a security) that may then be sold and resold to various investors. Each investor in turn acquires the right to enjoy the promised payments and interest rate until the bond matures or is sold to another investor.

For example, suppose that Mega Oil Corporation had wanted to raise cash in 1996. They might have created a bond, selling for $1,000, promising to pay $85 annually until 2016, and at that date repay the $1,000. Since $85 is 8.5 percent of the face value of $1,000, these bonds are named the Mega Oil 8.5s for 2016.

The Small Investor Comes to the Aid of His Country

Face
Value

The $1,000 price is called the *face value*. If Mega Oil needed to raise $20 million, they would have issued 20,000 bonds for $1,000 each. You could have invested $10,000 by buying ten of those bonds. Let us suppose that you did that. You could hold the bonds for twenty years. They would pay you 8.5 percent interest for each bond for each year. The value of each year's payment (for each bond) would be $85, which is 8.5 percent of $1,000. However, bonds are usually written so that interest is paid twice a year, so each bond would pay half of $85 twice each year. For your ten bonds, you would receive $425.00 twice yearly for twenty years. After twenty years, after the final interest payment, you would have collected a total of $17,000 (20 x 10 x $85) in interest, and then you would have received your original $10,000 back, too.

To summarize the example:

Initial investment: 10 x $1,000 = $10,000   You pay to Mega Oil at first

Income from interest: 20 x 10 x $85 = $17,000   Mega Oil pays to you over 20 years

Return of principal: $10,000   Mega Oil pays to you at the end

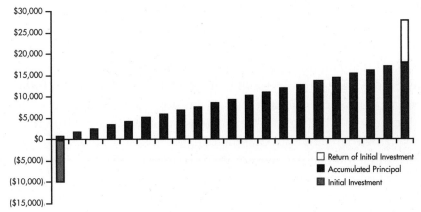

20 Years with Ten 8.5 Percent Bonds

Notice also that you have another chance of making a profit: while that $17,000 of income is coming to you at the rate of $425 every six months, you have an opportunity to reinvest it to make more. Now let's look at some real-life examples, a couple of bonds that we'll be returning to throughout this chapter, to illustrate a variety of important points.

In early 1994 Sears Roebuck and Co. (symbol S) issued a new bond to pay 6.25 percent until January 2004. The person who bought that bond new could plan to hold the bond for ten years, collect $31.25 every six months, and at the end of the term receive the $1,000 face value on maturity. This is the "Sears 6.25, '04" bond.

About the same time, Wal-Mart (symbol WMT) issued a new 7.5 percent bond of their own. The Wal-Mart 7.5 percent bond was to mature in May 2004. If you had bought it in May 1994, you would have ten years of collecting $37.50 every six months and receive $1,000 on maturity. This is the "Wal-Mart 7.5, '04" bond.

Characteristics of Bonds

Many people think of bond investing as staid and conservative. You might have an image of retired people or insurance companies leaving all of their money in bonds. This is true of many bonds. However, bonds can also be wild and exciting, gaining or losing large amounts of their value in a hurry. Bonds can be fairly simple to evaluate or extremely complex. The simplest bonds might be U.S. Treasury notes with no special provisions attached. The wildest bonds might be those issued by an Argentine corporation with a call provision, and a convertible option, where the issuer is in default. That would probably be a bond that you might buy for pennies on the face-value dollar and expect to have large probability of losing it all, or you might have a shot at huge profits if the company improves. ("Call" and "convertible" are peculiar contract provisions attached to a bond that are explained later in this chapter.) *Default* means a failure to pay a promised interest payment or final repayment. The Sears and Walmart bonds are examples of generally safe and secure investments that one might very well plan to simply hold until 2004 for the interest payments and return of face value.

Default

The best bonds are relatively safe and predictable if you just buy and hold, while some others offer extreme speculation. You can blend a mixture of risk and reward prospects to suit your personal investment strategy by selecting the right mix of bonds. Or you can stay out of the bond markets but use them as a standard of performance for other investments.

I have several standards of performance for my risk-oriented investing, and one of them is directly tied to the bond market. I feel that if my annual profit in the markets stays ahead of the total return I could have earned on long-term Treasury bonds, that is one indication of moderate success. I also use several other standards, but the bond markets offer one that is easy to check.

The Language of Bonds

If you are buying lumber at Home Depot, you should know the difference between a landscape timber and a slat. Well, in the bond markets, you need to learn a special language too. It's not difficult. We'll start here with the basics. In the example above, each individual loan (bond) had a loan amount, or face value, of $1,000. Most of the bonds that we will deal with have a face value of $1,000. Occasionally you may see a government bond or some other bond for a higher face value, but $1,000 is by far the most common.

Coupon
Rate

The interest rate specified for the bond, 8.5 percent in the Mega Oil loan agreement, is the *coupon rate* (or *coupon yield*). After a bond is issued, the coupon rate is fixed and unchanging for that bond. Coupon rates for different bonds vary depending on current interest rates in the economy at the time the bond is issued, as well as the length of the loan and the credit worthiness of the borrower. It is easy to find bonds still in circulation that have coupon rates of interest between 5 percent and 20 percent. The loan interest rate is called a coupon rate because in prior years the lenders actually got paper certificates for the bonds, and each certificate had the proper number of tear-off coupons that could be turned in to receive the interest. Such coupons are no longer used except for old bonds. These days the records are kept in computers that hold numbered accounts. The year of the final payment on the bond is the *maturity* of the bond. The time left to maturity is the *term*.

Maturity

The Sears and Wal-Mart bonds mentioned above have face values of $1,000 and maturities of 2004. The Sears coupon yield is 6.25 percent and the Walmart coupon yield is 7.5 percent. They both have maturity of 2004, but in 2001 their terms would be three years.

Term

So a bond is this: a loan agreement for a specified term, with a specified maturity date and fixed schedule of interest payments. It promises a constant series of interest payments and it promises to repay the original principal, usually $1,000 after the last interest payment.

When you buy a bond, you lend the issuer money and you get in return:

1. a loan agreement for a specified term, with a promise of a constant series of interest payments, and
2. a promise of repayment of the original loan principal at maturity.

Changing Prices and Yields

Bonds may be bought and sold another way, too. You might buy a bond in 2002 that matures in 2010, planning to hold it until final maturity. In 2007 it might happen that you need that money back. If for whatever reason you decide to sell your bonds before maturity, your broker will use bond markets where they are sold after initial issue, called the *secondary* (or *resale*) *market*. Current market conditions may affect the prices and rates of bonds in the resale markets.

Secondary Market

To fully understand price and yield changes requires more mathematics than you want to read in this book. In the real world, thousands of computers do the math, and all the brokers and newspapers have access to the information every day. Don't worry about the math, just follow the money.

It may happen someday that you decide to sell a 6 percent bond that you bought new for $1,000. The buyer gets almost the same product that you bought. You sell her the continuing interest payments and also the promised return of capital at the end of the term. But market rates and the time until maturity have changed, and you have already received some of the interest payments. Because of those changes, the buyer may offer you a lower price; suppose it is $950 and you accept that price. Let us see what has happened to the yield: the bond with a 6 percent coupon pays $60 per year, but for the new owner that is 6.32 percent (60 ÷ 950 = .0632) of her price.

Current Yield

At the time of sale, 6.32 percent is the new yield on the bond. That yield calculated relative to the current price is called the *current yield*. Current yield equals the annual interest payment divided by the current price. So the lesson here is that current yield changes with market conditions and the price of the bond, while the coupon yield is always the same fixed value.

Price also changes. In the above example, the price changed to $950. If you decide to sell your bond, the market will pay what it will pay. You cannot influence the price. The original $1,000 is guaranteed as the par value, or repayment value, but bond price is the current market value of the bond. It can be less than or greater than face value. Now let's look at some specific examples.

In September 2001, the Sears bond had a market value of $1,022 for a current yield of 6.1 percent (that's 62.50 ÷ 1,022). The Wal-Mart bond sold for $1,077 with a current yield of 6.96 percent. From early 1994 to September 2001, the prices of both bonds went above face value. There are many factors that affect the price and yield of bonds, and we will look at them in the rest of this chapter.

Market Rate

A *market rate* is the interest rate for which people are willing to buy and sell a particular bond on a particular day. The bond market is a free and open market, and people can ask or offer whatever prices they choose, but the price at which the bond is actually sold is the market price: a price at which both the buyers and the sellers of the bond agree. That market price determines the current yield for the bond. For example, one day people may be willing to buy and sell U.S. Treasury bonds that mature in 2007 and give current yield of 6.96 percent. However, no one is willing to buy for a higher price that would give current yield any lower than that, and no one is willing to sell for a lower price that would give current yield higher than that. Thus 6.96 percent becomes the market rate for that bond on that day. A New York City revenue bond might require 8.33 percent to bring about agreement among buyers and sellers, so that would be its market rate on that day. Each of those rates is likely to change the next day, and in fact it will probably change during the day as people hear news or rumors about the economy. Each of those rates is likely to change substantially over a period of months or years, as inflation or business conditions change.

Market Rate

Fixed-Income Investing

You often hear people talk about bond investing as *"fixed-income" investing.* The term is misleading. A bond is a fixed-income security, because the stated (coupon) payment is fixed for the life of the bond. But, as we have seen, that does not guarantee any fixed investment profit or loss if you buy or sell bonds that have not reached maturity. This term is particularly misleading when used to describe mutual funds that buy and sell bonds. If you buy shares in a bond mutual fund, that is called fixed-income investing, but you get no fixed income. You don't have any guarantee or expectation of anything being fixed. What you expect to get is the annual (and variable) profit of the fund, which is constantly buying and selling bonds that have not reached maturity. "Fixed-income" investing is a term that refers to the bonds themselves. It does not mean anything about the results for bond traders or mutual funds.

Fixed-Income Investing

Ratings

How will you protect yourself from the risk of market erosion of prices? You can't do anything after you buy the bond except sell it, because the markets are not responsive to your needs. However, you can do a few things about choosing the characteristics of the bonds you buy.

The risk of your investment is largely dependent on the quality and strength of the corporation or government that issued it. It is difficult for us to evaluate the relative strength of different organizations on our own. Two prominent commercial services do that for us, Standard & Poor's and Moody's. They regularly publish their most up-to-date opinions about the strength and quality of corporations, their stocks and bonds, and municipal bonds. The *bond ratings* scales are:

Bond Ratings

S&P (best to worst): AAA, AA, A, BBB, BB, B, CCC, CC, C, D;

Moody's (best to worst): Aaa, Aa, A, Baa, Ba, B, Caa, Ca, C.

These grades are broken down into finer points, too. S&P sometimes adds + or − to a grade to indicate that it's a little on the strong or weak side of that grade. Moody adds a 1, 2, or 3 to the grade. For example, Moody's scale includes: A1, which ranks better than A2, which is better than A3, which is better than Baa1, and so on. The corresponding ratings on each scale are nearly equivalent; that is, AAA is nearly the same as Aaa, and BB+ is nearly the same as Ba1.

Investment Grade

The first four grades (AAA to BBB, or Aaa to Baa) on each scale are considered *investment grade,* which means they are considered to be suitable for conservative investors and to have less fluctuation and risk. But remember that even an AAA bond is still subject to market value fluctuation. The ratings agencies assess the strength of the issuing corporation or government and the likelihood that the issuer will both pay the interest and repay the face value. They do not try to promise you anything about the future market value of the bond.

Junk Bonds

The grades below BBB or Baa are sometimes referred to as *junk bonds.* The pejorative term refers to the attendant risk. But notice that there are relative levels of junk. A bond rated Ba1 is only slightly riskier than a Baa3 bond, and it may carry nearly the same yield. By comparison, a C bond is much riskier than an AA bond and must offer a much higher compensating yield. As you can see, it is not enough to simply evaluate bonds as either junk or investment grade.

The Sears 6.25 percent '04 bond was initially rated BBB when it was new, but it had been upgraded to A– by September 2001. The Wal-Mart 7.5 percent '04 bond was issued new with an AA rating, and it has held that rating. The Sears bond is investment grade, but the Wal-Mart bond is very-high-quality investment grade. The ratings of those two bonds and thousands of others are constantly reviewed and revised by the ratings agencies when necessary.

Types of Bonds

Each individual bond is relatively straightforward, but the bond markets as a whole are extremely complex. There are many different types of bonds with different characteristics. Some bonds, even U.S. Treasury bonds, come with special conditions. The bond is a contract for repayment, and as such it may come with various contractual conditions. For example, some U.S. Treasury bonds come with a provision that says, in effect, "Maybe this bond matures in 2006 and maybe it matures in 2012; we'll let you know later." You should get a higher yield for a bond like that. Some bonds come with a provision that says, "This bond matures in 2013; however, if it is convenient for us, we may pay it off in 2007." That last one is a *call provision,* which means that the issuer can call (buy back) the bond before maturity.

Call Provision

These conditions may have a strong effect on the value and safety of your bond. If you buy a bond through a broker, ask him to explain to you any special conditions attached. If you buy mutual funds that buy bonds, make sure you know what kinds of bonds and what kinds of conditions fall within the charters of your funds (read the prospectus!).

U.S. Treasury Bonds

These are the safest bonds in the world, but they are not entirely risk free. While the U.S. government has never defaulted on its debt, there is the risk that you might someday have to sell under unfavorable market conditions. These bonds are given the strongest guarantee in the world and have the added advantage that the interest is exempt from your state and local taxes. If you sell the bond for a profit or a loss, this will affect your taxes and must be reported.

Notes and Bills

Treasury bonds are called *notes* when issued for two to ten years, and they are called *bills* when issued for one year or less. You have the opportunity to buy bonds directly from the Treasury if you want to avoid brokers. Look in the government pages of your telephone book to find a number for Treasury direct sales, call your regional Federal Reserve office, or see *www.publicdebt.treas.gov/bpd/bpdhome.htm.*

One distinction of U.S. Treasury savings bonds is that there is no secondary market for these. They are restricted to the buy-and-hold investor unless you return them to the Treasury.

Municipal Bonds

Municipal Bonds

Municipal bonds are bonds issued by local or state governments or by agencies acting under the auspices of a local government. Municipal bond yield is exempt from federal taxes and the taxes of the home state of the issuing agency. Because of the tax savings, they will normally have a lower yield than taxable bonds of equal quality do. Municipal bonds are usually found to have high-quality ratings, because we don't expect to see governments defaulting on debt. However, there is no uniform rule on this. Some cities, counties, and local government agencies do have low credit ratings. Even as I write today, there is a hospital revenue bond issued by Prince Georges County, Maryland, maturing in July 2024, that is rated B3 by Moody's. *(Revenue*

Revenue Bond

bond means that the revenues of the issuing agency or government are pledged to pay the bond.) The county government has not pledged its full faith and credit to that bond. You could buy that bond for about 68 cents on the dollar of face value and get about 8.6 percent return on the investment for twenty years. That might be a good investment for someone who wanted continuing income and was willing to face the risk of default.

The world of municipal bond investing is changing. There was a long-standing presumption that governments don't default on their bonds, and for many years people looked to municipal bonds as a source of stability and safety for the small investor. Then along came Orange County, California, apparently prepared to wreck all of that. To make a sad story short, the government of Orange County borrowed money from a lot of people and other agencies who were looking for a safe haven, then gambled with the money. The gamblers lost, big time! The other innocents stood to lose also unless Orange County would step up to their responsibility to stand behind their bonds. They did not. So a lot of people lost a lot of money. If you grew up thinking that municipal bonds were always a safe haven, wake up and look around.

Municipal bonds are also available with extra insurance on repayment. The issuing agency may buy insurance for their bonds from private companies set up for just that purpose. You pay a little more for that kind of protection. The value of this insurance is highly debatable. None of the private insurers have ever been tested in a real crunch situation, such as a massive default of local governments. Since the state and local governments are also rated by the ratings agencies, it might be wise to confine your bonds business to governments and agencies that have AA or AAA ratings, and forgo the insurance.

Corporate Bonds

A *corporate bond* is issued by any private business. The business must get approval and registration from the Securities and Exchange Commission to take the bonds to market, but basically they are just going out to get a loan for $10, $20, $80 million, or whatever. Corporate bonds usually pay higher yield than government or municipal bonds because they presumably carry higher risk and the earnings are fully taxable.

Corporate
Bond

Secured Debt

One way for a corporation to make their bonds more attractive is to provide some security beyond the company's promise to repay.

Bonds are called *secured* if the company pledges the value of some of its other assets in case of default. For example, a company that owns a lot of land and buildings might pledge that in case of default on the bonds, they would sell the land to repay the bond holders. Your home mortgage represents a secured debt. In the event that you fail to pay the mortgage, you promise to let the creditor sell the house to recoup their money. Other bonds that have no such asset-based protection are called *debentures*. Sometimes a large corporation might issue some

Secured
Bonds

Debentures

secured debt and some debentures. The debentures should pay higher yield than would the secured debt.

A company might promise that it would use its assets to pay off two bond issues, but it would pay one issue before paying the other. The bond that is first in rights of payment would be called *senior debt,* and the bond that was second or third in rights of payment would be called *subordinated.* A second mortgage on your home would be a subordinated secured debt.

If the company had issued all three types of bonds, with the same maturity dates, then the senior secured debt would be the safest and pay the lowest yield, the subordinate secured debt would pay more, and the debentures would pay even more.

Convertibles

Some corporate bonds, called *convertible bonds,* carry a provision that under specified conditions they may be traded for the company's common stock; in other words, they can be converted to stock.

What's the point? The conversion privilege is worth something to the buyers because it provides an extra choice of how to realize a

There Are Many Ways to Go, Including the Convertible

profit. Therefore the corporation can offer a lower yield on the bonds. Bond buyers may or may not find that appealing, depending on the terms of the conversion offer and the attractiveness of the company's stock.

Here is an example: say Wellfarm Corporation issues a $1,000 bond with maturity in 2018 and coupon at 10 percent. In order to make it more appealing to buyers, they offer a conversion option with the bond that says, "Anytime after January 1, 2008, this bond may be converted into forty-five shares of our common stock." Suppose the common stock is currently trading at $18.50 and for the past two years has varied in price from $16 to $23.75.

If you held the bond until sometime after January 1, 2008, you would have four choices:

1. Keep the bond; collect $100 annual interest, and plan to collect $1,000 face value at maturity.
2. Sell the bond—the conversion option would enhance the value and selling price of the bond.
3. Convert to the stock and keep the stock.
4. Convert to the stock and sell the stock.

The value of the stock may have gone up or down. If the stock is high, say, $34, your conversion stock would be worth $1,530 (45 x $34). That might look attractive, and it would be reflected in the current market value of your bond. The bond would have a $1,530 straight conversion value plus some value relative to the yield and the continuing conversion choice. Its price would certainly be above $1,600, and you might sell it in the bond market.

If, however, the stock has fallen, say, to $17, the forty-five shares would just be worth $765, which is not attractive. However, you would still hold a bond, which still had the value of a normal bond investment, and you could hold it for its bond value. The final analysis is that if the company were sound, you would never have less than the value of a normal bond, and if the stock were strong, you might have a great deal more.

Zero Coupon Bonds

Zero Coupon Bond

Remember my Florida Federal bonds? A *zero coupon bond* (I'll call it a zero) is a bond that does not pay its interest every six months; instead it saves up everything and pays it all at once at the maturity. U.S. savings bonds are like zeroes in many ways. There are tax complications with zeroes that you or your tax advisor must consider when you plan to buy them, when you sell them, and even while you are holding them. Your friends at the IRS call zeroes "Original Issue Discount Instruments," and they will be happy to give you a copy of their publication #1212, which lists a lot of them. That publication serves three purposes: to help you identify zero coupon bonds that are in the markets; to help your broker understand his or her responsibilities in reporting the investments to the IRS; and to explain tax rules related to them. Do not buy zero coupon bonds until you have read and understand the tax requirements.

All right, so how do they work? Let me show you the growth of an investment that is earning compound annual interest of 7 percent. Just for the sake of argument let us begin with $508.35. Look at the value if the interest is kept in the investment and compounds each year.

| after 1 year | $543.93 | after 5 years | $712.99 |
| after 3 years | $622.75 | after 10 years | $1,000.00 |

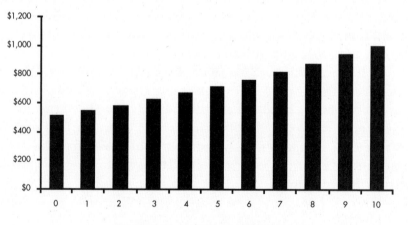

7 Percent Annual Compound Growth

What if they sold you a $1,000 face value bond for $508.35, but never paid you any interest? That's the zero coupon, and after ten years they would repay the bond face value of $1,000. Then you would have the results of 7 percent compound growth over the ten years. The price that you paid is $491.65 less than the face value, and that is the original issue discount.

A zero coupon bond is a bond that is sold at a discount on the face value and does not pay any interest before maturity. It will be priced to yield a specified equivalent compound interest on maturity.

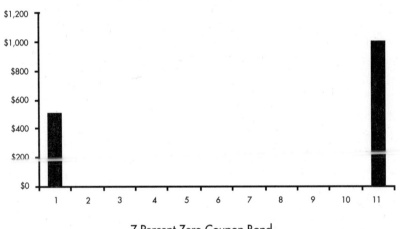

7 Percent Zero Coupon Bond

Call Provisions

Sometimes, when companies or governments issue new bonds, they want to build in an extra feature to protect themselves from the long-term repayment requirement. For example, ABCD Goldfish Corporation may want to sell bonds when the market rate is 13 percent. That would force them to pay 13 percent interest for the life of the bonds. If after a few years market rates fell to 8 percent, ABCD might like to issue new bonds at 8 percent, repay the old 13 percent bonds, and save a bundle on interest payments. They cannot do that unless you agree to sell back your 13 percent bonds.

A call provision is a contractual provision added to the bond contract that says you will agree to give up the bond after some specified date, at the company's request. If the bond has a call provision, you may have to give up your right to collect the 13 percent coupon sooner than the bond's maturity. You should get paid extra for that. ABCD might offer to pay you more than the $1,000 face value when they call the bond, or they might offer some other inducement like higher yield or convertibility to make the bond attractive to you. At any rate, you need to know if there is a call provision, and remember it was put in there for the pleasure of the bond issuer, not you.

Junk Bonds

These are bonds that carry a higher-than-average risk of default and usually bring along a higher yield. They are bonds with Standard & Poor's or Moody's ratings below BBB or Baa. A bond rated BB (or Ba) is only slightly junky and may pay only a slightly higher yield than a BBB. A bond rated C is very junky and should pay a very high current yield before you buy it. It has a high risk of loss.

Investment Grade Bonds

These are bonds for which the repayment of interest and principal is more secure than the average bond, according to the opinions of Moody's and Standard & Poor's. They are rated Aaa to Baa, or AAA to BBB. Investment grade does not mean that you should simply buy it and forget it. In August 2000, Enron Corporation had bonds outstanding of well over $3 billion total face value; right, *B* for billion. Those bonds were rated BBB+ (investment grade) in August 2000. In September 2001, they were still rated BBB+. By December 2001, Enron was bankrupt, and the bonds were selling among speculators at near 20 cents on the dollar and were likely worth less than that. The stockholders got nothing, zero, zilch. The bond holders could at least expect to collect some of the residual value of the company's assets.

Adjustable-Rate Bonds

Remember that I told you that bonds promise to pay a fixed yield throughout their lifetimes until maturity? Well, when it comes to adjustable-rate bonds, maybe they do and maybe they don't. Sometimes it is convenient to bond issuers and bond buyers to have the interest vary over the years. These are not the most common types of bonds, but they have their uses. Some bonds are written with a clause that says the yield will be one rate for the first few years and a different rate thereafter. In particular if the buyers think the issuer has a risk of defaulting or failing in business, then the buyers might demand that the bonds pay 6 percent for the first five years and then, if they are not paid off, pay a higher rate for the last five years. Any conditions you might imagine can be written into the bond contracts according to the needs and imagination of the corporation's financial officer.

Another case of interest is the U.S. Treasury Inflation Adjusted Security, also called *Treasury inflation-protected securities,* or TIPS. These are bonds sold by the Treasury that have a fixed yield plus an additional adjustable yield. The idea is that when inflation goes up, the adjustable yield will be increased in order to protect the bond holder from the effects of inflation.

TIPS

Buy and Hold

That's all folks! If you have read carefully to this point then you know more about bonds than 99 percent of your friends. If you have a good broker who can select them for you, and if you will simply buy and hold the bonds until maturity, then it doesn't need to be much more complicated than that.

Risk and Reward

So far we have explored a simple view of bonds that should be appealing to many of us. But in risk-oriented investing, bonds can be a great deal more exciting and complex than the first view we discussed above. Suppose that you and your broker do a lot of very fine analysis and you find and buy a batch of bonds that mature in the year 2009 and pay you $4,000 twice yearly in interest. So you're happy and content to hold them to maturity and plan on the steady income stream. But what if you have an unanticipated emergency need for the money? (This is a risk not only with bonds, but one that comes with every investment.) You are not worried, because there are efficient markets for bonds that will allow your broker to sell your bonds for a fair price.

The risk is that the fair price might be less than what you paid. If the bonds each cost $1,000 when you bought them at issue, the current market value might be considerably lower or higher depending on market conditions. There is a chance that you might sell your bonds for more than you paid, but for now let's look at the risk side: you might lose money on the sale.

Here's how that might work. Say you have 100 bonds with coupon rate of 8 percent maturing in 2009. That makes $4,000 every six months, right (8 percent of $1,000 = $80 per year for each of the 100 bonds)? The risk lies in current fair-market interest rates. If the markets, in their collective wisdom, have settled on a current interest rate of 10 percent, they will not buy your bonds that only pay 8 percent unless you adjust the price to meet the buyer's needs. In this case the bond market computers may have agreed that an 8 percent coupon bond maturing in 2009 is currently worth only $900. That leaves you looking at $100 per bond in loss. We will return to these bonds in a moment.

Here is the deal: If you buy good bonds and hold them to maturity, you may reasonably expect to collect the interest and return of principal that you bought in the bond. However, if for any reason you have

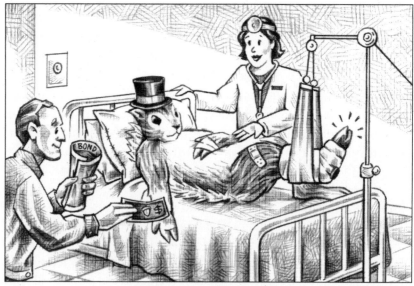

The Small Investor Is Laid Up

to sell the bonds before maturity, you are at the mercy of market conditions in setting the price of your bonds.

> The primary risk in bond markets is that market conditions may change the value of your bonds, and you may lose money if you have to sell them.

Here are some prices of $1,000 face-value bonds listed in a recent issue of *Barron's*:

- A 5.5 percent U.S. Treasury bond that matures in 2008 may be sold for $1,075; the current yield is 5.1 percent.
- A 6.75 percent AT&T bond that matures in 2004 may be sold for $1040; the current yield is 6.49 percent.
- A 6 percent Boston Celtics bond that matures in 2038 may be sold for $550; the current yield is 10.9 percent.
- A 7.5 percent IBM bond that matures in 2013 may be sold for $1,125; the current yield is 6.67 percent.

Each of them has face value of $1,000. Why are these prices adjusted up or down from face value? That is a more complex question which we can only begin to deal with in this book, but the first lesson is that bond prices do change with market conditions, and you have no control over those conditions.

You should value bonds in two ways when you consider buying or selling:

1. The bond gives a yield or a continuing stream of income.
2. The bond is a marketable security.

Both valuation methods are useful, and different investors may have good reasons for placing greater emphasis on one over the other. You should always consider both of them, although one or the other may seem more important to you at various times.

There are two views we use to judge yield: current yield, which means the coupon payment divided by the current price; and *yield to maturity*, which is the current yield with an adjustment to compensate for the gain or loss in the principal. There are two factors that affect the value of a bond: the interest payments and the final repayment. Current yield only considers the income payments relative to current

Yield to Maturity

price. Yield to maturity includes that, plus the gain or loss of principal when the face value is repaid. If the bond was priced below face value, then the yield to maturity would be greater than the current yield because of the gain on final repayment. If the bond was priced above face value, then the yield to maturity would be less than the current yield because of the loss on final repayment.

It is easy to calculate current yield. It is more complex to calculate the yield to maturity. Don't worry about the math. You don't need to do it. You can simply check in the *Wall Street Journal* or ask your broker for a bond's yield to maturity. Several websites (listed at chapter end) also offer that information.

Now let us return to the matter of those bonds that you sold for $900 each. For each bond, the buyer gets the $80 each year of interest plus some growth of principal (her or she will get back $1,000 at maturity), which is an extra $100 in profit. The current yield describes the interest payments according to the current price. In our example, the current yield becomes $80 ÷ $900 = 8.89 percent. As I stated earlier, current yield is the coupon payment divided by the current price. That may be either higher or lower than the original coupon yield.

Examples of current yield:

- If a 4 percent bond sells for $800, on that date the current yield is $40 ÷ $800 = 5 percent.
- If a 10 percent bond sells for $700, on that date the current yield is $100 ÷ $700 = 14.28 percent.
- If a 14 percent bond sells for $1,250, on that date the current yield is $140 ÷ $1,250 = 11.20 percent.

Each of the current yields will change whenever the price changes.

Now let's discuss another factor that can affect the bond. For our earlier example where the 8 percent bond sold for $900, the yield to maturity would depend on the date of sale. If the sale date were exactly eleven years before maturity, the yield to maturity would be 9.4 percent. This should seem reasonable, because the buyer gets the stream of payments worth 8.89 percent (current yield), plus $100 extra growth in principal with the $1,000 return of face value.

If the date of sale were exactly five years before maturity, the yield to maturity would be 10.5 percent. The extra $100 gained in five years is better return than $100 gained in 11 years.

When you need information on a bond, you easily can calculate the current yield yourself. For the yield to maturity, ask your broker or look in a financial publication. As an investor who is comparing choices, you should evaluate bonds by considering both current yield and yield to maturity.

Bond Listings

When you look in a newspaper, you may see bonds listed in several ways. The first trick is to be able to identify the bond. For Treasury bonds, the listing will show something like this:

Bond description	Bid	Asked	Yield
10¾ Aug 05	132:29	133:01	6.23

This means a 10.75 percent bond that matures in August 2005. The :29 and the :01 represent 32nds of a dollar, so 132:29 means $132 and $^{29}/_{32}$, or $132.906; the 133:01 means $133 and $^{1}/_{32}$, or $133.031. The bid and asked values are per $100 of par value. So for a $1,000 par bond, you would multiply by ten. The yield shown here is yield to maturity. What is the payment stream? It is 10.75 percent of $1,000, which is $107.50, paid twice each year as $53.75 for each $1,000 bond.

Now we can read the above example line: a U.S. Treasury bond with 10.75 percent coupon rate is maturing in August 2005 with buyers bidding $1,329.06 for $1,000 face value, and sellers are asking $1,330.31 for $1,000 face value. At the asking price, the yield to maturity would be 6.23 percent. The final payment at maturity is $1,000 per bond.

Here is another:

Bond description	Bid	Asked	Yield
7½ Nov 24	121:05	121:06	5.81

This is a 7.5 percent Treasury bond maturing in November 2024. Buyers offer $1,210.156 and sellers want $1,210.188 per $1,000 face value. At the asking price the yield to maturity is 5.81 percent. The payment stream is $75.00 yearly, paid every six months as $37.50. Again, the final payment at maturity is $1,000 per bond. Notice that the bid and asked prices are very close. For high-quality bonds, there is usually not much disagreement about the value of the bonds.

One distinguishing feature of bills (treasury bonds issued for one year or less) is that they are sold in $10,000 or larger face value. Usually the bills will be listed separately, and the notes will be listed with the longer bonds, but denoted with "(n)".

Corporate bonds are listed differently. They should show at least the following:

Name & coupon	Current yield	High	Low	Last
Cleveland Electric 8⅜ 12	9.0	94	91¾	93½

This is a Cleveland Electric Corporation bond with 8⅜ percent coupon, maturing in 2012. On the previous day, it traded between $91.75 (low) and $94.00 (high) and the last transaction was at $93.50, per $100 value. The final price on a $1,000 face bond was $935.00. The current yield is 9 percent. If you want to know the yield to maturity, call your broker or check the *Wall Street Journal.* If the sale was exactly fifteen years before maturity, and you paid the 93½ price, the yield to maturity would be about 9.1 percent. What is the income stream? 8.375 percent of $1,000 per year, paid half every six months. That is $41.875 every six months for each bond you hold. The final payment will be the $1,000 face value.

It would be instructive to pick up a newspaper and read a few of these listings, just to get the flavor of it. Be aware that no newspaper is likely to list all of the bonds in the market, since there are just too many of them. Small newspapers may not show any bond market information. Prominent papers will list the recently traded bonds. If you want to know about others, call your broker or head to your library's business reference section.

If you have read and understood everything up to this point, you have a basic working knowledge of bonds. Many people go through life and even invest in financial markets without ever knowing as much as you know now. The rest of the story is one complication after another. Financial people are clever and creative, so they invent all kinds of bonds, as well as things that act like bonds, bonds that can be changed into something else, and on and on. Each of those special cases would require its own separate study if you intended to invest with them. In the remainder of the chapter, we will look at some of the risks and special cases and mention how they differ and how they might be useful to you.

> You now have much more knowledge about bonds than most folks, but it is still only a little knowledge in the grand scheme of things. A little knowledge is a dangerous thing. So be careful out there!

Risk-Oriented Investing

Bond yield rates are set in more or less open market negotiations between all of the bond issuers and all of the bond sellers or buyers. This whole process is just like the way things operate in most businesses, in that everything is negotiable. When Big Soap Corporation decides that they need to raise $50 million through a bond offering, they talk to their preferred financial services company and negotiate an offering of the bonds. They discuss yield, term, maturity, seniority, and special conditions on the bond. But if they want to stretch out the term to repayment, they will have to raise the coupon yield. Repayment after a longer rather than shorter amount of time is a greater risk for investors, so the investment markets demand higher interest payments for longer-term bonds. Generally speaking, if all other factors are equal, an issuer's short-term bond should pay a lower yield than the same issuer's long-term bond.

Variations in Price: The Risks

When you buy a normal bond, you buy a promise of two things: the twice-yearly payment of interest and the final repayment of principal. Anything that threatens either of those is a threat to your investment success. Furthermore, you might want to sell the bond sometime to raise money. The sale price that you receive may be higher or lower than what you paid or what you would like.

So the threats to your bond investment are these:

1. The issuing company or agency might fail to make the regular interest payments.
2. The issuing company or agency might not repay the principal at maturity.
3. If you sell before maturity, the bond markets may dictate a lower price than what you paid.

What could threaten the payment of interest or repayment of face value? The issuer of the bonds might go bankrupt. Or they might decide that they are in such trouble that they just won't pay the interest. Or they might pay other people or other bonds before they pay yours and not have enough left to pay you. If the company is short on funds, they will pay their suppliers before they pay the bonds' interest, and they may have a clause that says some senior bonds get paid before subordinate bonds. Subordinated debt will be paid when they get to it, if there is money left to pay.

How can you protect yourself from these risks? You or your broker can evaluate the financial strength of the company and check the bond conditions to discover whether there is any senior debt. You might consider the long-term history of the firm's payment of their debts. You might consider overall economic conditions and the health of their markets. If the company relies on selling record-player turntables, this will not generate a reliable stream of income, so maybe you shouldn't buy their bonds. Fortunately, there is a lot of help available to you. Standard & Poor's and Moody's regularly evaluate companies and bonds to predict which are safe and which are not so safe. It is almost guaranteed that they can evaluate companies and bonds better than you or your broker can, so you should rely heavily on those ratings. The main point here is that if the rating for a bond is high (A or better), then you should feel quite safe that the interest payments will be met.

However, a high rating is not a guarantee that the company will meet its obligations to you. Penn-Central was one of the largest and strongest firms in the United States in 1969 and had the highest ratings from several rating agencies. Shortly thereafter, they went bankrupt after giving almost no warning to anyone, and the bond holders were severely hurt. Nearly up until the time of the bankruptcy, in June 1970, their bonds were rated as investment grade by the major ratings agencies. This is not intended as a criticism of Standard & Poor's or Moody's. They do a lot of fine work and give us a lot of valuable information. But when they publish their ratings, they do not guarantee the safety of your investments. They publish opinions, not gospel.

Bond Values and Interest Rates

To study risk further, we need to look at the relationships of bond values and market interest rates. For example, consider an AA (very safe) corporate bond that pays 8 percent (coupon yield) and matures in 2010. The original value was par, or $1,000. Suppose you want to sell it when there are six years left to maturity and at that time the prevailing market interest rate is 12 percent for AA-rated corporate bonds maturing in 2010. The market would impose a fair price on your bond so that the yield to maturity would become 12 percent. That means that your bond must sell for $836 to make a fair market. You would have lost $164 in the value of the bond due to the rise in market interest rates from 8 percent to 12 percent.

> When market rates rise, the price of preexisting bonds will fall, and when market rates fall, the price of preexisting bonds will rise.

Let's look at the same bond, but change the scenario. Suppose the current market rates on new AA bonds maturing in 2010 actually fell to 6 percent on the day of your sale. The market would impose a new price on your bond to make it pay 6 percent yield to maturity. However, in this case, your bond is paying more than new bonds coming to market are paying, so the market will bid up to higher prices to get your bond—$1,098. What did you get? You have had the interest payments for however long you held it, and you got more than your original investment back. What did the buyer get? The buyer got a higher coupon than new bonds, which would be only $60 per year. The buyer's current yield is 7.29 percent, and he is looking at a loss of principal since the bond will still only return $1,000 at maturity. The coupon payments plus the projected loss on the principal combine to give the buyer a yield to maturity of 6 percent.

Here is the essential characteristic of bond price fluctuation, which you must remember if you want to trade bonds or follow bond market action. Prices of existing (previously sold) bonds move opposite to current interest rates. How much do they move? Usually bonds with longer times left to maturity will react to interest movements more than will bonds with shorter times left to maturity. Here are some examples of bond prices and yields in August 2000 and September 2001.

For each bond, the prices and current yields have changed since they were new. The changes are due to ratings, prevailing market interest rates, time left to maturity, and the public's changing attitudes about each corporation and about buying bonds.

A *Lucent Corporation 6.5 percent debenture maturing in 2028* was rated A and priced at 89.375 per 100, in August 2000. That made the yield to maturity 7.41 percent. In September 2001, the rating had been lowered substantially to BB−, the price was 70.00, and yield to maturity became 9.62 percent.

A *Boeing Corporation 8.1 percent debenture maturing in 2006* was rated AA− in August 2000. The price was 103.125, and the yield to maturity was 7.44 percent. In September 2001, the rating was still AA−, the price rose to 112.67, and yield to maturity fell to 5.65 percent. In this case the price change was due primarily to two factors: Prevailing market rates had fallen, so the rate on this bond had to fall, too; and the bond was a year closer to maturity, so it was slightly safer than it had been before.

A *Standard Commercial Corporation convertible senior note, 8.875 percent, maturing in 2005* was rated BB− in August 2000. The price was 85.00 and the yield to maturity was 13.05 percent (that's a lot of yield). In September 2001, the rating was up to BB, the price was up to 98.12, and the yield to maturity was down to 9.36 percent.

These three bonds were affected differently by changing market factors. The most important prevailing influence was the market rate, which went down. Generally that would cause all three bond prices to rise, to lower their yields to maturity. However, the Lucent bond price fell dramatically, due to the lower rating and a loss of confidence in the company. The Boeing bond price behaved about as was expected. The Standard Commercial bond price was up more than would be predicted by the market rate changes. In the Standard Commercial case, the other strong influence was a substantial rise in the price of the stock. That made the conversion privilege worth much more than it had been before. All of those bonds maintained a constant $1,000 face value to be repaid on maturity.

In September 2001 the Sears 6.25 percent '04 had a price of $1,022, which gave a yield to maturity of 5.52 percent. The Wal-Mart 7.5 percent '04 had a price of $1,120, for yield to maturity of 5.89 percent.

Each of those bonds might appeal to different investors for different reasons, depending on whether the investor wanted current yield or yield to maturity.

Normally, earlier maturity bonds should pay lower yield to maturity than will later-maturity bonds of the same quality and terms. Whenever new earlier-maturity bonds pay more yield to maturity than new later-maturity bonds, the term used is *interest rate inversion*. For example, we would have an interest rate inversion if the government issued a new ninety-day Treasury bill that paid 5 percent, and a new ten-year Treasury note paying 4.7 percent.

Interest
Rate
Inversion

There are many theories and opinions about what inversion means and how investors should behave when an interest-rate inversion occurs. For our purposes, it is sufficient to say that an inversion is a warning that something strange is going on in the financial markets, and that we should be alert to more danger and change than normal.

The Costs of Buying Bonds

The fees that you may pay for buying and selling bonds vary a great deal and depend on the number of bonds you are buying. Here are

So You See, It's Very Simple

some rates that you would have paid with four well-known brokerage firms in late 2001:

- Broker 1 charges a flat rate of $7 for each bond you buy.
- Broker 2 charges a fee of $30 plus $4 per bond.
- Broker 3 charges $8 dollars per bond for the first ten, plus $2 per bond for each one after ten.
- Broker 4 will charge a flat rate of $75 for purchase of any number of bonds.

For a purchase of five bonds, the charges would be $35, $50, $40, and $75 for brokers 1, 2, 3, and 4 respectively. For a purchase of twenty bonds, the charges would be $140, $110, $100, and $75 for brokers 1, 2, 3, and 4 respectively. Brokers all make their own fee structures, and these get changed frequently. The examples above are typical. If you plan to buy only a few bonds, the fees may be considerable in comparison to your potential profits.

Bond Funds

There are mutual funds that buy and sell bonds, and there are many different ways in which they select them or mix them with other investments. If you plan to spend less than about $10,000, it is probably smarter and more economical to buy bond mutual funds rather than individual bonds (see chapters 9 and 10).

There are distinctions between buying individual bonds and buying bond mutual funds. When you buy the bonds, you control or choose your own rates and terms, subject to market availability. When you buy the mutual fund, there is no maturity date; you simply turn your money over to the investment company and they make whatever they can through working the bond markets. With individual bond purchases, you make your own decision about when to buy or sell. With the funds, you simply leave the money in the fund for however long you like. If you buy and hold a bond, there are no capital gains to be taxed until you choose to sell. With the fund, there may be capital gains or losses each year.

Interest Rates

Here is the truth. If you don't believe anything else I have said, believe this:

No one can consistently, accurately, and reliably predict interest rates.

Anyone who says she can do this is not your friend. Therefore, no one can accurately guarantee the market prices of your bonds. This leads to some lessons about investing:

1. The only guarantee you get is the guarantee of the government or the corporation that issued the bonds, which in turn is no stronger than that organization's finances and assets.
2. Planning for safety in bonds means planning to buy and hold.
3. Diversify by purchasing bonds that will behave differently in different situations and have varying maturity dates.

Planning to buy and hold does not mean that you have to actually hold them. It just means that you buy bonds that you think you would feel comfortable holding to maturity. Remember our earlier discussion about plans? You need a plan so that you know where you're going, but you don't have to stick with the plan if surprises develop later on. In January 1995 I bought some 7.25 percent U.S. Treasury bonds maturing in May 2016 at the price of 92.4062. Current yield was 7.8 percent. I expected to hold those babies to maturity. But luckily, pretty soon market interest rates started to fall and by July I could get 104 for each bond. Current yield was down to 7 percent. I decided to grab the profits and run. I made 3.9 percent on one interest payment plus 12.55 percent profit on the sale, so the whole thing paid over 16 percent in six months, a tidy return.

Recommended Further Reading and Internet Resources

Nichols's book is outstanding, and I would recommend it as your next resource to study if you really want to be up on bonds. It has ten times as much information as I had room for in this chapter and is quite well written.

Moody's Bond Record, in your library, frequently updated.

Moody's Credit Survey, in your library, frequently updated.

Nichols, Donald. *The Personal Investor's Complete Book of Bonds.* Chicago: Dearborn Financial Publishers, 1990.

Renberg, Werner. *All about Bond Funds.* New York: John Wiley, 1995.

Standard & Poor's Bond Guide, in your library, updated monthly.

The website to get all the news on U.S. Treasury bonds is *www.publicdebt. treas.gov/bpd/bpdhome.htm.*

Smart Money has a nice Web feature to let you see the variations in current yield and yield to maturity when the price and maturity of bonds vary: *www.smartmoney.com/onebond/index.cfm?story=bondcalculator.*

See *www.bondsonline.com* or *www.standardandpoors.com* for general research on bonds.

Chapter 7

Investing in Stocks

Small investors need to know:

- What is a stock market?

- Why do people go to that kind of market?

- Can everybody win? Does everybody win?

- Can I win?

- Do stock prices go up and down?

The Stock Markets . . . at Last!

All right! Here you are. You put up with the stuff about risk and diversification and bonds and the other sermons, but what you really wanted to learn about was the stock markets, wasn't it? Don't apologize, that's the most fun for me to write about, too. However, if you skipped any of the preceding chapters to rush into this one, shame on you! You are asking for trouble, and I will not be accountable for your subsequent grief.

Studying the stock markets will help you to be a better investor, even if you never intend to buy individual stocks. If, for example, you plan to put all of your investing money into mutual funds, you still want to be able to make some judgments about selecting stock funds, diversifying amongst them, and judging risk.

What should you reasonably expect from the stock markets? It's hard to say. I don't know you or whether you will work hard or buy large or small stocks, or utilities or software companies. But we can make a guess that you will get average results. That's what averages are for, after all.

The Small Investor in the Market

For a representation of some kind of average performance, we can look at the most widely reported index, the Dow Jones Industrial Average (Dow). It represents the stock price performance of thirty of the best-known companies with some of the most widely traded stocks. The thirty include GE, IBM, GM, AT&T, McDonalds, and twenty-five other such stalwarts of American business. The Dow is not a true mathematical average of stock prices, but an adjusted average that has been revised many times over its 100-year life. The numbers are widely reported and regarded by many as an indicator of overall stock market performance. The numbers do not reflect performance of all stocks in general, but they are probably a fair indicator of the stock prices of the largest and best-known American firms. Such large, established firms are collectively labeled *blue chips*.

Blue Chips

The Long View

The long-term view of investment in American stock markets is pretty good. That means that if you choose to invest in American companies by buying stocks and holding them for a long time, you can have a strong expectation that you will make good profits.

How good? We don't exactly know, but the evidence is that the profit would probably be better than from other long-term investments. How long is long term? Again, nobody can say exactly how long you'll need to hold onto any given stock or stocks. Statistically, the long run means however long it takes. If you don't have that long, you'll have to compromise. A fair view of the long run for many investors might be placed at five to twenty years. Many folks need to think about getting their money back after five to ten years.

Below, I am going to illustrate what kinds of results you may have gotten if you (the collective average you) had invested in the stocks at their average price each year, held them for five years and sold at average prices in the fifth year, or held for ten years and sold at average prices in the tenth year. It is unlikely that anyone would ever do that, or ever want to, but the calculations indicate something about the average results for the average investor who chooses to invest principally in large and well-known American firms on the New York Stock Exchange.

If, on the other hand, you invest in different kinds of stocks, say, only small companies, the Dow doesn't say much about the results you might expect. There are other published indexes that address the results and history of other groups of stocks: the Dow Jones Utilities Average; the S&P 500, which is based on 500 of the biggest firms rather than just 30; the *Wilshire 5000,* which covers most of the stocks publicly traded on American stock exchanges; and the *Russell 2000,* which includes 2,000 small company stocks.

Wilshire 5000

Russell 2000

The chart below shows what the results would have been if a person had invested $1,000 in the Dow Jones Industrial stocks on fifteen occasions during the past seventy-five years. It shows the results of buying at average prices each year and selling at the average prices during the year of sale. (The following chart contains some rounding.)

Year of investment	Value of investment if held for		Compound annual rate of return	
	5 years	10 years	5 years	10 years
1927	$370*	$950	–18%	–0.6%
1936	750	1,190	–6%	2%
1940	1,330	1,600	5%	5%
1945	1,270	2,610	5%	10%
1948	1,530	2,730	9%	11%
1952	1,760	2,360	12%	9%
1959	1,320	1,390	6%	3%
1963	1,270	1,290	5%	3%
1968	1,002	910	0.4%	–1%
1973	890	1,290	–2%	3%
1979	1,400	2,970	7%	12%
1982	2,560	3,780	21%	14%
1988	1,710	4,190	11%	15%
1993	2,420	*	19%	*
1996	1,780	*	12%	*

*Data not yet available

These numbers do not include brokers' commissions, which would drag down the profits a little, and they do not include dividends that the companies pay to shareholders. Dividend payments would increase the rate of return each year by anywhere from 2 percent to 7 percent. For example, during the years 1988 to 1993, the dividend yield on the Dow stocks averaged close to 3 percent. You might reasonably claim that the five-year compound rate of return for the 1988 purchase should be figured as 11 percent + 3 percent = 14 percent. But since the first table only addresses gains or losses on the stock prices, let's look at the effect of adding in dividend payments.

Dividends are handled differently by different investors, and for a variety of good reasons. Some folks want to take the money and use it for living or playing expenses. Others reinvest the dividends in more stock. Any calculation of the effect of dividends has to make some assumption about what the investor does with the dividends. Over a period as short as five years this can make a big difference. For the example below, I am going to assume that the investor takes the dividend as regular income and spends it.

Now the profits over the five-year and ten-year periods are increased. They look like this:

Year of investment	From price of stock held for		From price of stock and dividends received	
	5 years	10 years	5 years	10 years
1927	−63%	−6%	−34%	40%
1936	−25%	19%	2%	68%
1940	33%	60%	58%	114%
1945	27%	161%	56%	216%
1948	53%	173%	83%	225%
1952	76%	136%	100%	177%
1959	32%	39%	49%	74%
1963	27%	29%	43%	65%
1968	2%	-9%	21%	36%
1973	−11%	29%	16%	83%
1979	40%	197%	67%	242%
1982	156%	278%	177%	316%
1988	71%	319%	87%	360%
1993	142%	*	175%	*
1996	78%	*	92%	*

*Data not yet available

If Uncle Jack bought $1,000 worth of Dow stocks in 1959 and sold it in 1969 at average prices, he would have sold for $1,390. The gain from the stock prices would have been $390; the gain from stock prices plus dividends would have been $740.

Is there any lesson in this? Well, it's like beauty—it's in the eyes of the beholder—but let me suggest a lesson:

> On average, the patient, long-term investor who buys stock in large American corporations may expect to earn some profits on the stock values plus 2 percent to 6 percent each year from the dividends. And that is not bad.

Stock Markets

Corporations often want to sell stock to raise money. Investors want to buy stocks because historical trends indicate that is a good way to build a nest egg. However, the investors will not buy much stock unless they are certain that there is a dependable way to get their money back. Therefore, the corporations can't sell much stock unless a dependable *secondary (trading) market* exists. Luckily, through the collective genius of democracy and capitalism, such markets, or exchanges, do exist. In spirit, they're like a farmers' market. Somebody provides a space for the sellers and buyers to come together and charges a fee for the convenience. But in *stock exchanges,* the sellers and the buyers are generally not acquainted and are many miles apart, so the market is a place for a bunch of middlemen to set up shop and just bring the buy requests and the sell requests together. The middlemen are brokers. In the New York Stock Exchange or American Stock Exchange, brokers pay a steep fee for the privilege of coming in to do business. A stock exchange is a professional organization of the people and firms who offer brokerage services. There are many similar organizations in every economically strong country in the world, but in the United States the largest exchanges are the New York Stock Exchange (NYSE) and the American Stock Exchange (AMEX).

One stock market is a special case. It is the *NASDAQ* (National Association of Securities Dealers Automated Quotation) System. The NASD (National Association of Securities Dealers) is one of the prominent, nongovernment securities regulatory organizations, and NASDAQ is its creature. NASDAQ is not an exchange and is not like a farmers' market. NASDAQ is a computer network, frequented by people and agencies

Secondary Market

Stock Exchange

NASDAQ

The Small Investor Is in for the Long Haul

who use the network for stock pricing and sales information. NASDAQ labors under some controversy. People used to say that small investors were ill treated by the NASDAQ. Other people may say that NASDAQ gives small investors the best deal they could expect in trading small or new companies that aren't big enough to get into the NYSE.

I have traded stocks using the NYSE, the ASE, and the NASDAQ, and I have never had any cause to doubt the efficiency or honesty of anyone handling any of my trades. Given the complexity and volume of their business, and the strains on their computer networks, it seems rather remarkable that NASDAQ can offer all the service and information they do for the large number of low-priced, thinly traded stocks that they service. If you are going to buy and sell individual stocks, don't avoid stocks just because they are traded through NASDAQ rather than the New York Stock Exchange. If you are interested in small, new companies, you may find that they are not traded on any of the major exchanges, and you have to use NASDAQ. Also some titans like Microsoft and Intel are traded on NASDAQ.

Stock markets offer a combination of excitement, risk, and roller-coaster emotional rides unlike anything else. They can set you up for life, or knock you down. They may even contribute something to your social life, particularly if you have been at a loss for conversational entrées.

So investing in stock markets offers fun and possible gains. As long as you care to bring your money, there will be people there who are eager to trade with you. If you ever quit bringing money for whatever reason, they will pitch you out and forget you. The market that loved you as a player will not provide a friend or counselor in time of need. As is the case with much of our daily toil, many want to share your success, but only a few stick around to share your failure.

Investment Clubs

An *investment club* is a legal partnership. It consists of a group of people who have agreed to share their money, knowledge, and work in investing. If you want to know the rules, methods, or how to get started, contact the National Association of Investors Corporation (877-275-6242 or *www.betterinvesting.com*). They will send you information about how clubs work, how to get started, and clubs in your area. Investment clubs generally have fairly good records. They tend to put more focus on individual stocks rather than bonds or mutual funds. If you plan to buy stocks, but don't have the experience, then find an investment club in your area or start one. It is likely that some local broker or investment advisor would be willing to offer free advice to your club, since it provides a good way for them to meet potential customers.

Investment clubs offer another avenue for diversification, too. Everybody knows something about business. But some people know more about other businesses than you do. Think about an investment club where there were six members who each had five years' experience in one of the following fields: computers, telecommunications, the grocery business, retail sales, newspapers, and raising kids. What a wealth of knowledge and experience to help you analyze products or services! They would each bring different points of view to each stock you might analyze. It is almost guaranteed that the group would make better decisions about stocks than any one of the members would individually. The group working together would certainly recognize and evaluate risks better than any individual working alone.

Investment Club

> The investments you make with an investment club will always be safer than the investments you make alone. The reason is that the group, together, will always recognize and evaluate risks better than anyone working alone.

Whether you form a club or join an existing club, look for diversity in experience, social background, and education. Don't start a club with just engineers who all work for the same employer and have worked there for years—they have all started thinking alike. Be attentive that the members share the workload. Some clubs fall into a habit of letting some dominant person do all the research and bully people into buy and sell decisions. Such clubs would offer none of the intended benefits of investment clubs. Make sure that all of the members agree on and are comfortable with the contributions level ($20 per month? $100 per month?) and the general philosophy (e.g., aggressive investing, conservative investing, stocks only, stocks and bonds). It would do more harm than good to bring someone in who shortly became unhappy about the ground rules.

If you intend to explore stocks, and if you have the small investor's usual healthy fear and suspicion, there may be nothing better for you than an investment club.

Why Stocks?

It's easy: that's where the rewards are. But it's difficult: that is also where the most work and the greatest risks are. Make no mistake about it—in the long run, common stocks on the whole will outperform every other type of investment. That's the good news. The bad news is that you probably won't just go out and buy the market's average results, and among individual stocks there will be huge variations in results. Besides, in the very long run most of us will be dead.

Does the long run do us any good? Does it do any good for the folks who held a lot of high-tech or Internet stocks in 2000 and have lost 70 percent or 80 percent or 90 percent of their money? The answer is no: those people will probably never recover from the damage done to their financial security. Did it do any good for your grandparents who bought stocks in 1927, lost badly in 1929 and 1930, and then made hardly any profits until 1946? Did the long-term upward trend of the market do any good for people who bought Wang Labs in 1983 at $30 a share, or in 1987 at $15, or in 1990 at $4? (Answer: No, Wang went bankrupt.) There are many such horror stories of stock investments that went totally rotten to an extent that the long-term trend ceases to have any consolation.

Let's Play the Market

Play the market? Let's not. If you treat this as play, you will lose your shirt.

 "Playing the market" is a phrase created by stockbrokers to make you think it's not really risky. It is risky and you play for keeps.

Let's Work the Market

We are going to get into some ideas about managing (risk-oriented) money that is allocated for (risk-oriented) investments in individual stocks.

Back in 1990, I was sitting around watching Unisys Corporation (symbol UIS on NYSE). Unisys makes computers and related products and provides all manner of services and support to people who use computer systems. Their stock had been through an awful slide, from around $40 per share in 1987 to a low of $16 in 1989, and down to $1 in 1990. They were victims of slumping mainframe sales and of the popular story going around that mainframes were dead. Nobody liked Unisys. However, I knew that they had an active and productive service organization that stood to gain from the current trends in large companies toward outsourcing computer support. I figured that the service organization was a good bet and the death of mainframes was a hoax, and that somehow this company ought to be worth more than $1 a share. Pretty smart thinking, right? But I didn't buy. I couldn't ever make up my mind and get off the dime. At the end of 1991 UIS was $6 a share, and at the end of 1992 it was $10. Since then it has been as low as $6 and as high as $40.

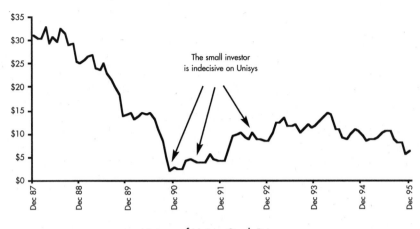

History of Unisys Stock Price

Lessons learned: First, it is possible to make good money in stocks, but there will come a point when somebody has to make a decision. It is not always easy. Second, there are some people, probably even some big-time money managers, who bought Unisys at around $30 a share in 1988 and finally sold low. Tough luck. It's a jungle out there.

Several years ago, in the early 1990s, Ford was clunking along (their stock, that is, not their cars). The country was in an economic slowdown and car sales were not holding up. The popular wisdom was that Americans could not build and sell cars in a competitive worldwide market. So there sits Ford. In 1989 the price of Ford stock had hovered around $50 a share and revenues had been $96 billion. In 1990 the price had fallen as low as $25 per share, and revenues were up a little. In 1991 the price bounced between $25 and $38, but it ended the year on a pronounced downslide. The revenues were off to about $88 billion. Net profits of the firm went from $4.3 billion profit in 1989 to $860 million profit in 1990 to $2.3 billion loss in 1991. Things looked pretty bad for Ford.

I took a look at it and had my own opinions. I thought they built good cars, and the company had a history of commitment to a strong dividend, which was interrupted by a dividend reduction in 1991. I liked it. So I bought Ford in November 1991 at $27.50. I sold it in July 1992 at $42 and collected $1.20 per share in dividend payments along the way. Good deal, right? At the time there were any number of prominent prognosticators who were preaching against Ford. In fact, I have a signed letter from one of them telling me to sell my Ford in the fall of 1991. But I held on and made a good profit. The people who held on longer made more. I ended up two years later buying Ford again at $29, but that was after a two-for-one stock split, meaning its value was comparable to $58.

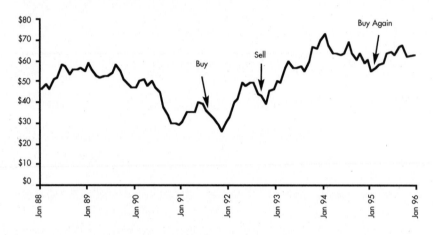

History of Ford Stock Price (presplit basis)

Lessons learned: First, it is possible to make money in stocks, but there will come a point when somebody has to make a decision. It is not always easy. Second, there are some people, probably even some big-time money managers, who passed on Ford until late in 1993 and missed the plum. There are probably some long-term investors who bought Ford at $48 in 1987 and still held it, in 2002, at a split-adjusted value below $40, so they have had a lot of grief with Ford. It requires some decisiveness to either buy or sell if you're going to take profits out of the market. Third, long-term investors in blue chip stocks do not always make profits.

You can look at the chart and make all kinds of judgments about whether I did well or not very well. However, I made decisions, I made commitments, and I made money. Good enough!

But sometimes even a blind pig can make money. In late 1992, I heard about a local company that was preparing for its initial public stock offering. I felt like writing a story, so I hustled the idea to the *Chapel Hill News* and went out to do my research on the company, Cree Research (symbol CREE on NASDAQ). I wrote a good story and learned a lot. I liked it. The initial price was $8, and by the time I finished my story it was $16, so I passed, and waited, and watched. Pretty soon it was $25, so I waited. Pretty soon it was $14, and I bought Cree at $12 in September 1993. Over the next eighteen months it really bounced around, but I liked the company and the people and I thought I partially understood their markets, so I bought more. The price bounced between $6 and $15, and I ended up making six purchases at an average price of $11. After my last buy, at $9.25, the stock went through the roof, to $20 per share. I had made plans to take some profits at $20 per share, but I changed my mind because of the strength and speed of the rally. It then increased to $25, then to $30; I sold some, just to get some money off the table. It had gotten to the point where nearly half of my total investments were in Cree, and that is just not good diversification for a small investor like me. It climbed further, to $35, then to $40. Then one day the market took an awful jolt, especially the high-tech stocks, and I decided to take some more money out. So I sold some at the market that morning and got $36.50. The stock climbed back up to $44, and the company split its stock.

Lessons learned: First, it is possible to make good money in stocks, but there will come a point when somebody has to make a decision. It is not always easy. Second, there are some people, probably even some big-time money managers, who bought Cree at $22 or $23 or $24 after the split. They might have held it for two or three years without ever seeing a profit. They might have become tired of it and sold at a big loss in late 1996 or early 1997. On the other hand, there were probably some people who bought Cree at $6 in December of 1994 and sold double the number of shares in the high twenties in late 1995. But it takes nerve and decisiveness.

Cree is an interesting case in high-risk speculation. Unlike Ford or Unisys, these guys had virtually never made a profit when I got in. The

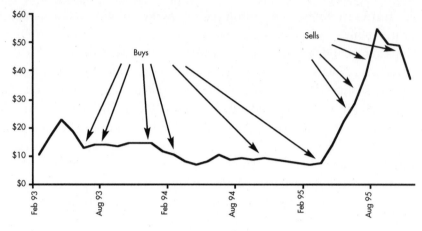

History of Cree Stock Price (presplit basis)

bet was on their potential. I put in as much as I was willing to expose to high risk, and I took money back out when I got nervous. They never paid a dividend and probably will not for a long time. Paying a dividend wouldn't make any sense. They should be putting their money into research and development, not just returning it to the shareholders. The market capitalization (the total value of the company's stock) at the time I was first buying was not over $80 million, and the staff and working digs were correspondingly small. But the potential for reward was immense. Since I sold out, in 1995, the stock has been on a wild ride. In comparable after-split-stock values, the stock has gone from around $5 to $6 in 1996 to a high of $28 in 1997, to a low around $8 in 1998, to a high of $160 in 1999, to a high of $400 in 2000, to a low around $48 in 2001. I bought some around $100 (current price comparison) in 2000 and sold a few weeks later for $70; then I bought again several times at between $12 and $18, and I'm ahead today. Don't know about tomorrow.

One of the first stocks I bought was Potomac Electric Corporation (symbol POM on NYSE) at $23.88. It was very big, safe, and secure and had an immensely strong track record on profits and dividend payments. The yield ran around 7 to 8 percent depending on price fluctuations. I planned to hold POM forever. In late 1993 all of the electric utilities were quite popular and the price had been pushed up substantially. But the dividend rate at that point fell below 6 percent. I was nervous about the overall stock market and decided to take some money out. I sold POM at $27.38 after having collected about $1.60 per share in dividends each year while I held it. Selling turned out to be a good move. It quickly went into a swoon, along with all the other electric companies and dropped to $22. I bought it again at $22 and watched it fall to $18 before coming back up to $27. All the while, on the second ride, I was collecting about 9 percent yield on my investment.

Lessons learned: First, it is possible to make money in stocks, but there will come a point when somebody has to make a decision. It is not always easy. Second, there are probably some people, probably even some mutual fund managers, who held POM all the way and failed to grab the profit when they had a chance. Even conservative, buy-and-hold, long-term small investors like us can sometimes make a profit by being decisive and taking some money back out of the markets.

Wait a minute! What did he just say? Did the author just claim to be a conservative, buy-and-hold investor? Then what about all that Cree business? Well, the truth is, the author diversifies. The author mixes up different kinds of investments. The author has more experience than you do and is willing to take more risks. But the author also keeps most of his money in conservative, long-term investments. In almost every case, when I buy a stock, bond, or fund, I have good intentions to hold that security for four years or more. But I keep my eyes open and accept that new information may change my view. I try to stay willing to admit my errors and get out, or admit my good fortune and take a profit. Think about that.

Buying and Selling

So I hope that the above examples, along with whatever you hear from the news and your friends, have convinced you that it is possible to make money and to lose money. Sometimes it may happen that two investors will buy the same stock at the same time, for the same price, and one will end up making it profitable while the other will not. This is because it's not just which stocks you pick, it's when and how you sell. More on that in chapter 8.

Even conservative, long-term, buy-and-hold small investors like us should be looking at the sell side. Because almost every stock is a winner and almost every stock is a loser. Sometimes you have to make decisions and take action if you want to be a winner.

It's a Stock Picker's World

Sometimes, especially if the major market averages are not moving much, you will hear commentators say, "It's not a stock market; it's a market of stocks." That means that you can't just safely go out and buy the average results of the entire market, instead you have to pick and choose stocks to buy in order to get ahead. But how?

The next few sections are going to review some of the popular notions about how you do this. There is no consensus on what works best. There are a thousand more or less reasonable schemes besides the ones I will mention here. This is an introduction only. I want you to get some idea of whether any of this makes sense to you. By the end of this chapter, you should have some well-formed thoughts about whether you will study some of these ideas in other books, seek other theories, or just chuck it all and avoid buying individual stocks. Find something that you will be comfortable with. I think this stuff is interesting and worth the risk; you may feel otherwise.

Investing in Common Stocks

Let's focus. Under *invest,* my big unabridged dictionary says first, "to array in the symbols of office or honor"; that's not what we want. The second definition says, "to commit money for a long period in order to earn a financial return." That's better. But see those key words *long period* and *earn.* That is not necessarily the stock trader's view, either the long period or the earning. Well, my point is that there are different views of the practice or art or work or fortune of investing, particularly investing in common stocks (the shares of ownership in the company).

You can do whatever you want, and I won't pass judgment, regardless, but let's distinguish between two popular views of stock investments. Any investor certainly wants to make a profit. Profits can be tied to two sources, the stock markets' changes in prices and the earnings of a company whose stock you own. Generally, when I invest, I look for companies that are likely to reward me on both counts. The first, stock market price changes, is in some sense an unearned reward, or at best a reward earned by your analytical insights into the stock. The second, company operational profits and dividends, is most assuredly earned by the management, labor, and sales of the company. Much of their fruits flow to the owners, the stockholders. Some investors devote all of their attention and plans to the price changes in the market. I think that is foolish, but it is certainly widely practiced and somebody makes a profit at it. Others, the more conservative investors, focus more on the earnings and dividends. They are expecting to derive profits through someone's labor, not rely on the more speculative variations in the markets.

You may sympathize with either view and manage your money accordingly, but you should consider both avenues to making profits and be aware of how other investors regard them.

Earnings and Dividends

What do you get when you buy common stock? You get to own a piece of the company. There is a document in the company's (or your broker's) records that says you are an owner. If anyone wants to buy your company, they may have to deal with you or your co-shareholders. You probably get the right to vote for the directors, but sometimes not. You also probably earn a share of the profits. The company earns some revenues from their sales, and after taking out the costs of administration, operations, and taxes, they should have a profit. That profit belongs to the shareholders and will go into two buckets: part into *dividends* paid to shareholders, and part for the company to retain to improve operations or initiate new product lines.

Dividends

Both of those two earnings buckets work for you, the shareholder. The dividend comes directly to you as cash, and the retained earnings increase the value of the company and your shares. Therefore many investors are particularly concerned about how the earnings and the dividends look compared to the price of a share.

P/E Ratio

The *price/earnings* (P/E) *ratio* is the price of one share divided by the total earnings per share. Generally speaking, lower values of the P/E ratio are considered safer than higher values. If a company's stock shows a P/E ratio of 10, each share of stock is earning ¹⁄₁₀ of its price. For each dollar you invest, the company earns 10 cents. If another company has a P/E ratio equal to 18, each share earns ¹⁄₁₈ of its price. For each dollar you put into that stock, the earnings will be about 5.6 cents.

> Stock buyers and sellers use P/E ratio numbers to estimate where prices might go. The rule of thumb: The estimated fair price for the stock = the estimated fair P/E ratio multiplied by the estimate of earnings.

Early in 2000, Emerson Electric (symbol EMR on the NYSE) was selling for $60 a share and had earnings for the prior year of $3 per share. That gave it a P/E ratio of 60 ÷ 3 = 20. Suppose some investors thought that 20 was a proper and fair P/E value for Emerson. In other words, they thought it was a fair buy at that level. If they forecast earnings for the next year of $4.50 per share, they would decide that the price could reasonably rise up to 20 x $4.50 = $90.

For those investors, this view of the P/E ratio would indicate that they should buy Emerson for $60 and have it rise next year to $90. Other investors would have other opinions, which is why the markets stay active.

At that time, General Electric had a price near $48 and earnings for the prior twelve months of $1.07 per share. That gave GE a P/E ratio of 48 ÷ 1.07 = 45. Some investors might have decided that General Electric did not deserve any higher P/E ratio than Emerson. These investors might also think that GE should have a P/E close to 20. They might think the fair price of GE should be closer to 20 x $1.07 = $21. This group would not buy GE at $48, and in fact they would sell it if they had it.

It takes all kinds to make a market. Given the price in early 2000 of $60 and earnings of $3, a sample of investors might consider these kinds of actions for Emerson:

Jake thinks that Emerson's P/E of 20 is fair, but the earnings next year will only be $4. He forecasts a future price for the stock of 20 x $4 = $80 and acts accordingly.

Sarah thinks that Emerson's P/E should be fairly set at 16 and that the earnings next year will hit $5. She forecasts a stock price of 16 x $5 = $80 for next year and acts accordingly.

Jim knows that the average P/E for all companies in similar business is 18, and he guesses that Emerson should get about the same. He figures that Emerson is really only worth 18 x $3 = $54 today.

Lynn buys Emerson stock at $62 just because she likes the products and their balance sheet. Eight months later, the forecasts become quite specific that Emerson will earn $4.20 in 2000, and the market still gives them a P/E value of 20. Then the stock price grows to 20 x $4.20 = $84.

Betty has held the stock for eight years and has no intention of selling. However, the mood of the market turns pessimistic, and all stocks get priced downward to lower P/E values. The market decides that now Emerson will only sell for 13 times the 1999 earnings of $3. So Betty's stock falls in value to 13 x $3 = $39. She is a long-term investor who sticks with Emerson because of their very strong long-term record. She is willing to wait and see what the long run will bring her.

Look at three fictional companies, ACO, BCO, and C3PO, which each earn $1 yearly in earnings per share. Suppose the market has decided, as the collective wisdom of all investors, that ACO deserves a P/E of 28, BCO deserves 19, and C3PO deserves 7. Then ACO should sell for $28 a share, BCO for $19, and C3PO for $7. If you think that the businesses and the prospects for those three were about the same, you should buy C3PO stock.

Imagine you have $5,000 to invest. In ACO that gets you 178 shares and earns $178 per year. In BCO, you could buy 263 shares and get $263 per year in company earnings. But in C3PO you would buy 714 shares and control $714 per year in earnings. If all other factors can be considered equal or nearly equal, the stock with the lower P/E ratio will earn more for the investor.

Many investors adopt a practice of not buying a stock unless the P/E ratio is below some value they consider safe. That imagined "safe" P/E value might be 8, 10, 14, the market average, or whatever they like, but it does influence the thinking and buying decisions of many.

For that reason, a low P/E ratio does help to support, or justify, the price of a stock.

The *yield ratio* (or simply, the *yield*) is the dividend per share divided by the price per share. Higher yield ratios are considered better than lower ones. Many investors adopt a practice of only buying stocks that have a yield ratio above some acceptable number. That imagined "safe" yield may be 2 percent, 4 percent, 6 percent, the market average, the yield on ten-year Treasury notes, or whatever they want, but it does influence the thinking and decisions of many investors. Therefore, a higher yield number helps to support the value of a stock and provide some assurance against loss of value.

Here are a few examples:

At the end of 2000, Bassett Furniture (BSET) had a price near $12, earnings for the past year of $1.49, and dividends for the past year of $0.80. Then at that time, the P/E ratio was 12 ÷ 1.49 = 8, and the yield ratio was 0.80 ÷ 12 = 6.7 percent.

At the end of 1991, Potomac Electric (POM) had a price of about $24, earnings of $1.87, and dividends for the year of $1.56; thus the P/E ratio was 24 ÷ 1.87 = 13, and the yield ratio was 1.56 ÷ 24 = 6.5 percent.

In 2000, Cree paid no dividends at all, so the yield was zero.

In 1999, Ford paid dividends of $1.88. At the end of that year the stock was at $46 and the yield was 1.88 ÷ 46 = 4.1 percent. In 2000 they reduced their payments to $1.80. At the end of 2000 the price was about $24, so the yield became 1.80 ÷ 24 = 7.5 percent. That yield might have seemed very attractive to some income-oriented investors, but look what happened: In 2001 the yield was just $1.20 and the price at the end of 2001 was near $20. The yield had dropped to about 6 percent, and the stock value had fallen, too.

High yield is generally thought to be desirable for many investors, but it does not guarantee safety. Do not buy stocks based on the yield alone.

An investor could use P/E and yield in comparing two companies such as Potomac Electric and Coca-Cola (Symbol KO). From this perspective, Potomac Electric may have appeared to be a sounder investment than Coca-Cola because it had much higher yield (6.5 percent compared to 1.4 percent) and much lower P/E ratio (13 compared to 28). That is only one way of looking at the stocks, and many other factors need to be considered, but it is a view that has a strong influence on some investors.

The numbers become important to investors who are only in it for the profit and who say that the most dependable sources of profit are earnings and yield. When Coca-Cola's P/E was 28, that meant that the investor would pay about $28 for each dollar of earnings. With a stock that had a P/E of 13, the investor would only pay about $13 for each dollar of earnings. Many investors feel that the stock price they pay to get a dollar of earnings should be a factor in their decisions.

If you were looking at two stocks, say KO and POM, as candidates to buy, you could do a little risk analysis, as follows. Both of these are large, profitable companies with long histories of solid earnings and dividend payments. With KO, I get lower yield now, and I expect faster growth of earnings and share price. With POM I expect larger dividends now, but more stable earnings and share price. Neither one of them will come with any guarantees.

You also want to consider the market's overall average yield or P/E ratio. Let's say that, on average, large blue chip companies were paying 4 percent yield with a P/E ratio of 15. What if the rest of investors decided that KO was no longer such a great growth vehicle? If the other investors decided that they had to have 4 percent yield or a P/E closer to the market average of 15, that might hurt the price of KO.

The stock market cannot change KO's earnings or dividends, so they change what they can, which is the price of the stock. For instance, if KO had earnings of $2 per share this year and dividend of 65 cents, in order to have a P/E of 15, they would need a price of 15 x 2 = $30. Investors might decide to reduce KO's price to $30, in order to reduce the P/E to 15. If the market decided to impose a yield of 4 percent on KO, then investors would reduce the price to $16. Both of those potential changes might be interpreted by some investors as showing a risk of lower stock price for KO.

On the other hand, if POM were to be purchased at a price of $24, with earnings of $1.87 and dividend of $1.56, and if the market were to reprice it to a P/E of 15 and yield of 4 percent, those would both tend to move the price up. The P/E of 15 would imply a price of 15 x $1.87 = $28, and the yield of 4 percent would imply a price of $39. Both of those might be interpreted as showing a possible price appreciation for POM.

This sort of analysis is summed up in the chart below:

	POM	KO
Actual market price	$24.00	$40.00
Earnings	$1.87	$2.00
Dividend	$1.56	$0.65
Current P/E	13	20
Current yield	6.5%	1.6%
Implied price if P/E has to be 15	$28.00	$30.00
Implied price if yield has to be 4%	$39.00	$16.25

This is of interest to some investors who think that in the long run many stocks will tend to be evaluated and priced equivalently. That kind of thinking would indicate that KO is overpriced and POM may be underpriced relative to other very large corporations. In the final analysis, a good stock picker has to do some figuring and thinking, and then decide whether there really is any good reason for KO to have a much higher P/E and a much lower yield than the average Dow Jones Industrial stock.

When "the market decides," it just means that most investors think that way and are acting accordingly. I do not intend to imply that the conclusions are necessarily correct, but that this is one way of looking at P/E ratios and yield ratios. Warren Buffett is one of the most respected and successful stock analysts of all time. It is instructive to read in his biography how he approached the analysis of Coca-Cola. (See Roger Lowenstein, *Buffett: The Making of an American Capitalist* [New York: Doubleday, 1996]). Buffet is a value-oriented investor, which means he is particularly attentive to the kinds of financial measurements represented by P/E and yield. But he is also a smart guy and realizes that there's a lot more to stock analysis than a set of numbers. Buffet's approach to buying Coca-Cola was strongly influenced by its market dominance. He is always influenced by consideration of the strength of a company's franchise (products and marketing) and its position relative to growth of its markets. For instance, he mentions that while Coca-Cola is very popular in China, the company has only begun to exploit that market and so one can see the strong possibility of immense increases in their sales and revenues.

The yield ratio tells you how fast your investment is coming back to you. If the yield ratio is 1.4 percent, then each year you get back 1.4 percent of what you have invested in the stock. When the yield ratio is 6.5 percent, then each year you could get back 6.5 percent of your investment. The astute and careful investor will also compare this with the yield return that one might get from a bond. A high-quality bond might return 7 percent or 8 percent with very little risk or opportunity for price fluctuation.

So what is best to buy? There is no automatic answer. For some people the choice is to buy Coca-Cola and pay the high price for earnings and yield, but expect steady, strong growth in earnings, yield, and share price over the coming years. The KO buyers accept a risk of share price loss that is implied by the high current P/E ratio. For some investors the choice is to buy Potomac Electric shares at a lower price and get strong assurance (from their history) that the dividend will be maintained at or above this good yield of 6.5 percent. Potomac Electric has a long, well-established history of raising the dividend year by year. The POM buyers accept the risk of share price loss that is implied just by being in the stock markets, but they are encouraged by the safe market of the company.

The high-dividend yield also helps to provide a prop for the stock. If it started to fall in price, the yield would go so high that it would certainly attract new buyers. For other buyers, the best choice is to buy a ten-year Treasury note that pays 5 or 6 percent, and rest secure in the government's promise to pay the yield every year and return exactly $1,000 at the end of the ten years.

As an independent small investor, you do not have to prove which decision is best or justify your decision to the world. Just find something that works well for you.

You may not want to be married to any particular guidelines or rules on how to use the P/E ratio or the yield ratio, but it would be foolish to ignore these factors. Both of them tell you something about the value of the stock and its relative attractiveness compared to other stocks.

Most of the financial news sources frequently publicize the market average P/E or perhaps the average yield for the Dow or the average for the Standard & Poor's 500 or some other group of stocks. Those numbers help value-conscious investors look at stocks relative to what other investments offer.

Compounding the Growth by Reinvesting Dividends

Look at two hypothetical investors Bill and Jane, who owned 100 shares of the same stock for ten years. Here are the numbers for the shares:

Year	1	3	4	5	6	7	8	9	10
price ($)	22	24	21	25	26	24	23	26	27
dividend	88¢	96¢	92¢	1.00	1.10	1.10	1.00	1.10	1.15

Bill collects his dividends in cash and spends them on current necessities. Jane collects her dividends and converts the money back into stock. Where do they stand at the end of the ten years?

Bill collected $1,013 cash for his 100 shares: $88 + 92 + 96 + 92 + 100 + 110 + 110 + 100 + 110 + 115, and he still has his 100 shares worth $2,700. A good, neat profit.

Jane bought new shares using the dividends:

Year	Shares held	Dividend earned	New shares bought
1	100	$88.00	4
2	104	95.68	4.2
3	108.2	103.87	4.3
4	112.5	103.50	4.9
5	117.4	117.40	4.7

Year	Shares held	Dividend earned	New shares bought
6	122.1	134.31	5.2
7	127.3	140.03	5.8
8	133.1	133.10	5.8
9	138.9	152.79	5.9
10	144.8	166.52	6.2

At the end of ten years, Jane owned 151 shares at $27 each for a total value of $4,077. Jane's investment grew by 85 percent, while Bill's had a total return of 69 percent gain. Of course, Bill also had some money from dividends to work with along the way. If Bill had reinvested the dividends elsewhere, he might be as well off as Jane, but if he simply spent the dividends, he would be way behind where he could have been.

Many investors have good and sufficient reasons to spend their dividends, and maybe you do, too. However, there is no denying that if you can reinvest dividends, the compound growth should pay off greatly in a few years.

Looking for Value or Growth?

The value theory of investing emphasizes that there are certain fundamentals about a company that will determine its ultimate success or failure. *Fundamentals* usually refer to basic business measurements like annual sales or profits or debt. *Value investing* leans on fundamental analysis that requires doing research in the company's financial reports and profit and loss statements. It requires analyzing the products or services of the company and its competitors. A value investor wants to know something about the management and their plans, as well as the company's history. A great book to read to pursue value investing further is *The Intelligent Investor* by Benjamin Graham (New York: Harper & Row, 1985). The bottom line is that if you want to make money, you'll have to do it the old-fashioned way: work for it. Graham's methods require work. They also require some understanding of financial statements and the ability to judge products and management. In-depth investment analysis is not a precise science and may require more background or more analysis than is suitable for some investors.

Fundamentals

Value Investing

There is a legitimate point of view that if you can't handle the analysis, then maybe you should just stay out of the stock markets. An alternate plan would be to join an investment club and share the burden with folks whose experience and education are different from yours. You might decide instead to find a good broker or advisor and follow their advice, or go back to school and study financial management or accounting.

Growth Investing

The idea of *growth investing* is sometimes described as the counterpoint to value investing. There is no real contradiction between value investing and growth investing, but the value-oriented investor will be more impressed by the financial ratios and the dividends and P/E ratio of a company, while the growth investor will concentrate his attention on the potential future growth of the total sales and earnings, as well as the stock price. The premise of growth investing is that trends in revenues and profits can carry a company into or out of a slump. For example, in 1991 Chrysler was a mess. The company's stock was selling for about $10. But then the automobile market started to come back. Anyone who could have discerned the future trends of car sales or of Chrysler's revenues and sales could have done very well over the next few years. The (strict) value investor would have rejected Chrysler throughout 1991 and 1992 and maybe wouild reject it even today. Some smart folks figured out the trends and the momentum in Chrysler's sales, stock price, and stock market volume early on and have made a pile of money.

Cree Research is an example of a growth-oriented investment. With small current sales or profits, it has nothing to offer the value investor, but if it ever gets up to $15 per share in revenue and maybe $1 a share in earnings, it will attract value investors plus all manner of growth investors, who will make assumptions about the trend's likelihood of continuing.

The growth theory can get you in trouble, too. Almost every medicine might be good for you if taken at the right time but can kill if abused. The same is true of growth investing. Many unhappy small investors could tell a sad story about their experiences in 2000 and 2001, if they were willing to confess. Here is one such story about Cisco Systems (symbol CSCO on NASDAQ). The lesson here is that a great company and a great investment are not synonymous.

Cisco was formed in 1984 to develop various computer communications devices. These people were geniuses. Cisco took the markets by storm through superior technology and marketing. In 1991, you might have bought 100 shares of their stock for around $3,000. If you had held it until late 1999, you would have had 14,400 shares, after several stock splits, worth $720,000. Not a bad day's work. Cisco was the great growth story. From 1992 through 1999, we saw their sales going up between 50 percent and 90 percent each year, which is astounding. Their profits increased 30 percent to 50 percent each year. The stock price went through the roof. A large number of investors made a lot of money investing in Cisco, and a large number of people thought the party would go on forever. It did not. In 2000 and 2001, their sales and profits kept rising, but investors looked at the P/E ratio above 100, with zero yield payments, and thought it was too expensive. The price quickly fell from near $160 in 2000 to near $15 in late 2001. At that time, their equipment sales had contracted enough that the earnings fell to about $0.15 per share, and the P/E ratio was still 100. Many investors were too discouraged or battered to consider buying Cisco again. Cisco still had great engineers, managers, and salespeople. They still had great products, but the stock was no longer considered a good deal. A lot of naïve growth-oriented investors were badly hurt by the collapse of Cisco.

You might have found that Cisco qualified as a value investment because of finances, management, markets, and almost everything except price, but the purist value investor is reluctant to buy stocks when the P/E ratio is much higher than the rest of the market. The bottom line of value investing is that most stocks represent good companies with good markets, but any stock can be just plain overpriced.

Investing for value and investing for growth are not antithetical. Some financial specialists prefer one over the other; others apply different methods at different times. A savvy stock picker will consider both. Anytime you prepare to make an investment, you should think about other things you might be doing with the money. If most of your money were invested in growth stocks, it might make sense to diversify some by making the value play, buying a couple with higher dividends and lower P/E ratios. That would have been productive strategy in 2000 and 2001.

Sectors

Sector

If you get into picking stocks, there will be many times when you are only concerned with a small part of the stock market. For example, you might be particularly interested in electric utilities. Electric utilities form a *sector* of the market. Other sectors would include perhaps only automobile companies or perhaps just department stores or just small cap companies. *Cap* is the standard market jargon for the total market capitalization of a company, the product of the price per share multiplied by the number of shares. It is, in a sense, what someone might pay if they tried to buy the entire company. Sectors of the market might include electric utilities, automobile, biotechnology, retail stores, small cap, medium cap, large cap, blue chips, growth, and so on. There are many different sectors. Any description that you might imagine for a group of stocks can define a sector.

Market Cap

Each sector requires its own approach to stock picking. Certain sectors are naturally full of value stocks, some are naturally full of growth stocks, some are composed of out-of-favor stocks, some tend toward higher or lower P/E values, and some tend toward higher or lower yield values. The electric utilities sector tends to show higher yield and lower P/E than others. The computer software sector is full of supposedly growth-oriented stocks that typically have high P/E and little or no dividends.

Top-Down Investing: Choose a Sector, Then Pick a Stock

Sometimes it is helpful to an investor to start out by selecting a sector before thinking about an individual company. For example, I have a personal bias in favor of electric utilities that operate in the southeastern United States. That gives me a sector of about fifteen stocks that I can study. Then my task is to find one of those fifteen in the sector that looks best, so I compare the P/E ratios, the yield ratios, the debt, the dividend histories, and the market area economies before making a choice. But in making that decision, I would not compare the P/E of an electric utility with that of Cisco. Once you make a decision to go into a specific sector, your comparisons should be with the comparable values in that sector. Or you may decide there is nothing in the sector that is good enough. There may be times when you have good reasons to be interested only in local banks in Alabama, so you study that sector to find one to buy. It's still OK if you decide that all of them are over-priced. That kind of thing has happened to me a couple of times when I was just too late in deciding to purchase stock. Other investors saw the reasons to buy paper companies and took action before I did, and everything got bid up to excessive prices.

You might also choose to focus on a sector before picking individual stocks in order to improve the diversification of your portfolio. The financial newspapers and stock advisory publications like *The Value Line Investment Survey* will give periodic reports on the average P/E, or average yield, or growth prospects for various sectors. Those numbers can help you pick the particular stock you want to buy. Or they might convince you that the entire sector is weak.

Sometimes the sector analysis can persuade you to stay away from a given stock. If one stock in a sector looks good but the overall sector is weak, it might happen that the market becomes prejudiced against the sector and takes the one good stock down with it. That is a judgment call that you or your advisor will have to wrestle with. If, for instance, at some time General Motors looked good to you while Ford and Chrysler looked bad, you would have to make a decision: is GM about to get socked with the same bad economic conditions that are hurting Ford and Chrysler, or is GM really doing a great job and stealing the market from the other two?

Large Cap, Small Cap

Usually a company with a market capitalization of more than say, $10 billion would be regarded as a *large cap,* and one with a market cap below $500 million would be *small cap* (and both of those numbers have changed a great deal since I wrote the first edition of this book). Beyond that, people have different ideas of how to define the two terms. What is important is the tendency of larger and smaller companies to behave differently.

Large
Cap

Small
Cap

Both large and small caps have certain characteristics and advantages. History shows that the smaller caps outperform the large caps over the long term, but they also carry greater risk. The smaller caps are usually more *volatile,* meaning the price runs up and down more, although there are great variations among individual companies.

Think about a situation where an engineer had a brilliant idea that led to a new product line estimated to have market potential of $20 million in sales, producing $6 million in profits. If he worked for General Motors (market capitalization of $28 billion), the increase in revenues is 0.003 percent and the increase in profits is 0.1 percent (calculated using year 2000 data). So, that one invention should not have a huge impact on the stock price. However, if he worked for Checkpoint Systems (CKP on the NYSE), the growth in revenues would have been 3 percent and the growth in profits would have been 32 percent. The invention would have had a dramatic impact on their stock price. Even without any great new invention, you could imagine a case where Checkpoint might have doubled their market share over a few years. It is difficult to imagine the behemoth GM doing that. However, the smaller companies are exposed to more risk, too. If a company only has a modest amount of capital goods to support their operations, a competitor could enter their market and take away sales easier than it could if the investments were huge. It is difficult to imagine a new American automobile manufacturer making much headway against Ford, GM, or Chrysler, but it is easy to imagine new strong competition for a fast-food chain, an auto parts manufacturer, or Cree Research, where the original investment would be smaller.

Generally, the small caps offer potentially greater growth, but also greater risks. This is probably an idea to practice in your diversification scheme, if you can stand the risks. Another approach might be to do your own stock picking among some blue chips or utilities and invest in a mutual fund that specializes in small caps. The mutual fund would diversify among 50 to 100 small companies and save you the trouble of studying a lot of them. Consistently, over my investing career, the small caps have brought both the greatest pain, by far, and the greatest profits, by far. Diversify!

Technical Analysis

Technical analysis is an attempt to learn from the numbers and the history of a stock. It relies on interpreting price history as a reflection of collective market judgment. It is easiest to see what is involved in the history of a stock by looking at charts of stock prices. You may not care to use it or study it, but many people do. It is worthwhile for you to recognize some of the words and ideas used in technical analysis.

Technical
Analysis

Technical analysts have studied the history of price movements and other measurements of market activity and found trends and patterns that they believe will help them forecast coming developments. Of course, no one should be so foolish that they promise certainty in such forecasting, but some analysts believe there is enough consistency and rational basis in the patterns to make them useful guides. Most stock market professionals agree that there is some validity in technical analysis, although the amount of validity is debated.

The following stock price charts, spanning from 1985 to 1995, tell a true story. The NASDAQ-traded company's name is withheld so we can concentrate on the technical analysis. In the middle of 1988, some analysts might have looked at the price chart and seen this:

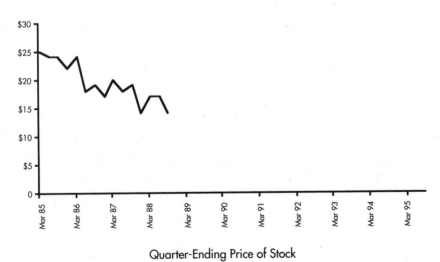

Quarter-Ending Price of Stock

This stock's record is not very pretty, but almost any stock is a winner if you can buy at the right time, and maybe this one is sufficiently low that it's ready for the big turnaround. Should we buy now? The technical analysts would take out a ruler and draw some *trend lines* on the graph:

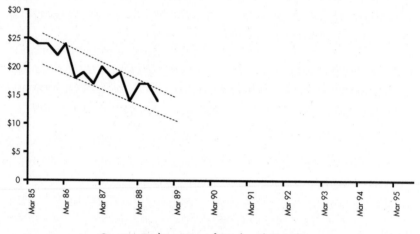

Quarter-Ending Price of Stock with Trend Lines

The trend lines draw attention to the succeeding lower values of each attempt to rally, and the succeeding lower values of each intermediate low point, leading to lower highs and lower lows. This is an ugly trend. Technical analysis would indicate against buying this stock in the middle of 1988.

If the analyst came back to the same stock in the middle of 1992, the picture (shown below) would show some new features. The downtrend continued and in fact got worse, as indicated by the new trend lines, but there is an interesting feature in the third quarter of 1991 where the upper and lower trend lines converge. That feature is thought to foretell the end of the downtrend. The graph here seems to confirm that. Some technical analysts would have felt very tempted to buy this stock in late 1991.

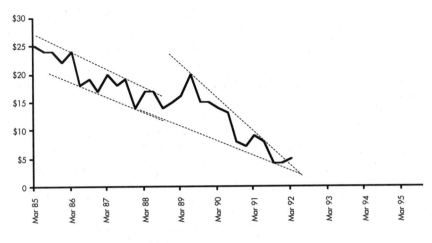

Quarter-Ending Price of Stock

If we leap forward, you can see that a new uptrend was established in late 1991 or early 1992. Also, in early 1995, the stock was breaking away from its 1993–94 trend. I have added a new line (the dotted curve), which is a *moving average* for the stock price. It represents the average price over the last four quarters.

Moving Average

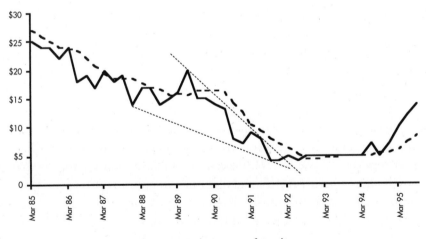

Quarter-Ending Price of Stock

One theory in technical analysis is that when a price moves significantly below or above its moving average, that is either a *sell signal* or a *buy signal*, respectively. In this case the chart gave an indication in late

Buy Signal, Sell Signal

1991 that the downtrend was over, and a strong buy signal in early 1995 by breaking out (jumping up) above its moving average. A confirmed technical analyst would be very eager to own this stock in early 1995. Within six months, his or her money would have doubled. However, notice also that the moving average line gave a buy signal in early 1989, so these things are not infallible.

Volume

Another interesting idea that comes out of technical analysis is volume momentum. *Volume* is quantity of sales in a specific period. *Volume momentum* is the theory that a price change on heavy share volume is more predictive than a price change on light volume. I don't think anyone disputes the validity of this theory.

Volume Momentum

Technical analysis is one of many tools that a stock picker might use. Some people say it is foolishness, and others say it can be relied upon for almost all buy or sell decisions. I say it is a tool. It won't do your thinking for you, but it might be useful enough to deserve some consideration. Some of us are skillful with a hammer, and some are not. Some investors are successful relying completely on technical analysis, and some are successful while ignoring it. You can decide for yourself whether it deserves any of your time and attention.

Dollar-Cost Averaging

Some people think that there is a magic method to guarantee that you'll come out ahead on investments. There is not. However, there is a method to take advantage of the long-term upward trend of the market if you can stay in long enough to outlast the short-term setbacks.

Dollar-Cost Averaging

Dollar-cost averaging means that you decide on some fixed amount that you will put into your investments every month, every quarter, or whatever time period you like. The benefits of dollar-cost averaging are that you have a regular practice and discipline in your investing, and price drops become opportunities to buy more stock with that fixed amount than you would have acquired at the higher prices.

Let us say that you have decided to invest $1,000 every quarter in your favorite stock, and the price of the stock over four quarters went like this: $18, $16, $18, $19 (we'll ignore brokerage fees for the moment). If you bought as many shares as you could with the $1,000 each quarter, and held any extra cash to put into next quarter's purchase, your four quarters' purchases would buy 55, 63, 55, 53 shares, respectively. At the end you would have 226 shares worth $4,294. This is better than you would have done if you had invested the entire $4,000 either in the first or the last month, and far better than you would have done if you had gotten scared and sold out on the price dip in the second quarter. The dollar-cost averaging procedure kept you in the market, and in fact buying more shares, when the price took the dip to $16.

However, if the price had gone down, say $18, $16, $16, $15, you would have ended up with 247 shares worth $3,705, which is a loss.

Dollar-cost averaging depends on the long-term uptrend in the price of the stock. If the uptrend is not there, or if you can't wait for it, dollar-cost averaging will not make you a winner. This method is applicable to any kind of investment as long as you can make regular fixed payments that are large enough to make the accompanying brokerage fees or sales loads not too painful. Accomplishing this is easiest if you work with an investment club or a mutual fund, but it also works with individual stocks if you can manage the discipline and fees.

There is no scheme, formula, or magic key to the stock markets that will make up for buying bad companies or for buying into long-term bear markets. But you say, "Aha! This is the new millennium, and there are no more long-term bear markets." I would respond, "It's extremely doubtful." Dollar-cost averaging in a bear market will lose money until the market turns.

Recommended Further Reading

Band, Richard. *Contrary Investing for the '90s: How to Profit by Going Against the Crowd.* New York: St. Martin's, 1991.

Dreman, David. *The New Contrarian Investment Strategy: The Psychology of Stock Market Success.* New York: Random House, 1982.

Engel, Louis, and Henry Hecht. *How to Buy Stocks.* New York: Little, Brown and Co., 1994.

Gard, Jim. *The Small Investor Goes to Market.* Berkeley, Calif.: Ten Speed Press, 1998.

Lowenstein, Louis. *What's Wrong with Wall Street.* Reading, Ma.: Addison-Wesley, 1989.

O'Neil, William. *How to Make Money in Stocks: A Winning System in Good Times or Bad.* New York: McGraw-Hill, 1994.

Zweig, Martin. *Winning on Wall Street.* New York: Warner Books, 1994.

Chapter 8

More on Stocks:
Selling, Losing, and Taking Profits

Small investors need to know:

- What does the smart money do?
- What does the dumb money do?
- If not "buy and hold," then what?
- How can I manage selling to protect profits or limit losses?
- What happens in stock market panics and crashes?

Good News

A lot of people make money by trading in stocks.

Bad News

A lot of people get badly hurt by trading in stocks. There are clever and ambitious people out there who would like to take your money. And bad stuff happens. Not all the time, of course, but sometimes. The miracle of capitalism is that while all of the money is changing hands, there is also real work going on; people keep building cars and houses and computers. So it is *possible* for everyone to win. But not everyone will win.

Brokerage Expenses

Brokers have to make a living, too. They are working for their bosses to generate sales and commissions, not just to feather your nest. Sometimes they may take a lot of commissions out of your account. They may be perfectly honest, but it pays to keep your eyes on those commissions.

The practice of creating excessive transactions in an account just to create multiple commissions is called churning. Almost any week, you can read in the *WSJ* about some case of disciplinary or legal action against a broker who has been accused of leading clients into excessive trading action in order to generate sales commissions. The majority of brokers are reasonable and fair businesspeople, but there are sharks who will get your telephone number and call you. When that happens, be prepared to give a very firm "no" to a very fast hustle. If you can't handle that, say your prayers, and lock away your money.

Check up on your regular broker. If you are willing to consistently let 6 to 10 percent of your portfolio disappear in commissions each year, why should your broker complain? Study your account statements month by month and year by year. Be vigilant about keeping track of

The Small Investor Reviews His Statements

how much you are spending in brokerage fees or account management fees, and know how much trading is being done in your name.

For example, suppose you had $20,000 in a brokerage account, and during the year you authorized the following six buys and three sells:

1. Buy 200 XYZ at $23   broker fee = $90

2. Buy 300 GHL at $6.50   broker fee = $60

3. Buy $4,000 of AZGTX   sales commission = $140
mutual fund with 3.5% load

4. Sell 200 XYZ at $21   broker fee = $90

5. Buy 200 ABC at $33   broker fee = $120

6. Buy 150 RST at $40   broker fee = $120

7. Sell 300 GHL at $8.50   broker fee = $60

8. Buy $2,000 of AZGTX   sales commission = $70

9. Sell 200 ABC at $37   broker fee = $120

That makes nine trades in a year. Perhaps they were successful. But the total fees were $870, which is over 4 percent of your capital. It will be tough to make a living that way. The figures above are representative of what brokers might charge. With some discount brokers you might expect to pay half as much, but you wouldn't get any help. With full-service brokers, you might pay higher fees and get the support that goes along with it. But no matter where or how you trade, the brokerage fees can be a significant percentage of your money, and you have to watch where they are going. *You* have to watch and control the fees; no one else will do it for you.

Bear Markets, Panics, and Crashes

In any market, goods change hands and prices go up and down. Most of the time we expect to see fairly orderly and rational changes in stock prices. We expect that either we, our brokers, or the gurus on the mountaintops can make sense out of what is going on and relate the price changes to economic news. But sometimes things run wild and you may run into manias, panics, and crashes. The crashes will be widely publicized, and everyone will be talking about them, but the manias and panics are not always as clearly defined. It is important to recognize the manias and panics because they are the warnings of coming crashes.

A mania is an excessive and unjustified rapid increase in prices. Sometimes, especially when the market has been going up strongly for a while, people seem to fear that the opportunity to make a lot of money is running away from them. Even professional money managers can worry that they may not be keeping up with their competitors. Then they may rush to buy just for the sake of buying. The panic phase can set in after investors have spent all of their ready cash, and people realize that price levels are excessive. If too many people want to take their profits quickly or need to get out of the markets and back to cash, that may set off a panic of sellers. In 1996 the American markets, especially the NASDAQ, started on a buying mania that went on, with occasional pauses, for four years. Some people thought it would go on forever. Eventually, during 2000 and 2001, it came to a grim halt and reversed, and many small investors were slammed to the mat in a selling panic.

The Small Investor Gets off the Bull

Experienced stock market seers had been predicting for years that the end was near, the market was overpriced, and trouble was just around the corner. They might have had good reasons for thinking so, but the market just kept on marching along. No one can foretell with certainty when market psychology will reverse. I listened to all the commentators and analysts and read all the market press, and I am certain that not one guru in a hundred knew when we fell off the cliff. Except a year later, they all said, "I told you so."

The smart money on Wall Street is supposed to be in the hands of people who usually make money, avoid the big trouble, and hear the hot news first. The "dumb money" is supposed to be in the hands of people who usually get into a hot stock too late, waste too much on brokerage fees, or buy last month's winners just when the smart money wants to sell.

It may be that the stock market downturn of 2000–2001 was just another transfer of money out of dumb hands into smart hands. It is too soon to make a definite judgment call on the outcome of this downturn, but if a lot of working people suddenly decided to stop or decrease their contributions to retirement plans, we would find out in a hurry. Even if they just decide to switch the money out of stocks and back to money market funds, the stock markets would go into a great swoon or possibly an actual crash.

A panic occurs when many investors decide they have to sell in a hurry. A crash occurs when the results of the panic get out of hand, and prices fall precipitously.

The next six paragraphs were written in 1995 as part of the first edition of this book. We have the benefit of hindsight now, but the ideas remain just as valid today as they were then.

It well may be that we are in a buying mania phase now, and possibly have been for several years. The rate of increases of prices of all stock markets in the U.S. for this sustained period is unprecedented. Even the mania before the 1929 crash only lasted a couple of years, and although the bull market of 1935 and '36 roughly doubled prices, that was a lull between two storms. The Dow Jones Industrial Average lost about half of its value between the first quarter of 1937 and the first quarter of 1938, and did not recover the loss until 1946. The current markets have roughly quintupled, from 1,000 to 5,000 on the Dow in thirteen years; 1995 action appears to be beyond all precedent. There may be good strong economic factors to support most of that price rise. Many commentators say there are, but we may also be in a buying mania. One of the dependable signs of a mania is that people start to feel compelled to rush their money into the markets. They feel as though the markets may leave them behind, and that there is not much time left to grab the prize.

One of the things that we might worry about is whether this is smart money or stupid money coming into the markets. Certainly, the prices that people pay for stocks are running up well ahead of the rewards that they take out. A lot of the new money is coming from retirement accounts. When must those retirement-oriented investors start withdrawing their money to buy food and pay medical bills? Whenever they need to take money back, it must come from either dividends or sale of stock. The dividend rate for most of the major American markets is so low that few will find it satisfactory for long.

It is important to see the distinctions between real money and stock ownership. Stock ownership can show all kinds of wondrous "paper" profits based on current market prices and percentage increases in share profits, but when people have to pay the mortgage or send the kids to college or pay for surgery, they must have real money. That means that stock must be sold or the dividends must be substantial.

But you may hear that it's different this time. Sure it is. It was different last time, too, but it never supported stock prices that only paid 2.3 percent average yield from dividends, like now. If this market keeps going up, one of three things must happen: Dividends must be substantially increased, the companies must demonstrate that their underlying values are greater and will produce greater earnings, or investors must settle for a lower dividend yield and earnings level. In the past, the investing public has never settled for as low a dividend yield and relative earnings power as they are buying now. Not for long, anyway.

What might persuade our fellow investors to stop buying stocks? What if the interest rate paid on long-term—high-quality bonds got up to 8 percent, 9 percent, 10 percent? That would certainly draw some money away from the stock markets. What if inflation got out of hand and people could no longer keep putting money into their retirement programs? Any of those things, or a hundred others, might cause the supply of new money into the market to fall off. Then the next seller would have to lower his price in order to attract new buyers. That might be the start of an orderly retreat of prices, or it might degenerate into a panic or even, perhaps, a crash. In 1987, the market (Dow price average) went up from about 1,900 to near 2,800 in less than a year. The yield fell to about 2.5 percent, while good long-term bonds were paying much higher. When the selling pressure was strong, the market panicked, crashed, and lost approximately one-third of its value in a few days.

Neither I nor anyone else can tell you with perfect assurance how close we might be to the end of a mania, or the next panic. But it certainly pays to be cautious when the yield is at or near an all-time low and stock prices have been pushed up rapidly to all-time highs. Think about what kind of defensive measures you can use, or how you will manage your selling tactics to get money out.

The Small Investor Joins the Bears

Selling—Attitude and Discipline

Smart selling is the toughest lesson any investor has to learn. Why? Because buying is fun and exciting, but selling is difficult and stressful.

> **WARNING**
>
> You will never be a successful investor until you work out your selling discipline, and practice it.

If you had bought 200 shares of what was then NationsBank (now Bank of America) in October 1991 and sold in June 1994, you would have earned $796 in dividends and made about $3,400 on the stock price. You might have paid between $100 and $300 in commissions. Some clever small investors held on until the end of 2001 and expanded their profits to over $25,000 on an initial $5,400 investment.

If you had bought 300 shares of Ford in January 1988 and sold in January 1995, you would have earned $2,252 in dividends and about $2,400 on the price of the stock, and you would have paid maybe $100 to $300 in brokerage commissions. A smart operator might have sold in early 1994 at about $33 per share. The lost 1994 dividend would have been $270, but the extra price appreciation would have been $1,200, netting an additional $900 for a well-timed sell.

If you had held 200 shares of IBM from February 1990 until April 1994, you would have earned $3,220 in dividends and taken about $10,000 in loss on the price of the stock. The disciplined investor might have sold in December 1991. Then the dividends would have been only $1,936, but the loss would have been only $4,000. Net advantage from that smart sale looks close to $5,000. But few people have the discipline to sell at a terrible price and take a $4,000 loss. What's the point?

> **🔑**
>
> Earnings from dividends are significant, but that should not mean that we neglect the potential profit or loss from the price of the stock. Managing your potential profits or losses into real profits and minimal losses requires selling discipline.

Buy-and-Hold

What about buy-and-hold? *Buy-and-hold* is a popular strategy that has some merit but also has some deficiencies. The idea is to buy good stocks, probably in blue chip companies with good fundamental business characteristics, and then just hold onto them and enjoy the fruits of the long-term upward trend of the market and the labor of the company's employees. Good plan. But like most good plans, it works when it works and fails when it fails.

What are the expected advantages of the buy-and-hold strategy? There are several that make good sense. You reduce trading costs by making fewer transactions. You focus on companies that are more stable and predictable. You make long-term commitments, and you do correspondingly more careful analysis before you buy. You sleep better. You spend more time paying attention to your spouse and children.

So, you see, buy-and-hold is a wonderful plan . . . when it works.

What are the potential disadvantages of buy-and-hold? Not many, but they are potentially fatal. For example, your broker or advisor will tell you not to worry about the current string of losses, because you are a buy-and-hold investor (she says with an approving tone). So you forgo the necessity of evaluating the effectiveness of the broker, you sleep better, and, well, you neglect your investments. You may fail to rebalance or reap profits when it is beneficial. You may fail to pay attention to business and economic conditions. Even if your purchase of the first stock was brilliant and successful, there may come a time when business conditions change or when another stock opportunity is better.

Buy-and-hold is fine, when it works. Buy-and-hold is better than a series of frequent trades that erode your principal through trading fees. Buy-and-hold may even be better than no plan at all. But what is really good is smart selling. And it is difficult. Of course, we cannot expect that everyone is going to be sharp enough to identify those three optimal selling decisions (like the ones for Ford, NationsBank, and IBM above). It's not that easy. But there are people who make good money in the financial markets. They don't make it by wearing bags over their heads with "Buy-and-Hold" written on the outside.

Working stocks is like playing bridge, in a sense. In bridge everyone likes to talk about bidding, because it's fun and easy. The difficult work is in playing the hands, and not as many people know much about doing that. It's the same thing with stock picking. It's fun, and you can always speculate on success or the potential for success. The harder part of the work comes in selling, and not as many people care to study that.

Some people fall into a self-imposed trap of treating selling as an admission of failure. Either you quit and give up on the potential gains you foresaw when you bought it, or you admit that your great gains could have been better, if only you had known then. We do get attached to our stocks. Everybody does. Almost every person who trades stocks loves to try to convince others that the last pick is the real gem, the best of all possible current investments. The point of sale is always some kind of emotional trial, both for our winners and our losers. If you are going to buy any kinds of investments, then learn two demanding lessons:

#1: Selling is important to your profit and loss results.
#2: Selling is difficult and complicated and stressful.

Selling

There is no single well-defined discipline or formula that will make everyone a smart seller, just as there is no one investment strategy or buying formula that makes everyone a winner. It doesn't do you any good to read about the best possible selling strategy if you don't have the inner fortitude to follow through on it. However, there are some ideas that are worth looking at, and maybe one or two of them will work for you.

Variations on Buying & Selling

BUY OR SELL AT YOUR PRICE

It is OK for you to specify a price that you want to obtain on any order. You can tell your broker to sell Sears (symbol S on NYSE) at $45, and the broker will do his best to complete the deal at that price. However, if the stock is currently being bid up, it might happen that the market is offering $46 just when you come in at $45, and you might lose a dollar per share by specifying $45; on the other hand the best offer might be $44.75, which leaves you holding the stock. The advantage of buying or selling at your specified price is that you can be confident that you will get your price or no deal. The disadvantages are that you may pay more than you needed to on a purchase or sell too low on a sale. You might also simply miss the deal when it could have been completed at very close to your price.

MARKET ORDERS

You can instruct your broker to buy or sell a stock at the current market price level, whatever it is. The *market order* is the most common way of entering orders. It has advantages and disadvantages. On September 20, 1995, AT&T announced the breakup of the company into three new independent companies. I thought that was a great idea. I saw the news before the market opened, called my broker, and told him to buy AT&T at the market price. I knew that the price had been hanging between $48 and $55 for a long time, but I didn't have any idea what would happen to it that day. I just wanted to buy it. I ended up buying it for $63 a share. If I had said to buy at $55, I would have been shut out. If I had said to buy at $65, I would have paid too much. At that time I was willing to trust in the collective rationality of the New York Stock Exchange and a good service history with my broker. The advantage that I gained was getting the stock I wanted at a fair price. The risk was that I might have paid a higher price than I had expected.

If you are dealing with very large and well-known companies on the New York Stock Exchange, this sort of risk will usually be acceptable. If you are dealing with small cap companies for which the price and liquidity are highly variable, this might be too much risk. Netscape (symbol NSCP on NASDAQ) went to market in September 1995 after an initial public stock offering that set the price at $28 a share. On the first day of public trading, people went crazy over it. This was certainly part of a buying mania for high-tech stocks. The price got up to $75 and quickly retreated. Some people who put in market orders to buy got the stock at over $70 and were facing a $20 per share loss by the end of the week.

> Use market orders when you have a high degree of confidence in the market you are using, in the stability of the share price, and in the customer service history of your broker.

The most common use of the market order happens when you consider buying a particular stock, and you ask your broker what bids

---

Market Order

and offers are currently active in the market. The answer might be, say, that the stock is at $34.25 bid, $34.75 asked. If you feel that is a fair range, you can put in a market order to buy the stock. That means that the broker should buy the stock for you at the best price that he can get. Usually the broker will be able to confirm within minutes that you have bought it at $34.50 or a price close to it. If the stock were volatile that day, you would expect the worst case to be that you buy a little higher, perhaps at $35. Market sell orders work the same way—the broker should get you the best price he can, and it should be very close to the stated range.

LIMIT ORDERS

Limit order

You can tell your broker that you want to buy or sell a stock at a certain price or better. That is called a *limit order*. For example, if GM is selling today at $47, you might decide that you would be happy to sell at $50, but you don't want to sit around watching CNBC all day to see when it hits. So you tell your broker to sell 200 shares of GM at $50, a limit order. The broker, or the stock exchange specialist, has to watch GM and as soon as someone offers $50 he or she should try to sell your stock. If the stock is going up, your broker might even get $50.50 for it. The limit sell order can be used to try to ensure that you get out of the stock position, but only if the price rises enough to give the price you want. It does not give guaranteed results.

> A limit order does not guarantee that you will get the price you want, even if trades were made at that price.

If somebody ahead of you sold GM at $50, and then there were no more buyers at $50, you would not get your sell price even though the target was hit. This occurs only rarely. One of our advantages as small investors is that if the market hits a certain price, we can generally feel safe that there is enough action and sales volume at that price to soak up whatever we want to buy or sell. If the manager of the AIM Equities Blue Chip Fund is trying to move 50,000 shares of GM, he has no such assurance.

STOP ORDERS (OR STOP-LOSS ORDERS)

A *stop order* is related to a limit order, but there is an important difference: the stop order becomes a market order when the target price is achieved. The stop order is basically a protective, or defensive, order to keep the market from running away from you. For instance, the first time I bought IBM, at $85.25 in 1992, I was lucky and it ran up to $100 in a hurry. I didn't want to sell, and I didn't want to take much risk, so I put in a stop-loss order at $93 to save me from losing all of the profit. Pretty quickly the price plunged and my broker sold it and got a price of $92.88. So I made a good profit on a short-term holding. If I had not had the stop loss order in, it is very likely that I would not have even known about the drop in price until it was down to $85 or less. You see, I, like most of you, have a life to live. I can't sit around watching the markets all the time. The stop-loss order sets a broker in place to act for us.

Stop
Order

Notice that the price I received for IBM was lower than the $93 that was in the order. The stop order says to the broker, "If the price hits $93, sell this boy at the market." But on that day, if I had insisted on $93, I might never have found a buyer.

There is one more potential catch with the stop-loss order: you had better be serious. Don't put in a stop loss-order and think you will have a chance to back out. You may have to live with some mistakes. For example, in the summer of 1992, the stock price of Hewlett-Packard (symbol HWP) was going down the drain. I recognized this as an opportunity and bought at $61.25. However, at the time I was very nervous about the market in general and was trying to be defensive. To protect against too much erosion of capital, I put in a defensive stop loss order at $54. HWP continued to slide and pretty soon hit $54, and my broker got me out at $54. Good service, bad judgment. The stock immediately turned around and a year later it was near $80. If I had had the nerve to avoid the stop order, or if I had had the nerve to set the stop at $52, I would have kept the stock and made a good profit instead of $8 per share loss (counting commissions). Tough luck. A year later, I held IBM again, purchased at $67.38, and put in a stop loss at $54. We hit the stop and got out at $53.75—right at the worst possible time. After I sold IBM, it quickly went back up to over $90. I got what I asked for: I avoided the risk and avoided the profit. So you'd better be serious about the stop-loss order before you put it in.

There you see three transactions made through stop-loss orders, two with IBM and one with Hewlett Packard. One made a good profit; two made substantial losses. You don't get any guarantees in the stock markets, only opportunity. And the opportunity cuts both ways. But in those three cases, I was practicing a selling discipline that was an absolutely essential ingredient of my personal investing strategy.

> When you hold a stock, it is perfectly reasonable to plan to hold it for a long time, but you should not just stick your head in the sand. Watch your stocks. Determine where you want to take profits or cut losses. Then take action to make those things happen.

Mental Stop

We should also discuss the concept of the *mental stop* (also known as the road to ruin). This is when an investor makes up his mind to sell if the market price falls to a certain level, but he does not actually place a stop order with his broker. Instead, he keeps his eyes open, planning to put in a sell order when the stock falls to some critical price. Fine, but remember, the road to ruin is paved with good intentions. With a mental stop, you run at least two risks. The first is that the market may get away from you. You plan to sell at $25 and the stock hits $20 before you hear about it. Or you plan to sell at $25 and you see the report of sales at $24, but by the time you get to a telephone, the stock is down to $22. Now what? There will be a gut reaction to not sell: "Don't accept this terrible price. Wait for it to come back to $24 or $25." Good luck! It won't come back.

The second risk is that you'll wait too long. People who wait are likely to find themselves in a mess. The markets will never wait on you. The most dangerous words in the language of any investor are "I'm just waiting for it to come back to my cost level, and then I will sell it." People hold losers forever waiting for them to come back. If your dearest friend says to you, "I am just waiting for it to come back up to $25," tell her, "Don't wait. Sell it. Let go of the worry. Find something else." If she ever again says, "I am just waiting for . . . ," counsel her to get out of the stock markets and look into Gamblers Anonymous. If you hold a stock that you have truly lost confidence in, sell it!

> The mental stop is a cancer on your selling discipline. Cut it out.

There is a popular theory that says, "Cut your losers, and let your winners run." It means get rid of the bad stocks and hang onto the good ones. But we know that every stock has the potential to be a winner or a loser. What to do? Well, I told you what to do with stocks that you have no confidence in, but what about the good stocks that are down in price? It happens all the time. Almost every stock that I have ever held was down in price at some point. I had an average cost of $12 in Cree and it fell to $6. What to do? It went back up to $60. What to do? It fell back down to $40. What to do? Well, if you had a good reason for buying the stock in the first place, reexamine whether it still satisfies your criteria. If it does, then maybe you should hold on. A stock that was good at $27 may still be good at $22. It can be a difficult call. If it were easy, everyone would be rich.

TAKING PROFITS

Whenever you own a stock that goes up, you will imagine that it could go up forever. But profits come from collecting dividends or selling, not from watching. Whenever you buy a stock, you should have done enough work that you have some idea about the markets, revenues, and profits of the firm. That knowledge should enable you to imagine a good price level that is fair for the stock. When you buy, set an idea of the price you expect to achieve before selling. If the price gets close to that level, either give your broker a limit sell order (to sell at X price or better) or reexamine the company's results and see if that is still the proper target price. At any rate, don't just sit idly by, expecting that the price will grow forever, beyond your original hoped-for value. The price may keep going, or it may not, but you should have some idea about reasonable expectations just as you did when you bought it.

It is no disgrace to take profits; some people make money that way. It is no disgrace to take losses; some people stay healthy that way. The only disgrace is to put your hard-earned money into the stock markets and forget about it. Even if you practice buy-and-hold, which may be right for some people, you should not buy and forget. In 1997, a lot of people bought British Airways stock (symbol BAB) at prices of $100 to $125 a share. The ones who just bought it and forgot it had some real pain (60 percent loss) as a result. They may all come out well—I hope they do—but they'll have experienced some pain along the way. If you expected to hold a stock for a long time, but it takes a dive, should you just hold on? If you expected to hold a stock for a long time, but it has a dramatic run-up in price, should you sell and grab the profits? Maybe yes, maybe no, but you should never just ignore the situation. The toughest part of the whole business may be making decisions and taking action.

The Small Investor Collects Profits

You can set up fixed guidelines, if you don't want to keep working at reevaluating your stocks. Suppose you tried this as a rule: When buying a stock, put in a stop-loss order at 10 percent below the buying price and a sell order at 20 percent above the buying price.

For example, you might buy MASCO Corp. (symbol MAS on the NYSE) at $30. Give your broker a stop-loss order at $27 and a limit sell order at $36. If the stock ever falls to $27, the broker will sell it at the market price; if it ever rises to $36, the broker will sell it for the best price he can get, at or above $36.

With that rule, all of your stock purchases will fit into one of three classes: they fall 10 percent and you get out with a 10 percent loss, they go up 20 percent and you make a 20 percent profit, or they stay within −10 percent to +20 percent of the purchase price and you just hold on until you feel like reevaluating them. With that rule, in a generally rising market you might expect to make fairly consistent profits, and in case of a generally falling market, you might expect to restrict your losses on each stock to not more than 10 percent plus whatever brokerage costs you have. (Of course this is based on average cases—exceptions will occur. But it's a pretty good rule of thumb.)

I do not recommend that everyone should adopt the rule above. It is only an example of how an investor might try putting some discipline and structure into his or her selling strategy.

Even if you did adopt this rule, or any other, you would still have some risk of long-term substantial losses. There are no risk-free investments. If you buy bad stocks and consistently lose 10 percent on each and pay brokerage fees, you might lose almost all of your money pretty quickly.

Hustlers

This very morning, as I sat here writing, a stockbroker called me. It was some guy I have never met, although he had called once before. He wanted to do me a favor—put me into "the single best idea" his firm had going this morning—and he was going to make only a small ($50) commission on the buy. He didn't tell me what commission they would extract on the sell. I wonder how big it might have been.

His best idea was Calloway Golf (symbol ELY). "Jim," he says, "have you heard about Gerber Food and Dr. Pepper? They were recently bought out and the stock went through the roof. Well, American Brands is currently sitting on a large cash stockpile and they need to buy a golf equipment manufacturer. We are convinced that American Brands is going to take over Calloway Golf." Insider buying is strong. The CEO and president of Calloway recently bought large amounts of the company's stock on the open market; the aver-

The Small Investor Gets Hustled

age daily trading volume has recently doubled, and there is a massive short squeeze going on.

Short
Sellers

Short sellers, or *shorts,* are stock traders who make a bet on a stock going down. In a short sale, they will borrow stock they did not own to sell at current prices. They expect to later buy it back at lower prices to close the loan of stock. If they can actually buy it back cheaper than they sold it, then they make a profit on a "sell high, buy low" deal. He says, "The shorts will have to buy in their sales to cover, and that will put immense upward pressure on the stock price." He said he needed to "put me in 1,000 shares," then a little later 500 shares, then a little later 200 shares. He said we could use a stop-loss order to limit the losses in case the stock fell.

This was where he was giving me very shaky and unreliable advice, although maybe he didn't understand it. A stop-loss order is an instruction to your broker to sell a stock at once if the price ever falls to a certain value. It is intended to limit your loss to whatever it might be at a certain point. In fact, a stop loss is not guaranteed to get the stated price for you, but only to sell the stock after it hits that price.

Then he wanted to know my overall investment portfolio size. I said it was none of his business. Then he wanted to know if it was at least $300,000. I said it was none of his business. Then he said, "Are you really that small?" I said it was none of his business. He said, "Good day, Jim," and hung up. All through the pitch, I kept telling him I would not buy anything until I had done my own homework, and I wasn't going to do it on a schedule to please him. He never seemed to hear that. You're right, I could have hung up in the first thirty seconds, but right away I knew I was going to use the example here.

This was a hard sell. At least in my league it looked like a hard sell. The guy said a number of things that sounded like legitimate reasons to buy Calloway (its price that day was $15.50). His claims that I could verify quickly and easily were true. But I passed.

Why did I pass? Well, first thing is, when you get to a certain point, somebody has to make a decision. To buy, to sell, somebody has to make a decision. I don't let strangers just call me out of the blue on Monday morning and make my decisions for me. I also have a fixed practice that I don't buy on impulse, no matter how great the story sounds. In fact, I almost never buy a stock unless I have spent several weeks, maybe months, thinking about it and gathering information. I practice the same advice I write. And finally, if someone offers us a deal that sounds too good to be true, that means that we just don't understand all of the risks yet.

Go look in today's newspaper, or call your broker. How's Calloway today? Did I avoid a loss? Did I miss a great opportunity? Either way, I don't intend to worry about it, and I won't feel any pain over it. I will go on about my investing practices in the same old slow and cautious way. It works for me and Mrs. Investor. Find something that works for you. Don't let anyone rattle you into decisions before you have examined the facts. Adopt your own rules or practices for safety and stick to them.

Gurus

John Wayne played the American hero better than anybody. Peter Lynch managed mutual funds better than anybody, and John Elway won football games better than anybody. In your business there are some people you know who are simply the best, or among the best. It's also true in investing.

There are a few people in the world who are generally acknowledged as masters of investing, and among them are a number who are master stock pickers; we call them our *gurus.* We would all pay a good price for their advice. But we don't have to. It's free. Many of them regularly appear on TV or in newspapers and magazines and give away their opinions about some current good buys in the stock markets.

One supposes that this enhances their reputations for selling their mutual funds or personalized advice. If you want to be cynical, you might even guess that their published views are self-serving—maybe they have already bought the stocks they are recommending and want you to rush out and bid up the prices. But let us adopt a more charitable view. These people are already wealthy, by my standards at least, and they probably enjoy having a chance to show off before a mass audience. So the point is you *can* get advice from real experts for free. It would be foolish to ignore it. But it might be equally as foolish to follow their advice blindly.

In July 1993, *Barron's* ran an article from a continuing series they call their "Roundtable." Once every six months or so, they call together some of the biggest names in the business to have a wide-open discussion on the economy and where the markets might be going. One of the things you can pick up in those articles is a list of recommended stocks. In the July 1993 article, one of the experts recommended 50-Off Stores. (Don't worry about which expert recommended it. Those folks really are good, but nobody promises 100 percent accuracy in picking stocks.)

50-Off Stores (symbol FOFF on NASDAQ) is a chain of small discount stores that sells mostly apparel, along with a few other odds and ends. During 1989 and 1990 the earnings had been between 20 cents and 33 cents per share and the share price bounced around between about $1 and $4. In 1991 the earnings doubled, but the stock price flew up to over $25. In 1992 it hit as high as $32 at one point (a growth stock). Well, the company was doing very well, but with a P/E ratio over 30 and no yield, it looked pretty expensive. Definitely not a value-oriented investment. From early 1992 until mid-1993, the price fell pretty much

Guru

in a straight line to $6 per share. Sales were up but earnings completely disappeared. They had a net loss for 1993.

Well, the "Roundtable" expert came in and reviewed the situation. He saw something that seemed to foretell a turnaround and prescribed buy at $6. The stock finished 1993 above $8, fell to $3 in early 1994, and finished 1994 below $4. The company died in 1997 with the stock valued below 10 cents.

OK, fair enough. This is risk-oriented investing and nobody ever said it would be easy. As small investors we have to remember that not every investment is equally attractive to everyone. What may offer fair risk and better diversification for one investor may be viewed as poison by another. In fact, in deference to that great man's track record, we should say that 50-Off was a reasonable risk and considered buy for him or for his mutual funds at the time. That doesn't mean that it was a good recommendation for everyone who heard about it. The expert had no doubt considered the risk level and cash level and current mix of stocks in his portfolio. For some reason the risk/reward potential of 50-Off looked appealing to him. That does not mean that it represented good diversification and a good risk/reward mix for us.

When the small investor learns that Mr. Hot Money is buying a stock, this should be taken as just part of the never-ending avalanche of available information. The small investor should consider how and where he heard about it. Is it, in fact, a reliable source of information? If so, maybe you should check it out. Find out some of the reasoning behind the position. If you can't learn the supporting reasoning, you have nothing more than rumor.

After you get that far, you have to decide whether this particular stock fits any of your own needs. Check your own current stock holdings. If you already own one firm in the same business, maybe you don't need another. What's good diversification and fair risk for Mr. Hot Money may be a walk on the wild side for you. Even if it is still interesting to you, do your homework. Check the *Value Line* report on the stock. If you use a full-service broker, ask for their opinion on the stock. Check the date on their report. You'll be surprised at how much old research gets handed around. Write to the company or go to their website and ask for their latest annual or quarterly reports.

Buy or sell advice from some "market expert" may well be good advice for somebody, sometime. That does not mean it is good advice for you. The person giving the advice doesn't know you or your needs.

And take your time. If you think you have such hot information that you have to buy right now, you are kidding yourself. Except in the rarest instances, we small investors will not get information when it is hot. If the stock is good today, it should be good tomorrow. Gurus serve a valid role in this world. They stimulate conversation. They make money and they spend money. But it does not necessarily follow that you should turn over your thinking to them or follow them blindly.

Beating the Averages

It is not profitable to give too much time and attention to how everyone else is doing. Take care of your money and let the others take care of theirs. What do we care what the averages are doing? What do we care how the mutual funds in general are doing? If you find out that the Dow Jones Industrial Average was up 14 percent last year, that won't put any money in your pocket unless you owned the right stocks. And if you find out the Standard & Poor's 500 was down 11 percent last quarter, that won't take any money out of your pocket. Forget the averages. Take care of yourself and your money. I finished 2001 with a better investment return than 95 percent of the mutual funds being sold, but who cares? That knowledge is not going to make a nickel for me next week, nor will it preserve my hard-earned gains. I still have to practice the defensive role of the cautious and insecure small investor.

Recommended Further Reading

The book *Investors Beware* is pretty much anecdotal and may be a bit one-sided in view, but the author has some experience in the business and has presumably seen much of what he reports. *The Intelligent Investor* is one of the true classics of this business and is a must-read for anyone who expects to buy individual stocks.

Allen, John. *Investors Beware: Protecting Yourself against Stockbroker Abuse while Protecting Your Money.* New York: John Wiley & Sons, 1993.

Graham, Benjamin. *The Intelligent Investor.* 4th ed. New York: Harper-Collins, 1994.

O'Shaughnessey, James. *What Works on Wall Street.* Rev. ed. New York: McGraw-Hill, 1998.

Schwager, Jack. *Getting Started in Technical Analysis.* New York: John Wiley & Sons, 1999.

Chapter 9

Mutual Funds

Small Investors need to know:

- What is a mutual fund?

- What are the benefits, costs, and risks?

- How can I buy mutual funds?

- How do they report their gains or losses?

- Where should I look for more information and research?

To Begin with—What Is a Mutual Fund, and Who Cares?

Part of what separates us from the professional money managers is that we have our own lives to live, and other priorities apart from the financial markets. You might do as well as the average money manager if you wanted to commit eight hours a day for two years to studying markets and you could get your hands on a few million dollars for educational purposes in the Wall Street "laboratory." But you don't want to. You can't. You won't. You're reading this book instead. You want to keep your money management as simple as possible and not devote too much time to it.

When I set out to manage my own money (versus just throwing it out there), I had a lot of motivation to overdo the research angle. Managing money, writing about it, and doing market research all happen to be fun for me. Even with all that, it took a year before I felt comfortable enough to be 75 percent invested. During that time I bought nineteen stocks, sold six of them (five at a profit), and bought three rather conservative mutual funds. Buying the mutual funds was the easiest part. I carefully studied each stock that I bought for weeks or months before the purchase, and I followed that with at least weekly reviews. You may be willing to do that much work. Some may even enjoy it. Others want an easier way.

Mutual funds were invented to solve several concerns of the individual investor. Their track records have been good. To a great extent, mutual funds achieve better results with less work than stocks do for small investors. The biggest and most famous of them all was the mighty Magellan Fund of Fidelity Distributors Corporation of Boston. Magellan, primarily under the guidance of Peter Lynch, achieved an average compound rate of return of over 18 percent for ten years. That's an incredible return; those guys made money faster than the government could spend it!

In 1965, individual investors owned over 80 percent of the value of U.S. stocks. In 1991 that had fallen to just over 50 percent. Today mutual funds, pension funds, and other institutional investors control much more of the markets. In 1960 there were 4 million individual accounts in mutual funds; in 1980 that had grown to 12 million; and today there are over 90 million. The total value of assets in mutual funds today is over $7 trillion, and that is not play money.

What Is a Mutual Fund?

A *mutual fund* is a pool of investment money under professional management. Many investors put in their money; a few professionals manage it. Compared to doing all of your own investment management, the expected benefits of investing in mutual funds are:

- less work for the individual investor,
- less risk for the individual investor,
- a good chance of making more profit for the individual investor.

To see how the risk factor works out in recent results, I looked at all the stocks (about 7,000) and all the mutual funds (about 11,000) that are available for screening on the Yahoo! Finance website. (If you need good screening tools that is a good place to look, and it's free.)

Mutual Fund

In late 2001, for results during the past year, 30 percent of the stocks were down 25 percent or more, and 17 percent of them were down 50 percent or more. With the mutual funds, 11 percent were down 25 percent or more, and just 1 percent were down 50 percent or more. These results bear out the very reasonable presumption that buying funds is less risky than buying stocks.

But suppose you just deal in "blue chip" stocks. Say you confine your money to companies with market cap of $10 billion or more, and the funds that buy those stocks. Of these, 21 percent of the stocks were down 25 percent or more, and 6 percent were down 50 percent or more. With the mutual funds, 16 percent were down 25 percent or more, and just 3 percent were down 50 percent or more.

You may say, "Yeah, but you were just evaluating the results during a nasty bear market." Right—that's when you need protection! Any way you slice it, the mutual funds are less likely to bring you large losses. That is not the same thing as saying that they will necessarily bring you large gains, but they do have better diversification and the safety that comes with it.

All of us should consider using mutual funds instead of direct purchases of stocks and bonds. But there is an area of concern to keep in mind. The mutual fund business is changing so rapidly that it is becoming difficult to balance the benefits against the costs of mutual fund investment. So you get a kind of "good news, bad news" situation: the advantages of mutual funds and the risks involved in new developments. I'm sorry about that, but there are always some tough points to consider.

How Does a Mutual Fund Work?

Money Market Account

A good starting point is to look at a bank money market account. The *money market account* is a type of mutual fund where all of the investors' money goes into a pool for buying short-term bonds. The bonds belong to the bank, not the depositor. The bank probably earns 3 to 7 percent annually on the money and pays out a little less to account holders. The majority of the account holders have little interest in investing directly in bonds. They prefer to let the bank do the work.

A mutual fund management company (also known as an *investment company*) is similar to the bank: They want to hold and invest your money; they plan to make a profit with it, and they will keep part of the profit.

Investing in a mutual fund resembles buying shares of any company that would use your money to run their business and pay you some dividends out of the profits; you might also profit from share price appreciation. With mutual funds, the share price is based directly on the assets that the fund owns. If you own General Motors stock, it is difficult to determine each day just exactly what the company is worth, but by contrast, if you own shares in the Vanguard 500 Index Fund (symbol VFINX, a fund that buys the companies of the Standard & Poor's 500 Index), you can use a well-understood, consistent formula for determining the fair price of the shares each day. We'll get to that later.

One big difference between stocks and funds is that for most mutual funds you do not sell your shares in an open market—instead, you sell them back to the fund company. The company stands ready to buy back (or redeem) shares at the current asset value at any time (with a few exceptions, such as closed-end funds, discussed later in this chapter).

The advantages of buying mutual funds are efficiency, professional management, and diversification (lower risk). We will look at each of those advantages separately. They are factors that you should consider in evaluating funds you might buy (more on choosing funds in chapter 10).

Mutual Fund Efficiency

One risk to your investment money is that the fund company might keep too much of it for themselves by charging high fees. Sometimes they do; however, the mutual fund will usually manage the investments at lower costs than would a lot of small investors acting independently. If a thousand of us each had $5,000 to invest in the stock market, over three years we might end up buying and selling five to ten stocks each. Acting separately, we might each pay $300 to $1,000 in commissions for purchases and final sales. That means between 6 percent and 20 percent of the principal is gone in fees. That makes it extremely difficult to end up with a profit.

The Small Investor Takes the Easy Way

But look at how it would work if we put all the money into a mutual fund. The investment company would manage all of that for us. They would collect the entire $5 million (1,000 x $5,000) and keep track of 1,000 separate accounts for us. They would apply their greater research and experience to invest the money in perhaps 50 to 200 individual stocks. And the fund management would track and analyze the stocks for us. They would buy and sell hundreds of stocks over the three years to try to maximize profit. They would also take care of the brokerage fees. And the fund would provide constant research and management service. In exchange for providing this service and the potential gains, they might charge us from zero to 3 percent of the amount invested when we buy in and maybe 1 percent in annual management expenses. That looks like 3 percent to 6 percent of the investment amount gone in fees.

So the three-year comparison is:

	Investment activity	Total fees
Acting alone:	buy or sell 5 to 10 stocks	fees total 6% to 20%
In the fund:	buy or sell hundreds of stocks	fees total 3% to 6%

The numbers above were just made up for the sale of this discussion; however, the numbers are realistic. They represent fair estimates of what might happen with some mutual funds. With mutual funds, economies of scale should act to benefit the individual investors.

Mutual Fund Diversification

Remember that in chapter 3 we talked about the problem of diversification for the small investor. There was a difficulty in choosing to spread your money among several stocks due to high brokerage fees. But we can get excellent diversification through a few mutual funds. For example, if you wanted to invest $50,000 on your own, you might buy five to ten stocks and four or five bonds and sell some of them to buy new from time to time. Quite aside from the research involved, that could cost $500 to $1,000 each year (or easily more) in brokers' fees. But $50,000 might be distributed among four mutual funds as follows:

- $10,000 in a blue chip fund holding 100 stocks,
- $10,000 in a small-capitalization fund holding 100 stocks,
- $15,000 in a bond fund holding 50 bonds, and
- $15,000 in a mortgage fund with investments in government-guaranteed mortgage certificates.

In this way you would only need to select the four mutual funds. The fund managers would take care of the work, time, and expense of diversifying, and the buying and selling of stocks or bonds. The initial commissions would total anywhere from zero to $1,000 and the ongoing yearly expenses would total maybe $300 to $600. Over a few years, you'd pay lower fees than you would buying the separate stocks and bonds. With the mutual funds, there are several ways to hold down the costs, which we will address later.

Mutual Fund Management and Research

The mutual fund should be able to bring stronger analysis and management to the investments than the individual investor would. Instead of the $5 million total investment we talked about before, an operating mutual fund would probably have a much larger amount to work with. If they had $500 million of investors' money and produced $10 million a year in revenue for the fund's management, they could hire a few bright, energetic analysts to do their research. In addition to the analysts, a senior manager would have final authority over what the mutual fund would buy or sell. That overseer should be a seasoned financial expert who had proven his or her good judgment and decisiveness in years of Wall Street guerilla warfare. Once again, we have to allow for variations from one fund to another, but you can see that the mutual fund generally gets better research and better decision-making wisdom than the individual investor does. Before you buy a fund, check that presumption by reading the fund's objectives, reviewing their current portfolio, and reviewing their performance record over the past five years.

Mutual fund performance has been an area of ongoing dispute. Certainly the longest-lived and most-advertised funds have been generally successful. But that is a biased sample, and it rides on a trend of rising markets over the past fifteen years. Research has been done that concludes that stock mutual funds generally do not outperform the overall market averages. On the other hand, you have the indisputable real-world example of the Magellan Fund that shows that choosing the right fund can be extremely profitable. My own conclusion is that for those of us who decide to get into the markets, picking a mutual fund is easier than picking a good stock or bond, is less risky, and has as good a chance at success.

In late 1995, I checked a random sample of thirty mutual funds investing in stocks or bonds or both.

	Past year	Prior 5 years compound rate
Average result	-2%	+8%
Best result	+20%	+18%
Worst result	-13%	-1%

In late 2001, I did the same check, but using only stock funds:

	Past year	Prior 5 years	Prior 10 years
Average result	-13%	+7%	+10%
Best result	+26%	+18%	+17%
Worst result	-72%	-5%	0

So the results appear to be all over the place. The results for the prior five- or ten-year terms are biased because the worst funds from those periods have gone out of business, so the worst results have been removed from the available data. During the five-year period from late 1996 to late 2001, the Standard & Poor's 500 Index rose at an annual rate of 9 percent per year, and, during the ten years from late 1991 to late 2001, it rose at an annual rate of 11 percent per year. There are all kinds of reasons for arguing that these figures are or are not representative, but I will suggest a useful, if simplistic, reading of the data:

> Year by year, good mutual funds are likely to do better than stock investments you would make on your own, and bad mutual funds are likely to do worse. Over longer periods of time, mutual funds that stay in business are likely to return a decent profit, requiring much less work and stress for the average investor than would be required of someone doing their own stock selection.

The Small Investor Can Relax and Enjoy Life

Finding a Good Mutual Fund

There are more than 10,000 mutual funds. Selecting one or two to buy can be a daunting task, but it is simpler than picking individual stocks. What are the differences between the funds, and how are they labeled? Funds can be studied by the kinds of things they invest in, the way they structure fees to shareholders, their risk levels, and other factors. In fact, there are clever and ambitious people in New York right now who are inventing new mutual funds with original features that can be advertised as filling a niche for some class of neglected investors. The more you study, the more variety and complexity you will find. Remember Rule #2: Don't get bogged down in a search for perfect information.

Types of Mutual Funds

The reason there are so many mutual funds is that a lot of companies want your money, and every one of them can invent 20 or 50 or 200 different funds with different investing methods that might appeal to some group of investors. The most obvious description of funds can be made according to the kinds of commodities they buy. Some examples are stock funds, which invest in various stock markets; bond funds, which invest primarily in bonds; balanced funds, which buy stocks seeking a combination of income and growth; and funds of funds, which invest in other mutual funds.

The Stock Fund

The simplest idea is the stock fund. A stock fund will typically invest between 60 and 95 percent of its money in stocks. Each fund will have a *prospectus* that describes the fund's rules and objectives. The fund is required to show the prospectus to each new investor so you know where the money is going. The statement of the fund's objective in the prospectus should help you gauge the risk and reward associated with a given fund.

Here is an example of some information (lifted out of context) from the prospectus of the Axe-Houghton Growth Fund, which was

Prospectus

one of the USF&G family of funds. It is no longer in business. This excerpt is not a complete or adequate description of the prospectus of the fund; it is an example of typical information that may be found in a prospectus.

INVESTMENT OBJECTIVE AND POLICIES

The Fund's primary investment objective is long-term capital growth. The Fund also seeks to protect capital values. The Fund's investment objective is a fundamental policy and may only be changed with the approval of shareholders. Other investment policies and practices are not fundamental and may be changed by the Board of Directors of the Company without shareholder approval. Due to the uncertainty inherent in all investments, there can be no assurance that the Fund will be able to achieve its investment objective.

The Fund's assets are normally invested in common and convertible preferred stocks. It is anticipated that the Fund's portfolio will be heavily weighted in stocks of companies that have above-average earnings growth potential. In selecting such stocks, the Fund's investment adviser will consider factors such as the issuer's financial condition, management, earnings momentum, and the position of the issuer in its industry. Investments are sometimes made in securities not currently paying dividends but believed to have good income and growth prospects. Under normal circumstances, at least 65 percent of the value of the Fund's total assets will be invested in stocks.

Some key phrases to pick up in the passage include "long-term capital growth"; "normally invested in common and convertible preferred stocks"; and "at least 65 percent invested in stocks." This fund may fairly be described as a stock fund. If you were interested in this fund, you could look at some Internet sites listed at the end of this chapter and get a lot of information about its performance, fees, recent investments, and objective. You could examine the fund's holdings to see that it conforms to the full statement of objectives in the prospectus and to see if their particular selection of stocks appeals to your risk and reward standards.

Among stock funds there are many, many variations. Here are examples of a few you'll be running into:

BLUE CHIP FUNDS

These are stock funds that focus on large, solid, well-known companies; they probably hold GE and Potomac Electric and Merck (symbol MRK). Examples include the AIM Blue Chip Fund and the USAA S&P 500 Index Fund.

SMALL-CAP FUNDS

These funds focus on companies whose market capitalization (total market value of all shares) is below a threshold value, such as $400 million or $800 million. Each manager sets her own limit on what is small cap. They probably own a mix of well-known and lesser-known companies. They might own Alabama Power Corp. (symbol ALQ, market cap $200 million) or Brown Shoe (symbol BWS, $233 million) or Crown Cork and Seal (symbol CCK, $170 million). Examples of small-cap funds include the Alger Small Cap Portfolio and the Berwyn Fund. One of them might possibly hold Wal-Mart stock (symbol WMT) with market cap of $240 billion. How can that be? Well, if the manager was very smart twenty years ago, he might have bought Wal-Mart when it was a small cap, and just held the stock ever since.

GROWTH FUNDS

These funds may not give much attention to company size; they focus instead on growing revenues and earnings. Part of the theory is that a high price for today's earnings may be a bargain for next year's. These funds might hold Coca-Cola, Philip Morris (symbol MO), and Office Depot (symbol ODP), plus some companies that are not yet household names. Examples include the AIM Weingarten Fund, Delaware Growth Opportunities Fund, and the Capstone Growth Fund.

INCOME FUNDS

These are the counterpart to the growth funds. The income funds are designed to serve investors who are more concerned about immediate income than pie-in-the-sky several years away. The investors who like income funds may be retirees who want to collect regular income from their nest eggs or other investors who don't believe that long-term earnings can be forecast reliably. Examples include the Capstone Government Income Fund, the Fidelity Equity Income Fund, and the Pioneer Equity Income Fund.

You may have observed that most of the funds' names are suggestive of the style of investing.

> Do not assume that a fund's name is a good indicator of the investment strategy—many funds are deceptive in that regard.

If you want to buy a small-cap fund or a utilities fund, don't just rely on the name. Check the prospectus and objectives to see what they are buying. Check some of the Internet sites at the end of this chapter to see what stocks they currently hold. Check some of the major ratings services such as Morningstar or Lipper Analytical Services or Value Line to see how they have classified and described the fund. Lipper Analytical Services may be the most objective on that question.

Fee Structure: Load or No-load

Some funds require you to pay a sales commission when you first invest. This kind of fee is called a *load,* or front-end load. It must be shown in the prospectus and may be as high as 8.5 percent in the most extreme cases. The commission is expressed as a percentage of the value of shares purchased.

Load

The term *no-load fund* means a fund that does not charge a sales commission. Don't be naïve—the no-load funds find other ways to get you to pay.

No-Load Fund

If the fund has a 3 percent load, the fee will be 3 percent of the amount that goes into the fund. For example, if you want to spend $5,000, they will split this into two amounts: $4,854, which actually goes into fund shares, and $146, which is the sales fee. The fee, $146, is 3 percent of the $4,854 amount invested. If you actually want exactly $5,000 worth of shares, they will charge you an additional $150 (3 percent of $5,000) for the sales fee.

Almost everyone classifies funds as being load or no-load, although this distinction is becoming blurred as the investment industry invents more ways to split up their fees into confusing options. Some funds may also require a back-end load, which is a percentage fee based on the amount the investor redeems when he sells his shares. Usually the simplest view of load or no-load refers to a front-end load.

If you want to buy a fund with a 4 percent front-end load and a 1 percent redemption fee (back-end load) and you send them a check for $8,000, they will first deduct $308 from the $8,000, and buy you $7,692 worth of shares. That works out so the fee ($308) is 4 percent of the amount invested ($7,692). Two years later, if you decide to sell after your shares have appreciated to $9,000 in value, the fund will deduct $90 (that's 1 percent) from the redemption amount and send you a check for $8,910. In this case the fund will be advertising that it appreciated 17 percent over the two years ($7,692 grew to $9,000), whereas your actual profit was just 11 percent ($8,000 grew to $8,910).

One of the absolute curses of the mutual fund business has become their tendency to develop new ways to describe hidden costs and present them in the prospectus in difficult-to-understand ways. If you plan to buy a mutual fund, read the prospectus. Read the section on fees especially carefully. If you don't understand it, don't buy the fund; they don't deserve your business. If you are working through a broker, ask for a written summary of all of the fees that the fund charges or takes out of earnings. If he won't do it, or if the summary is confusing, take your business elsewhere.

The Family of Funds

Mutual funds can be grouped according to the managing investment company. For purposes of planning your investments, you might want to focus your attention on which investment company runs the mutual fund. Fidelity Investment Company operates over 200 different funds. They are spoken of collectively as the Fidelity Family. Others include the Dreyfus Family and the Oppenheimer Family. There are two reasons why an investor might want to keep all funds in the same family. First, the investment company would probably send a unified report, which would make it easy to compare and total the results of several investments. Second, the investment company would probably give you a break on fees if you transferred your money from one of their funds to another. The downside is that you might miss out on some good opportunities by staying in one family.

The Risk Level

When you begin to consider the risks associated with mutual funds, you find a "good news, bad news" scene. The good news is that there is a reasonable presumption that the professional management and the diversification they provide should avoid most of the worst risks that you would encounter alone. You can assume some degree of safety relative to the type of investments they use. In other words, investing in an international stock fund should be safer than buying foreign stocks on our own, but it would still be riskier than buying an American blue chip stock fund. The bad news is that there is no clear and simple measurement of risk that can be relied upon. In an ideal case, we would like to see a scale of values from 1 to 10, 1 being the least risky. Then we could look at the scale and say that the Amoeba Fund has risk rating 8 and the Protozoa Fund has risk rating 4, so the Protozoa Fund is safer. We would like all of the magazines and newspapers and brokers to provide those numbers to us so that we could evaluate risk. No such luck!

What you can find, though, are fairly consistent opinions about the relative risk levels of different funds. For example, the Morningstar mutual funds reports will rank funds by risk level using five grades, very high, high, medium, low, and very low, based on the funds' previous volatility history. *Kiplinger's Personal Finance* magazine uses a volatility ranking from 1 to 10 (10 indicating the highest volatility). These publications are not totally consistent. I have found occasional contradictions among them, but since there is no certain scientific method of determining risk, they do give us the best indicators available.

My advice is not to expect any guarantees on risk level. What you can expect is some amount of reasonably consistent opinion on the volatility of a given fund compared to other funds that have similar investments. The websites listed at the end of this chapter give a lot of helpful information and would all be good places to study when trying to find a fund that is right for you, however, they all shy away from talking about risk. They do include some search criteria, including "beta" or "the Sharpe ratio," which are numbers that have some relationship to a fund's volatility or risk/reward measurements, but it is highly unlikely that many investors, including professional fund managers, have any clear idea what those numbers represent. ("Beta" is defined on page 258. The *Sharpe ratio* is a number calculated from statistical parameters that gives an indicator of the investment's previous return compared to its volatility. Don't worry about it.)

Sharpe Ratio

So why do they present beta and the Sharpe ratio and such? The reason is that there are well-known formulas to calculate those numbers. The websites and publications can handle the formulas with their computers. But it is very difficult to describe and understand risk using a formula. The publications do what is easy for them and what gives some appearance of describing risk.

Bottom line on risk of funds:

> You will not find any useful, clear, and simple indicators of funds' specific risks.

Morningstar and Value Line publish helpful opinions about the level of risk as compared to the reward for individual funds. That is probably the best you can expect, except for the thinking you do on your own.

The Socially Responsible Funds

When I looked into this group, I learned something about doing my homework on mutual funds. Even though these funds share a common label, there are a lot of differences between them. They offer you different fees, different objectives, and different results in profitability. Even though each claims to be "responsible," each also has different ideas about the stocks they buy and the ways in which they try to be socially responsible.

Socially Responsible Funds

Here is a group of funds that advertise themselves as supporting the public interests. They choose to adopt the labels *"socially responsible"* or "environmental." The label is helpful because it indicates that there is something at work beyond just the profit motive. The label is also misleading because one investor's concept of what is socially responsible may be another investor's Three Mile Island. Is it more socially responsible to support oil-driven power plants or nuclear-driven power plants?

There is an arguable point of view that all investing is socially responsible. It supports businesses that create jobs. You don't have to feel guilty about non-socially-responsible investing. On the other hand, there is an arguable point of view that no investing is socially responsible. It avoids direct support of all-too-obvious immediate public needs. The money could go to charity or political action committees or a landscape architect. Once again when push comes to shove it's your money and you make your choice.

A few socially responsible funds are:

- The Calvert Social Investment Fund
- Delaware Social Awareness Fund
- The Smith-Barney Social Awareness Fund
- The Domini Social Equity Fund
- The TIAA-CREF Social Choice Equity Fund

There are others. It's unlikely that any two investors would agree on which is the most responsible. Even though all of these funds fall into the category of "socially responsible funds," they vary in their objectives and investments.

The Smith-Barney Social Awareness Fund selects companies that make a positive contribution to society. Their recent holdings included IBM, J. P. Morgan (symbol JPM), and Alcoa (symbol AA).

The Calvert Social Investment Fund chooses companies that are environmentally sustaining, equal-opportunity employers, responsible corporate citizens, and makers of safe, healthy products. Their recent holdings included Microsoft, IBM, and Home Depot (symbol HD).

The Delaware Social Awareness Fund selects companies that avoid activity in nuclear power, tobacco, gambling, or other areas they have determined to be objectionable. Their recent holdings included AOL/Time-Warner (symbol AOL) and Eli Lilly (symbol LLY).

Even if you are socially responsible, you probably also want to make a profit. The following table shows some of the expenses and results for those five funds. The performance numbers indicate annualized total return (dividends and capital appreciation, after deducting expenses) in the one year or five years ending November 2001.

	Costs		Performance	
	Load	Annual expense	1 year	5 years
Calvert Social	4.75%	1.2%	−6%	6%
Delaware Social	5.75%	1.5%	−13%	*
Domini Social	0	1.0%	−14%	10%
Smith-Barney Social	5.0%	1.2%	−11%	10%
TIAA-CREF Social	0	0.3%	−14%	*

*Means not yet 5 years old

Over the past year, they have generally followed the stock markets results for large-cap stocks. The above information is not enough to show you whether any of these funds is a good investment for you. The point is you need to do more homework than simply asking for a socially responsible fund. These funds would not have the same appeal to all investors. When you decide to invest in these or any others, you should read and compare the prospectuses and the recent results of several funds. There is a helpful website dedicated to socially responsible investing: *www.socialinvest.org.*

How Do I Get Started?

Individual stock prices are set directly by the market action during each day, but the funds' prices are a little different. In order to understand the pricing mechanisms you need to know about two numbers, called the public offering price and the net asset value.

Public Offering Price

The amount you will pay for a share of a fund is given by the *public offering price* (POP), which is computed at the close of each business day for each mutual fund. The public offering price is the net value (per share) of the fund's investments, plus a little extra for the sales commission, if they have a load.

Net Asset Value

Net asset value (NAV) is the sum of values of everything the fund owns, minus the liabilities, divided by the number of shares outstanding. The public offering price is equal to, or slightly higher than, the net asset value.

Think of the net asset value as the intrinsic worth of each share, and public offering price as the market price, which is either the same or slightly higher than the net asset value.

Suppose you bought a fund called the Fine Fund, and it had net assets of $260,300, and 29,750 shares outstanding. Then the net asset value of the Fine Fund, on that day, would be $260,300 ÷ 29,750 = $8.75 per share. This value is good from that day's market closing until the markets open the next morning.

To get the POP, for public sales, the fund management would calculate the NAV based on stock market prices at the end of the day, adding an adjustment to compensate for the sales load. If Fine Fund had a sales load of 2 percent, the POP would be $8.92. For each share you bought you would pay $8.75 for actual share value and an additional $0.175 for the sales fee ($0.175 is 2 percent of $8.75). For no-load funds, the POP is equal to the NAV. The essential rule to know is that you can buy shares at the cost of POP and redeem them at the price of NAV.

Your cost to buy shares = number of shares x POP
Your redemption value = number of shares x NAV

When the fund has a redemption fee, or back-end load, that will be deducted from your redemption value.

Buying and Redeeming Mutual Funds

If you decide to buy a mutual fund, it can be as simple as buying an individual stock. You can call your broker and tell him you have $2,000 to buy the Fine Fund. The broker will purchase the shares at a price determined by the POP at the close of trading on that day.

Suppose the NAV at the close of that day was $8.75. If there was no initial sales charge (no load), then POP = NAV and your $2,000 would buy 228.6 shares (2,000 ÷ 8.75 = 228.6). If there was an initial sales load of 2 percent as we calculated above, you would buy shares at the public offering price of $8.924. You would get 224.2 shares (2,000 ÷ 8.924 = 224.2). In either case, each of your new shares would have equal value with everyone else's shares, $8.75, the net asset value. You can find the values of POP and NAV for many funds listed in the daily business sections of newspapers. Just as with a stock purchase, your shares will be worth more or less the next day, but they will have the same value as everyone else's shares.

Let's say it's a no-load fund, and two years later you still had your 228.6 shares—but you looked in the paper one day and saw that the current NAV for Fine Fund was $9.136 (based on the previous day's market prices), and you decided to sell. At the close of business on the day you sold, let us say Fine Fund held:

	Total value
1,300 shares of A Corp at $10.50	$13,650
3,500 shares of B Corp at $42.50	$148,750
6,000 shares of R Corp at $14.10	$84,600
$39,000 in cash	$39,000
Total	$286,000

The net assets on that day would be $286,000. If there were 31,300 shares outstanding and no debt for the fund, you would calculate the NAV as:

NAV = $286,000 ÷ 31,300 = $9.14 per share.

You could redeem your shares that day, at the close of market trading, for $9.14 per share—just like anyone else who held shares that day. Your 228.6 shares would bring $2,089.40 (228.6 x $9.14).

You May Trade with a Broker or the Fund Management

If you want to buy or redeem mutual fund shares, you have to deal with someone who is in that business. That must be either the management of the fund or another party with whom the fund has set up a business relationship for buying and redeeming shares. That other party is probably a stockbroker. This is not as simple as we would like it to be, because the brokers will not all handle all of the funds you might like. We talked about this problem in chapter 4 as part of our discussion on finding professional help. If you plan to buy mutual funds, you might review that section.

Profits and Losses

With a mutual fund investment, you, a broker, and the investment company are going to get their hands on your money. The ideal case is where everyone wins—and in the stock and bond markets that is possible. Let's get an idea of how everyone will make out.

Funds Expenses

The fee structure for mutual funds is getting more complicated all the time. *Read the prospectus!* If it's not clear, don't spend your money on that fund (Rule #1). Serious people around Wall Street say that the quality and clarity of the prospectus and earnings reports tell a lot about the quality and thinking of the fund's management. If you don't understand the fee structure, beware! What kind of financial managers would not show their fees clearly?

Mutual funds' fees come in three forms:

- load (up-front, advanced, sales fee, front-end): a one-time fee charged when you buy shares;
- expenses (ongoing, annual, operational, management, 12b-1 fees): various kinds of ongoing annual charges; and
- back-end load (redemption fee): a one-time fee charged when you redeem (sell) your shares.

All mutual funds will charge one or more of these fees. That's fair—they have to make a living, too. The manager deserves to earn $300,000 a year if she is really good, and all of their analysts have to make $60,000 because they live in New York or Boston.

Don't worry about what they keep—concentrate on what you keep. Remember Rule #4 (It's not a contest).

Let's look at an example. Imagine that we have the choice of two funds, A or B. You put $10,000 into A; I put $10,000 into B. Imagine further that the account values progress as shown below for the next three years:

	Fund A	Fund B
Front-end load	0%	4%
Amount invested	$10,000	$9,615
Annual fees	0.4%	0.5%
Redemption fee	1%	1%
Value after 3 years	$11,000	$12,000
Return on redemption	$10,890	$11,880
Profit	$890	$1,880
Total 3-year expenses	$230	$670

Fund B was much more expensive, but it was still a better investment. You should be happier making money along with the fund management, rather than just muddling along with a cheap ride.

But it would be irresponsible to ignore the expenses. Let's look at the three types. First, we consider the infamous front-end load. The mutual fund management may charge you a fee right up front just to set up your account. For this you get in the game—you get your name in their records and you get their earnings reports. The load will be somewhere between 0 and 8.5 percent, charged when you buy shares.

Second, along the way they may take out various expenses to keep their business operating. These expenses get all kinds of obscure names (including 12b-1), which don't mean a whole lot. It would be impossible for us to review all of the kinds of fees—indeed, it would fill a whole new book! Just make sure you get a clear statement of the fee amount. It should be less than 2 percent a year, on an ongoing basis. That'll be in the prospectus. I'll mention it again: *Read the prospectus!* Even as I write this, I have in hand two annual statements from large well-known mutual funds. Both of them show an "investment advisory fee" along with about eight to ten other obscure fees. Both of them will no doubt advertise that their investment advisory fee is fairly small and will leave the customer to figure out for himself where the money is actually going.

Third, some funds have a redemption fee. The redemption is taken from your share value when you redeem (cash in) your fund shares. Sometimes the redemption fee will go away after three, or four, or five years. That will be stated in the prospectus. The logic in this is that it would be difficult for the fund to manage its business if too many people were buying and selling too frequently. They encourage you to leave your money in place for a few years.

Here is a view of some hypothetical fund results, just to help you learn what to look at. (Finest Fund and Magnificent Mutual Fund are fictional examples.)

EXAMPLE OF ONE YEAR WITH THE FINEST FUND

The Finest Fund charges a 2 percent front-end load, 1.5 percent annual expenses, and 1 percent redemption fee. If you had $10,000 to spend on the fund, initially $196 would go to the broker (salesperson) who sold you the fund, and $9,804 ($196 = 2 percent of $9,804) would be invested in stocks (or gold or whatever the fund trades). In the first year the $9,804 of stocks might grow to $12,000. Then the fund would rake off 1.5 percent for annual expenses, that is, $180. That would leave $11,820.

So the $9,804 has grown to $11,820 assets in the fund. The fund will report that as a 20.6 percent gain (after taking out expenses). Your actual investment value has grown from $10,000 to $11,820, which is an 18.2 percent return, but the fund only looks at the part of the money they had to work with after taking out the front-end load.

EXAMPLE OF FOUR YEARS WITH THE MAGNIFICENT MUTUAL FUND

If you were to put up $10,000 to buy shares in the Magnificent Mutual Fund, you might find something like this: their prospectus shows 3 percent sales load, 1.25 percent annual expenses, and 1 percent redemption fee. Suppose that over the next four years stock prices, as indicated by the S&P 500 Index, show returns of +6 percent, +2 percent, −10 percent, and +8 percent. And let's say that the management at Magnificent Mutual is good enough to buy stocks that give +9 percent, +8 percent, −4 percent, and +15 percent in the four years (that means they are pretty good).

After holding this investment for four years, you could sell and walk away with $11,879. That is a real gain of $1,879 (which is 18.79 percent) in four years, about 4.4 percent compound annual gain.

Is this any good? The investment company has taken a total of $850 in fees over the life of your investment. Let's look at the results three ways:

1. The compound annual gains in values of the stocks they bought gave a total 30 percent gain in the four years, but this ignores fund expenses.
2. Counting expenses, the fund's reported results for four years are +7.6 percent, +6.7 percent, −5.2 percent, and +13.6 percent. That gives an increase in share values of 24 percent in four years.
3. The results for the investor: $10,000 became $11,879, an 18.79 percent gain in four years.

When you look at it this way, it appears that the fund has raked off a lot of money for poor results. But that is not the whole story. It is more realistic to look at the changes in the S&P 500 Index over four years: +6 percent, +2 percent, -10 percent, and +8 percent. That gives a four-year total growth of +5.1 percent. If you had taken your $10,000 to a pretty good stockbroker, paid brokerage fees, worked hard, and been lucky, you might have realized a gain over the four years of between 0 percent and +10 percent.

By using the Magnificent Mutual Fund you came out ahead (up almost 19 percent) with less work and lower risk. You made good money—they made good money—who is to worry? Of course, if your return from the fund had been much less than the standard of performance, you should have considered moving that investment. This has been a purely hypothetical example, but it will give you an idea of how to interpret the funds' statements of results.

Dividends: More Profits

So far we have taken a simple approach to fund profits and just looked at changes in net asset values. There is also another way to profit from funds also. Since they are buying stocks or bonds, they will frequently collect some dividends (or interest). Those dividends will be paid out to the shareholders in cash or reinvested as additional shares if you request it. That again will add to your total return from the fund. When the fund management reports their results, they will always report the paid-out dividends as if all of the dividends had been immediately reinvested in new shares. You don't have to reinvest the dividends. You could keep them or spend them, but many investors will reinvest and the fund management will do their arithmetic on that basis. Just remember when they claim annual growth of +9.3 percent, this means growth of assets plus dividends reinvested, minus their expenses. For a growth fund, expect the growth of assets to be somewhat greater than dividends; for an income fund expect the dividends to be larger than the growth of assets.

Getting Your Money Back

Getting your investment and gains back out of a mutual fund can sometimes be a problem. It should not be. It will not be a problem for you if you address the issue in the beginning.

> Don't put any money into a mutual fund until you know the procedures and the timing for redeeming the shares.

In order to regain your capital, reap the profits, or perhaps recognize a loss, you will have to redeem some or all of your shares. Funds have different procedures and rules for handling redemptions. The basic idea is simple enough—they cancel your shares and send you a check. However, in practice it may not be quite that easy, and it may take longer than you care to wait for your money. The time to resolve this problem and avoid unnecessary hassles is when you first invest in the fund. In January 1992, I asked PaineWebber to transfer funds from an IRA money market fund to a new account I had set up with another broker. In September, they were still sending me statements showing that they were trying to complete the transaction (yes, I said September). The amount of money involved was insignificant, but the delay was aggravating.

In the prospectus, the rules must be spelled out in detail regarding what you have to do in order to redeem shares. If you purchase the funds through a broker, she should be able to take care of the redemption.

When you buy the shares, ask about the requirements and the time period for redeeming shares and getting your money back. There will normally be a delay of a few days for them to process your request.

If you purchase the shares from the fund, they will require either a written request or a telephone call in which you provide adequate identification before they will return the money. In either case, there will be some sort of procedure meant to prove that the request comes from the true owner of the shares. There are several ways they can verify the authenticity of the request. You just want to make sure that it's all set up in advance. Don't wait until the day you need the money and then begin an 8- to 15-day process of sending letters back and forth to establish the redemption. When you first buy the shares, make sure that all signature cards, code words, and whatever else may be required are set up immediately. Then you will know that you can cash in quickly (within a few days).

Changes in the Mutual Funds Industry

Lots of brokers, investment managers, and newspaper columnists like to talk about mutual funds. Whenever they need to get down to brass tacks, most of the hard data comes from past performance. Sure, everyone keeps saying, "Past performance is no guarantee of future results," but it is obvious that they want you to believe that past performance is an indicator of future results.

It should be clear to any investor whose eyes haven't glazed over that the investment companies and the brokerage firms are, in effect, advertising that "mutual funds have been very, very good to us for the past fifteen years; therefore, buy more mutual funds." How often do they advertise their risk levels? How often do they advertise what's in the portfolio? Never! (Well, hardly ever.) They only advertise past performance.

Examine that logic before committing any money. The question to ask is: "Should we believe that the performance of the past fifteen years is an indicator of future results?" My answer to that question is generally no. My personal investment strategy says that the world and the financial markets have changed too much in that time period. The mutual funds industry has certainly changed enormously. The old rules and the old methods may be no longer reliable. I invest in a few carefully selected mutual funds because of what I see or believe about the current economy and future business prospects, and because I want to diversify—not just because the funds industry has had a good track record.

The game has changed. Huge changes are occurring all around. Some of those changes are fundamental to the economy and the markets and will affect all investors. We don't have time to roll out six chapters on economics, but we can look at the investment industry.

I have already mentioned the rapid growth of funds, both in numbers and in total assets. Do you believe that the industry is capable of producing enough talented managers and analysts to staff the new funds and manage the new money according to the standards that we require? Look at any other business or industry that has grown very fast. You may have worked for one. Do they usually succeed in developing competent new management as fast as is needed? Do some folks have to get on-the-job training? Is that what you want from your money managers? (Answers: No, yes, no.)

If 1,000 new funds are created in the next two or three years, as there probably will be, we can guess that many of them will have new and unique objectives. It would be foolhardy to assume that all of those new

The Wolves Are at the Small Investor's Door

funds will have strong management, capable and well-trained staffs, good profit potential within their niches, and adequate safety through diversification. It may be—but the smart money will not bet on the field.

Given all that, I still think that, for most small investors, advantages outweigh the risks. But caution is advised. Please work hard at selecting the funds to buy. Read the next chapter and refer again to chapter 5.

Closed-End Funds

Closed-End Fund

There is a separate class of funds that operate differently from most that we will discuss. The *closed-end funds* do not sell and redeem shares whenever customers want. Instead, they sell shares once to raise investing capital, and then those shares may be sold on the open markets, along with stocks, just like the shares of any other publicly owned company. Investing in a closed-end fund is very much like buying individual stocks. The investors can determine a net asset value for the shares, but the selling price of shares is fixed by market demand as it is for stocks. The selling price will generally be around the net asset value, but it may vary by plus or minus 10 or 20 percent. Sometimes people speak of "open-end" funds to indicate those that sell and redeem shares on demand, but the common usage of "mutual fund" assumes an open-end fund. The closed-end funds are frequently just referred to as investment companies or publicly traded funds. The (open-end) mutual funds are by far the more common in the press reports and in individual investors' strategies.

There is a popular myth about closed-end funds that you don't want to believe. Some writers claim that if a closed-end fund is selling below its net asset value, then that is a gift and you should buy it, because you get ownership of assets that are worth more than what you are paying. BALONEY! That is a naïve view of markets. If you buy the shares of a closed-end fund, you get the shares. You don't get ownership of the fund's assets. The shares that you purchase are worth whatever they will fetch in the open market, and that is the current market price. If the assets are worth more, that might be an indicator of underlying value in the investment; but it does not mean you can now, or in the future, be certain of realizing that value when you sell.

There is no way to describe all of the types of funds. Just assume that if there is anything in the world that moves through markets, there may be a mutual fund that buys and sells those things. That fund will give you an opportunity for an indirect investment in those things. An interesting exception is the zero coupon bond—there are tax complications that make zeros especially unattractive for mutual funds.

Recommended Further Reading

The business magazines *Money*, *Smart Money*, *Kiplingers*, and *Fortune*, and other specialty investment publications, such as *Morningstar Mutual Fund Reports*, *The Value Line Mutual Fund Survey*, *Investor's Business Daily*, and *Barron's* will continue to give the best up-to-the-minute opinions in mutual funds. If you like a lot of facts and figures and history on mutual funds, you'll find enough to keep you busy for weeks at the Investment Company Institute site, *www.ici.org*.

Jaffe, Charles A. *Chuck Jaffe's Lifetime Guide to Mutual Funds*. Cambridge, Ms.: Perseus Publications, 2000.

www.socialinvest.org

www.quicken.com/investments/funds

www.smartmoney.com/funds

www.morningstar.com

cbs.marketwatch.com

www.yahoo.finance.com

Chapter 10

Selecting Mutual Funds for Diversification and Asset Allocation

---

Small investors need to know:

- Does past performance mean anything?

- Where can I get more information?

- How can I diversify with mutual funds?

- How can I evaluate and choose among mutual funds?

Should I Buy Mutual Funds?

You have to decide for yourself where to put your money, but there is a good case to argue that, for most small investors, a large chunk of our risk-oriented investment capital should go into mutual funds. The questions that naturally arise are, "How do I mix mutual funds with the other parts of my investing?" and "How do I select the funds?"

This chapter will deal with those problems. The main themes are why to buy funds, how to use them for diversification, how to understand the reports and reviews that are offered in many different reference sources, and how to evaluate the funds. Luckily, there are a lot of people eager to write about these themes. There are more sources of information, and probably more good, readable, reliable sources, than any of us could keep up with.

Past Performance Is Not a Guarantee of Future Results

During the year ending November 30, 2001, the average fund investing in American telecommunications companies lost 41 percent of its value. The funds invested in science and technology lost 42 percent on average. The funds tracking the S&P 500 Index lost 14 percent. There were some bright spots, but a lot of people lost a lot of money during those twelve months. So I'm going to tell you to buy mutual funds, right? Right!

From 1997 to 2001, most funds investing in American stocks made money. They gained 7 percent compound annual return on average. Investors who owned sector funds specializing in financial services or biotechnology made much more. The income funds made around 7 percent. Even most of the weakest mutual funds during that period were profitable or had just small losses for the five years. The performance of 1997 to 2000 was not a good indicator of funds' performances in 2001.

So what are you going to do? You have by now read about stocks and bonds and mutual funds, and you have an understanding of some of the basic ideas. Time is running out. There are only a few pages left in this book, and I can tell you that the last chapter is not going to help you make much money. It is time to make some real decisions on mutual funds. You may decide to toss the book in the trash and go back to your garden or your spouse. Very well, go—I wish you well. But if you think you are going to stick with, or at least try, some investing in financial markets, you have to take a hard look at some mutual funds.

It would be difficult for the average small investor to build a reasonably safe and diversified investment portfolio without using some mutual funds. You may also buy stocks or bonds or some other things, but if you are a true-blue small investor, you need to diversify. Small investors like us probably don't have enough money to fully diversify through the stock markets, and we almost certainly don't have enough time or research tools to buy and track more than a few stocks. In order to do a good job in buying 10 stocks, you might have to study 50 or 100. That would be a tremendous toll on your time and attention. You may want to acquire a mix of stocks and stock mutual funds plus bonds or bond mutual funds, but without mutual funds you probably will not attain adequate diversification.

Allocating Your Money

You still have the question of how to allocate your investment capital. I cannot tell you exactly how to do that because I don't know your circumstances. Some of the books and magazines mentioned throughout this book offer guidelines for people of similar age, finances, expectations, other assets, plans for the money, and so on. By all means look at them. *Smart Money* has run fine articles of that nature. *Consumer Reports* also offers similar advice.

There are variations in opinions on the asset allocation problem. Some financial advisors say that people older than fifty should keep most of their money in safe bonds or bond funds. But lately it has become more acceptable for the retired investor to continue to plan for growth of capital in order to keep ahead of inflation and provide for a longer retirement. That would point toward putting more money into growth-stock funds and accepting the risk of being in the stock market. So the published advice you will see is contradictory. The answer for you is a very personal decision. It depends on your retirement income, life expectations, and other financial circumstances. The retired couple who owned their home could presumably stand more risk than a similar couple who did not.

The same kinds of variations apply to any other category of investors, whether old or young, married or single, parents or not. It is all very personal.

Different Kinds of Funds

In the last chapter we looked briefly at types of funds, and we saw that there are different ways to classify them. There are more than 10,000 mutual funds and the number is increasing, so you have a lot of choices out there. In fact, you have enough choices to satisfy almost any whim, and enough choices to create a lot of trouble. Luckily, it is not necessary to study all of those funds to make your choices. Each time that you wish to buy a fund, it will probably be sufficient for you to look over performance results for ten to twenty of them. That's easy. The results are widely published in many newspapers, magazines, and websites. Out of the funds that you look at, you might pick a few to study closely, and out of that last group, you will probably find more than one that suit your needs. In order to get into this process, we need to further explore the classification of funds.

When you set out to find a mutual fund investment, you want to consult to your PIG. Many services are available through newspapers, magazines, and the Internet that will help you evaluate funds for protection (risk level), income (yield), and growth potential. Most of the websites listed at the end of this chapter will allow you to describe the fund characteristics you want and get back a list of perhaps a few funds (or perhaps hundreds) that satisfy those requirements.

Just to illustrate the point, in November 2001 you could have gone to the Lipper website *(www.lipperleaders.com)* and asked for "Lipper Leaders" for consistent return that invest mainly in large-cap growth stocks. You probably would have gotten back a list of about 100 funds. If you further required each fund to be a Lipper Leader for preservation of capital, the list was narrowed to one fund, the Orbitex Clermont Fund (symbol CLERX).

You can go to the *Smart Money* website *(www.smartmoney.com)* and use their "Find Funds" page to search for funds. I used it to ask for funds that had both year-to-date and five-year annualized returns of 5 percent or better, and had beta between 0.8 and 1.2, and had front load not over 3 percent, and allowed an initial investment for an IRA of $500. That gave me a list of 229 funds—too many to study.

I then required that the funds only invested in bonds—123 left. I then required that the funds should have at least a four-star Morningstar rating, which got down to 42 funds, and then said I just wanted funds that bought intermediate-term government bonds.

At last, with all of those conditions in place, I got a list of 6 mutual funds that satisfied all of my requirements. So that gave a good group of funds to examine more closely, and I know all six of them have a number of good qualities. It would take a long time to sort through all the available funds for those particular criteria without using the Internet resources. Other websites offer similar search features that you can use to search for funds with all kinds of special requirements that might be of interest.

That funds search was an example of a *screen*. A screen is a computer-based search method that allows you to specify particular criteria that you want in investments, and then let the system search through thousands of funds or stocks or bonds, to produce a list of investment possibilities that satisfy your requirements.

You need to look at a lot more than the fund's name and category to figure out what it actually does and whether it might be right for you. Recall that the socially responsible funds differed in their statements of investment objectives, their selection of stocks, and their results. Any category of funds you look at will have considerable variations.

Loads and No-Loads

Fees are important, but the distinction between load and no-load is becoming blurred. The mutual funds industry tries to deceive us as to what the expenses are, but *mutual fund expenses* will hit you in one or more of these three ways:

- up-front fee when you buy the fund, called a load, or front-end load;
- ongoing expenses as they operate the fund; and
- redemption fee when you sell, called a deferred fee, or back-end load.

The front load is sometimes described as a "normal load," which probably means 4 percent to 8 percent depending on whom you are talking to, or a "low load," which means less than 4 percent. Either way, it comes directly off the top of your money. If you buy $1,000 worth of a fund that has a 4 percent load, and for the first two years it reports total return of 5 percent and 8 percent, respectively, then the investment cost you $1,042 because of the load. At the end of the two years, you would have $1,134, which is a compound annual rate of return on your $1,042 of just about 4.4 percent. That's OK, but it's not really good. The front load eats a big hole in your profits. A 4 percent back load would give nearly the same result.

Many investors and advisors have a firm rule that they will not touch any funds with a sales load or redemption fee. They argue that there are plenty of other choices with equally attractive objectives and historical results, so why pay the fee? That's pretty good thinking, but it may not be right for you. For example, a full-service broker firm has to make a living at the business. In order to get some income they may want to sell you funds with a load, which is a sales commission. If the load is not present on the front end, it may be replaced by a redemption fee when you sell. And if you don't see either a front-end or back-end load, there will probably be a 12b-1 fee, which is used to cover sales expenses for the fund. The front sales load and redemption fee are pretty obvious. The 12b-1 fee is sneaky because you probably won't see the expense; the funds management company will just take it out of the assets along with their other operational expenses. Just don't forget that the brokers, their sales force, the fund management, and their sales force are all hardworking professional people who have to make a living at the business. Read the prospectus to find out where the expenses lie.

Given all that, it still makes sense to look for funds with reasonable expenses. For most small investors, it is probably true that no-load is the preferred way to go, but not with blinders on. For example, here comes the American Funds Company Growth Fund of America (symbol AGTHX), which does carry a 5.75 percent front-end load (ouch!) plus a solid 0.7 percent expense ratio. It may look expensive, but they have been very good over a long time period. For the three-year and five-year periods ending December 1, 2001, they earned compound annual rates of 14 percent and 17 percent, respectively. That performance was balanced by a 13 percent loss during 2001, which was a bad time for most funds. So take a hard look at sales loads and expenses, but remember that the payoff is in what you keep, not what they keep. If everybody makes good money, you should be happy.

More Classifications of Funds

In the *Mutual Funds Quarterly* printed by *Barron's* with data supplied by Lipper Analytical Services, there are forty-four distinct objectives used to classify the funds shown with their definitions of the objectives. For example, they show:

- Balanced funds: The goal is preserving principal; on average, the funds maintain approximately a 60:40 ratio of stocks to bonds.
- Convertibles funds: They invest primarily in convertible bonds and convertible preferred stocks.
- Emerging markets funds: They invest primarily in stocks of emerging market nations. ("Emerging" is a very loose term; it may include the third world or new or growing capital structures or new financial markets.)
- Gold funds: They have at least 65 percent of assets in gold, or gold mining, or mining-financing-related equities.
- Growth funds: They invest principally in companies whose earnings are expected to grow faster than other companies' earnings. Often, they expect their earnings to grow faster than the average rate for companies in the Dow Jones Industrial group or the S&P 500. They may buy stocks of the faster-growing Dow companies, but not all of the thirty industrials.
- Income funds: They seek high current income through stocks, bonds, or money market investments; they have no more than 60 percent in stocks and no more than 75 percent in bonds.
- Specialty funds: These are just funds that defy any of the other forty-three classifications and do not normally stay within any particular size for stock capitalization.

I recommend the review of mutual funds in *Barron's* for your further study. It is published after the end of each calendar quarter. Certainly, *Business Week* and many other periodicals give similar reports.

The Value Line Mutual Funds Survey, available online or through mail, is another valuable resource for funds research that offers a view of funds classifications. It offers thirty-one different objectives, which are often, but not always, in agreement with the Lipper categories. They differ because of the ways each service approaches describing funds. Value Line classifies each fund according to the fund's own statement of objectives. The Lipper classification is based on their independent analysis of what the fund actually does with the money. For that reason, the

Lipper classification is probably more useful to you whenever they differ. For a great many funds, their classifications will be the same. Some of the Value Line classifications include:

- Large-Cap Value or Large-Cap Aggressive Growth (largely S&P 500 stocks);
- Asset Allocation Global Funds (mix of foreign and American stocks and bonds);
- Short Maturity Corporate High-Quality Bond Funds; and
- Non-Japan Pacific Area Stock Funds.

Their thirty-one categories give a pretty good range of choices for focusing your mutual fund asset allocation and diversification.

When you are searching for a mutual fund, the *Value Line* research and analysis would be a valuable starting point, but if you get to the point of actually putting your money on the line for a particular fund, then it would also be wise to check the Lipper category to see what they say the fund does.

Diversifying with Mutual Funds

Pay attention here! There are two guidelines for diversifying with mutual funds:

1. *Most small investors* should be doing most of their investing through mutual funds because it is too expensive and too much work to do it all through purchase and resale of individual stocks and bonds;
2. *All small investors* must use mutual funds to round out their portfolios and obtain decent diversification.

Number 1 is a general guideline to make things easy for you. Number 2 is a requirement, unless you have the time and expertise to do a lot of financial analysis. So, now, we can look at some examples of how this works.

One strategy for your investments might involve picking some individual large-cap stocks yourself and using mutual funds to get the diversification into other stock and bonds. Suppose that the investor had $52,000 that she planned to put into risk-oriented investments in the financial markets. The following could be a beginning strategy for her:

1. I will initially keep half of my money in cash, until I see how things are working and develop a better comfort level.
2. I will find two or three large-cap value stocks and invest $10,000 in them (in total); this will require considerable time and effort in research.
3. I will select one mutual fund from the small-cap growth list and one from the small-cap value list and invest $4,000 in each.
4. I will find a bond fund that specializes in investment-grade bonds and invest $8,000 in it.

The money is allocated as $26,000 temporary cash reserve, $10,000 for stock picks, $8,000 for stock mutual funds, and $8,000 for bond mutual funds.

Maybe the funds selection part of the investment plan looks easy. You could look in Morningstar, pick a fund with five-star rating from each of the two categories small-cap growth and small-cap value, and buy them. That would *not* be a wise approach to funds selection. What would be wise is to look at all of their top-rated funds in each area, consider their load expenses and other expenses, and contact them by phone or website to get copies of the prospectuses and recent annual or semi-annual reports. *Read the prospectuses!!!* If you don't have time to read them, give your money to charity. Look at their current holdings as shown in the reports. Read their objectives and fees as shown in the prospectuses. Look at the recent and longer-term total-return figures for each as reported in a recent issue of *Business Week,* the *Wall Street Journal,* or any of the dozen other periodicals that regularly report those numbers. Read the opinions about each fund in *Morningstar Mutual Fund Reports* or *The Value Line Mutual Funds Survey.*

You can do all of that with a few toll-free telephone calls, a trip to your local library, the purchase price of a few magazines, and perhaps eight hours of research. That is not too much work to do if you are going to put $8,000 at risk.

You might go through the same process again in choosing the bonds fund, but you might start with Morningstar or *Business Week* or a website that gives information on bonds funds.

All of the reference publications that I have mentioned here offer good helpful starting points. None of them offers a good place to turn off your brain and snooze.

Internet Research for Mutual Funds

There are many Internet sites that offer tons of information on mutual funds. Many of them offer fund screens.

If you want to know what funds are offered by a particular investment company, that information is easily available. If you want to know which corporate bond funds had the best performance during the past year, that information is easily available. If you want to know how long the manager of a particular fund has been there or what specific bonds a fund holds or what percentage of the assets is concentrated in the ten largest holdings, all of that information is available.

Do not forget the earlier warnings about Internet research. In many cases the information available online is old. It may be six to nine months old. It may be too old to be of any use. It may also be simply wrong. The companies providing the websites always state that they do not guarantee the accuracy of the information. In many cases you cannot tell how old the information is.

So, given all that, does that mean don't use the Web? No, I don't mean that! Use the Web! It is worth its weight in gold to mutual funds buyers, but be aware of the potential shortcomings. If you see interesting information, then ask yourself whether it would matter if the source was ten weeks old. When you get ready to put your money on the table, do some double-checking first. There is a selection of good websites at the end of the chapter.

Asset Allocation Funds

Diversification is complicated. Among the investors I talk to it is probably the least understood part of their strategies. You know you have to diversify. Diversification can get difficult, but many people and businesses are eager to take that burden from you, for a price. If you use a full-service broker, he will certainly offer to simply manage your money for you and provide the necessary diversification. Another way to get diversification with fewer headaches and low expenses is to use asset allocation funds.

Asset allocation funds use a mix of investments and change the mix according to what they believe offers the best chances at any given

Asset
Allocation
Funds

time. The mix may include stocks, bonds, money markets, gold, options, futures, or almost anything else. You have to read the prospectus to see where each asset allocation fund draws the line.

A recent edition of *The Value Line Mutual Funds Survey* lists thirty-one asset allocation funds. In late 2001 they included:

- Advantis Spectrum Fund A (1.8 percent current yield): 5.5 percent front load, 74 percent invested in stocks and 26 percent in bonds
- Brinson Tactical Allocation Fund (1.7 percent current yield): 1 percent front load, 1.5 percent expense level; had a strong performance record from mid-1996 to mid-2001
- Fidelity Asset Manager (3.6 percent current yield): no-load, 0.5 percent annual expenses, 56 percent in stocks and 39 percent in bonds; the management had broad flexibility in choosing domestic and foreign investments.
- Vanguard Asset Allocation Fund (4.4 percent current yield): no-load, listed as 60 percent in stocks and 40 percent in bonds; the stock investments were of the S&P 500 class, and the bonds were long-term U.S. Treasuries.

Those yield numbers were current in late 2001. Every quarter they change.

Some of the asset allocation funds emphasize market timing in switching from stocks to bonds, or switching among different stock market sectors. They might at one time be 90 percent invested in stocks and six months later have half invested in bonds and half in cash.

Other asset allocation funds have more specific rules about where they put your money. Such a fund might say they will always have 40 percent to 80 percent of the money in stocks, 10 percent to 60 percent in bonds, and the balance in cash. You have to read the prospectus to see which kind you are buying.

There are two asset allocation funds that I have used for part of my investment strategy. They offer several features that I do not actively practice in my other investments. Those features include the following:

Market Timing

- They actively seek to switch money between markets at the best times, which I do not (that tactic is called *market timing*).

- They invest in, among other things, precious metals and options, which I do not.
- They actively seek to work contrarian strategies, which I do not.

Contrarian style is just what the name implies. It advocates choosing investments that are currently out of favor (e.g., low priced) and holding them until they return to their normal price levels.

Contrarian

So those funds offer very specific methods of diversification for my investing, and they offer features that I do not care to pursue on my own.

The asset allocation group may have something to offer you. However, here again you cannot simply close your eyes and throw a dart at the list. These funds, just like the socially responsible funds, the growth funds, or any other group, have a wide range of characteristics that might or might not be good for you. Some of the asset allocation funds are regarded as high-risk funds, and some are quite low risk. Among the group there are very great differences in how they choose to allocate and great differences in how much yield they pay.

Do the homework. Do the research. Read the prospectuses!!! Be a smart little investor. If you spent six years earning that money, don't risk it on a sudden whim.

Allocating Your Investments

There are other approaches to asset allocation that may be good for you. You might like to select a combination of funds, or stocks and funds, that produces an asset allocation mix that appeals to you. You might even decide to work your own strategy in switching money between different investments. There are some investment companies that will allow you to switch money between various funds at little or no cost.

One approach to choosing your mutual funds is to decide which areas you do not want to work on yourself. You may look in Moody's bond manuals and the newspaper fixed income (bond-reporting) pages and decide they are just too tedious for your further attention. In that case, you should find a mutual fund, or two or three, to handle the portion of your investments that is dedicated to fixed-income (bond) investing.

The Small Investor Allocates His Assets

The mutual funds you study and buy should be selected to complement the other parts of your investment strategy. If your personal stock picking is going to focus on small-cap stocks that carry a higher risk, your mutual funds ought to balance that with some safer funds, such as utilities funds or municipal bonds funds.

You may choose to study blue chip stocks and specialize in them for individual stock purchases. That's enough to keep any two people busy. Then it might be best, for diversification, to buy a mutual fund that specializes in small-cap stocks and one or two more that buy bonds. You might think that health care is a promising avenue of investment, but perhaps you simply don't know enough about it to evaluate the best stocks. Then it would be easier and safer to choose a mutual fund to handle that for you. You can find plenty of good mutual funds that specialize in drug companies, health maintenance organizations, or biotechnology, or ones that span the entire health care field.

There are millions of different ways individual investors might approach the job of selecting funds. I cannot list all of them, so instead let's look at some basic ideas and examples. In the following paragraphs there are some ideas and questions that you might use to get started. Then we'll look at some specific (fictional) examples of how various investors proceed. Probably none of my examples will exactly fit your situation, but they should suggest approaches to help you get started.

You should have some idea now of what kinds of investing appeal to you and how much you are already involved in financial markets. The small investor should answer these questions: Am I going to invest in individual stocks? Stock funds? Individual bonds? Bond funds? Specialized and hybrid funds such as sector funds, balanced funds, or asset allocation funds? How much money do I already have invested in any of those, and how much more do I want to put in? How do I intend to manage risk?

We will start by addressing those questions in two ways. One way is to allocate money across risk levels and then try to pick investments that work for that allocation; another is to select specific types of investments and then try to manage risk within those types.

An example of the first approach is that an investor might decide to put 25 percent of his money into very safe investments, 25 percent into low risk, 25 percent in medium risk, and 25 percent in investments seeking higher reward with possibly high risk. Now, for the next step, he has to choose some investments. They might be allocated as $10,000 in a bank CD, $10,000 in a municipal bonds fund, $10,000 in an S&P 500 Index stock fund, and $10,000 in a small-cap growth stock fund.

In the second approach, another investor might decide to keep $4,000 in his savings account, $15,000 in mutual funds, and $10,000 in stocks or bonds that he selected on his own. Now, for the second step, he has to find investments that will give the proper risk management within these classses.

Case study: Jack Sprat is a thirty-eight-year-old chemist with a reasonably secure career at a large drug company where he has worked for eight years. He is single, owns his home, and can manage his debts and mortgage reasonably well out of his current income. In his company 401(k) retirement plan, he has $25,000 worth of his company's stock and

$15,000 in money market funds. He has no other investments, but he has an additional $12,000 of savings that he wishes to allocate to investing. He feels that the company stock is quite safe, so he doesn't want to let go of any of it. That leaves him with the $15,000 in the 401(k) money market account and the $12,000 savings to work with. The $15,000 has to stay in the 401(k). The other two choices his company offers in their 401(k) plan are a long-term bond fund with a good history and an asset allocation fund. Jack sees that he has a diversification problem: Too much of his financial safety is dependent on the success of his employer, both in his job and the company stock; however, he has made a decision that the company and his position are solid.

By holding all of that company stock, Jack has already messed up his diversification strategy, but we'll see what he can do.

He decides that he needs some investments with potential higher return, and he certainly needs exposure to economic considerations outside of the drug business. He decides to take the $15,000 in the 401(k) and split it between the bond fund and the asset allocation fund. The bond fund is low risk, and this particular asset allocation fund has some investments that put it in a relatively higher risk category. Now, what about the other $12,000? Jack wants more exposure to the stock market, but he does not want the work and trouble of studying individual stocks. That means he will use mutual funds for getting stock market opportunities. He could decide to use a blue chip stock fund and a small-cap growth fund for $6,000 each.

Jack's investment plans could now be summed up as follows:

Low risk	Medium risk	High risk
$7,500 in bond fund	$7,500 in asset allocation fund	$6,000 in small-cap fund
		$6,000 in blue chip fund
		$25,000 in company stock

That leaves him with very large exposure to the safety and success of his employer, plus large exposure to the volatility of the stock market.

Types of investments	Amount invested
individual stocks	$25,000 (the employer's stock)
mutual funds (4)	$27,000

The bond fund and the asset allocation fund carry some diversification protection. In total this appears to be a medium-high-risk investment strategy, with particular dependence on his current employer. If it works for Jack, then OK, it works. This is a plan, which is far better than no plan at all. At the very least, in working this out, Jack has had to think through his current situation and make some decisions about risk level and types of investments to use.

As an investment advisor, I would encourage Jack to seriously reduce his investment in the company stock, but his plan is better than no plan at all.

Case study: Paul and Mary are in their early sixties, are both retired, and have $73,000 in savings along with current retirement income of $2,400 per month. That retirement income is secure for the rest of their lives, and they figure that they need about $2,000 per month to just get by. They have no experience in financial markets. Their investment goals are safety of their principal, the $73,000, and some growth opportunity. They began their investment strategy by deciding that $55,000 must be kept in very safe investments and that the other $18,000 must be moderately safe but should offer some growth opportunity. They know of a small company in their town that they believe is a good investment, and they've done enough homework to decide to invest $8,000 in the stock of that company.

They think of that as a moderate risk investment, but it may be fairly high risk. They should not allocate any more of their money to individual stock selections. Now the risk picture looks like this:

Low risk	Medium risk	High risk
$55,000 yet to be allocated	$10,000 yet to be allocated	$8,000 small-cap stock

They are already outside of their strategic planning framework, but people do, unfortunately, fall in love with the stocks that they pick. Paul and Mary need to be conservative with the rest of the money. The $10,000 could buy them two mutual funds chosen for safety and total return prospects. They choose a large-cap growth fund and a balanced fund, for $5,000 each. Each of the funds should be chosen with an eye for high safety ratings, consistent good return, and low volatility over the past five years, without management changes. The low-risk money will be allocated among bond funds and less risky stock funds. They choose to keep some money in a money market fund and for the rest use a low-duration bond fund, a long-term investment-grade corporate bond fund, and an income fund that uses stocks and bonds. (*Duration* is a very complicated bond characteristic. It is related to the term, but not the same as the term. You need only note that "low duration" generally means safer than others. Low-duration bond funds should be very attractive to conservative investors.) As a result of Paul and Mary's decisions, the money is allocated like this:

Duration

Low risk	Medium risk	High risk
$10,000 money market	$5,000 large-cap stock fund	$8,000 local company stock
$14,000 low-duration fund	$5,000 balanced fund	
$15,000 corporate bond fund		
$16,000 income fund		

And all of the dividends or yield will be reinvested in the funds.

This is a plan. Maybe not the best plan, but it is most certainly better then no plan at all. Notice that they have not selected any tax-exempt investments. At their income level, their tax rates are low enough that the tax savings would not be good enough to compensate them for the lower return from tax-exempt investments. Notice also that they have not invested in any limited partnerships involving parking lot developments (see chapter 1, under "Common Errors or Traps for Small Investors"). First, they don't know anything about the parking lot business, and second, limited partnerships are usually high-risk ventures with uncertainty about when investors might be able to retrieve the money. The parking lot business is good for somebody—

else, where would we park? But it is not good business for Paul and Mary. Ditto for limited partnerships.

> **Case study:** Sally and Jim are a well-off (at least by my standards) forty-something professional couple. Their combined income is $135,000 (before tax). They live very comfortably on that and save $1,600 a month, of which $600 goes into Sally's 401(k) at work and the rest goes in a bank money market account. The balances are currently $37,000 in the 401(k) and $49,000 in the money market account. Sally and Jim are traditional small investors. They have the essential fear and suspicion of financial markets, and they have little prior experience with investing. They have decided to look for a good, solid combination of growth and income, with a balance between conservative and moderately risky methods. It is worthwhile for them to keep the profits tax free. They agree to take some of the $49,000 from the money market savings and put it to work in more aggressive investments.

The first view of their planning looks like this:

Low risk	Medium risk	High risk
$37,000 in the 401(k)	$17,000 from current savings	$17,000 from current savings
$15,000 current savings in money market account	$250 per month added to investments	$250 per month added to investments
$600 per month added to 401(k)		
$500 per month added to money market savings		

The $37,000 in the 401(k) and all income-producing selections are tax-sheltered. The mutual funds selected with an eye for high growth and low distributions are taxable.

Sally's 401(k) offers six investment choices: company stock, a growth stock fund, a short-term bond fund, a long-term bond fund, a money market fund, and a balanced fund. All of those would be taxable if they were outside of the 401(k), but in the 401(k) they are not taxable as current income. She buys equal parts of the company stock, the growth stock fund, and the long-term bond fund.

What should Jim and Sally do about picking individual stocks in this situation? They are both smart, self-reliant, professional people. They think they can handle stock selections, and they want to give it a try. Keeping in mind their lack of prior stock selection or other market experience, they agree to buy two stocks initially and reevaluate their performances after six months before buying any more. They decide that because of their technical and business experience they can reasonably evaluate and buy one stock in the retail stores sector and one in the transportation industry. Those both fall into the high-risk category, and they also want to buy a technology-oriented mutual fund. For the technology mutual fund they will start with $5,000 and add $100 per month. The other $150 per month in the high-risk area will be held aside while they explore more ideas.

The medium-risk $17,000 and $250 per month will be allocated equally among four mutual funds chosen for a balanced approach to safety, diversification, and growth potential. They have decided to use an asset allocation fund, a world growth stock fund, a small-cap growth stock fund, and an S&P 500 Index fund.

Is this a plan? Yes, it is. Is this the best plan in the world? Probably not. Does the plan, however, address their needs and their situation and show that they have evaluated their investing goals and their risk orientation? Yes, it does. Is this better than no plan at all? You know the answer.

Let's review the outcome for Sally and Jim, since it is more complex than the others.

Planned investment	Income producing?*	Is it taxable	Current/future amount
company stock in 401(k)	no	no	$14,100
growth stock fund in 401(k)	no	no	$12,500
long-term bond fund in 401(k)	no	no	$10,400
ongoing contributions to 401(k)	no	no	$600/month
retail sector stock	no	yes	$6,000
transportation stock	no	yes	$6,000
high-tech fund	no	yes	$5,000
higher-risk area contributions			$100/month

Planned investment	Income producing?*	Is it taxable	Current/future amount
asset allocation fund	no	yes	$4,000 + $50/month
world growth stock fund	no	yes	$4,000 + $50/month
small-cap growth stock fund	no	yes	$4,000 + $50/month
S&P 500 Index stock fund	no	yes	$5,000 + $100/month
maintained in ready savings account			$15,000 + $500/month

*Yes or no means significantly income producing or not; the investments within the 401(k) produce yield that stays in the 401(k) and is not counted as current income.

There is not much there that will be taxed until they start to withdraw money from the 401(k) in twenty years.

But as any architect, football coach, or teacher can tell you, having a good plan is not the same as having the job done. Sally and Jim, Jack, and Paul and Mary now have their real work set out for them. They have to evaluate the stocks, bonds, or mutual funds they wish to use as investments. The focus of this chapter is on funds.

Evaluating Funds

In the earlier sections of this chapter, as well as in chapter 9, we have talked about choosing the funds that are best for you as a small investor. We have talked about selecting the funds with the best or most interesting features. That is not easy. There are so many funds and ways to analyze them. Sometimes the differences are obvious and important, sometimes subtle or trivial. In this section we will look at some of the ways you might try to evaluate and discriminate between funds.

When you are evaluating any fund or funds that you might be interested in purchasing, try using the items below as a checklist of factors to look at. We will start with a list of the criteria and then follow up with more explanation of each.

1. Objective: What does this fund do with the money?
2. Management: Who is running the show? Are they any good?
3. Size: How much money does this fund currently have under management?

4. Risk: How much volatility does the fund exhibit, and what are the causes of its volatility?

5. Fees: How much of your money are the managers planning to take?

6. Reports: Does the fund give clear reports of their results and fees?

7. Past performance: What are their profit or loss results over the last few years?

8. Taxes: Is the fund's practice going to generate current taxes for you?

9. Income: Is the fund going to generate current income for you?

10. Current holdings: What do they have in the portfolio now, and is that attractive to you?

11. Diversification: Does this fund bring better diversification to your portfolio?

The Small Investor Evaluates the Field

1. The Objective or Class of the Fund

The first questions should always be, Why are you looking at this fund, or any fund? What do you want? What kinds of investment service do you need? Then consider whether the fund suits your needs for diversification, tax avoidance, risk and reward balance, and whether it buys stocks, bonds, options, and/or futures. Are the stocks large cap or small? Are they growth or value oriented? That last distinction is often not obvious because different managers may have different ideas about what makes a value stock. The main sources of help in answering this question should be the prospectus, the annual report that lists their current holdings, and the evaluations put out by the *WSJ*, Morningstar, or whatever periodical you like to read for reference.

Bond funds come in a great many different flavors. Some are volatile, and some are highly predictable. Some produce high taxable current income, and some produce little current income.

2. The Management and the Strategy

This is tough; obviously, when you give them your money, you are only buying their management skill. But how can you evaluate the managers? If you watch the various financial news shows on television, you will hear about different managers and sometimes see an interview with one of them. That is helpful if you happen to catch the person who manages a fund you are interested in.

Another way to evaluate them is to look at the past performance. If a manager has been with one fund for ten years, that ten years' performance of that fund says something about that manager. However, if the fund has a new manager, the past performance may not mean anything to you as you make your current investment plans. Two helpful sources are the Morningstar reports and *The Value Line Mutual Funds Survey.* Both of those will attempt to evaluate the current management and investment strategies, giving you at least two opinions, and they may be the best information available. If you read *Barron's* or *Kiplinger's*, or some other financial publications, you will see frequent in-depth interviews with fund managers or analyses of specific funds that may hit the area you want to see. Evaluation of a fund manager can be useful if you have good information, but sometimes that information is not easily available. Some people would advise you not to buy a fund if you don't have adequate information about the management. That will have to be your call, because available information about a fund's manager is frequently sketchy at best.

3. Fund Size (in Current Assets)

It is not clear whether size means much. Some people think that if a fund is too small, it cannot properly diversify. On the other hand, if a fund is too large, it may become just a proxy for the market, or the managers may not be able to properly track all of their investments. A strategy that was highly effective for $80 million and 30 stocks may be less effective for $800 million and 200 stocks. If a fund is successful because of one person's brilliant analysis and insights, she may be stretched too thin when the fund grows to a larger size. It is arguable how these factors play out in real life. Many investors started to shy away from the great Magellan Fund because of its size. Magellan was, however, successful over a long time frame after it got to be the biggest.

A Mutual Fund Can Grow Out of Hand

4. Risk

The risk level of a fund is always highly debatable. Funds and their managers are subject to all of the same risks that we have looked at throughout the book. Most of the publications that we have mentioned say something about the risk level of different funds, and they don't always agree.

There is a reasonable argument that the funds will manage the risks better than we can individually. For example, consider a high-yield bond fund. That means a fund that is probably 75 percent invested in junk bonds and pays a high current annual yield. If you bought just one of those junk bonds, you would need a lot of experience and research to see and evaluate the risks. And could you judge the likelihood that the bond rating might be changed sometime soon? Probably not. But the fund manager and all of her elves have databases and experience and they evaluate bonds for a living. They would almost certainly do a better job than we in selecting junk bonds to buy. Beyond that, you or I might buy one or two junk bonds. If one of them defaulted, we would have a large problem. The mutual fund might buy 100 junk bonds; if one of them defaulted, that would be less of a problem. This is the classic example of diversifying within an asset class to spread the risk. Just because a fund buys a lot of securities where each individually has risky characteristics does not mean that the fund is too risky.

The sector funds may also inherit risk that comes with their territories. Suppose you buy just one high-yield electric utility company stock. If prevailing long-term interest rates rose very much, that stock value would fall. You can mitigate that risk by diversifying your investments. But if the fund manager has an objective that says 80 percent is to be invested in electric utilities, he cannot diversify away from that risk.

You may therefore choose to avoid that fund. Or you may not. Even when you foresee a risk of rising interest rates, there is the chance that you are wrong, and the utilities funds may give you a useful balance and diversification to guard against your own bad judgment.

A well-chosen mutual fund might also give you a reasonably easy entree into an area of the markets that you were hesitant to enter on your own. Small-cap stocks generally bring along higher risks than blue chip companies do. The small company's management may have trouble dealing with growth, or it may be easy for a competitor to come into their markets and compete effectively. At the very least, it is more difficult to get good up-to-date information on small caps. So this might be the ideal area to use a mutual fund. A fund that specializes in small-cap stocks will spread the risk through diversification and also have better sources of information than we have.

We talked about risk and volatility in chapter 3. It would be nice if we could all agree on a neat measurement of risk. Reporting a good, solid, agreed-upon number for risk seems to be too difficult. Many fund analysts and writers settle for using beta, the Greek letter ß. Why a Greek letter? The fund analysts and writers want to put an air of mystery and scientific pretension around it. *Beta* is a number that may be calculated and assigned to a stock or a mutual fund as an indicator of volatility. The calculation depends on some statistical parameters that measure how much the security price moves up and down relative to how much a particular index is moving up or down. Don't worry about the math; that is the work of gnomes. Instead you may want to focus on two questions: How should I interpret beta, and is it truly indicative of anything?

Beta

The key to understanding it is that beta equal to 1 indicates average volatility compared to the index. Beta greater than 1 indicates more volatility than the index, and beta less than 1 indicates less volatility. As for whether it really means anything, that is the stuff of doctoral dissertations. For our purposes, it is enough to consider your peace of mind and comfort level with your mutual funds. The funds with higher values of beta are going to cause you more anguish and more joy as they run up and down. The funds with lower values for beta are going to be your steady riders; they should not go up and down quite as much as the overall market does.

Take special note, however, that beta equal to 1 does not necessarily mean safety, or even low volatility. It means that in the past this mutual fund (or stock) has been about as volatile as the rest of the market. If the entire stock market goes into a dive, the beta-equals-one funds will probably dive right along too.

This may or may not be of any value to the investor. After all, a basketball bounces up and down more than a cannonball, but that does not mean that the basketball is more dangerous. The essential thing for you to know is that there is a calculation that produces a number called beta, and that many people use that as a substitute for figuring out what the real risks are.

Many financial publications leave out any discussion of risk for stocks and mutual funds. The reason is that evaluating risk is difficult and complicated and they don't want to lose your attention. Many publications and websites just show values for beta, or they allow you to screen for different values of beta, which helps to gauge volatility, or at least see the historic volatility, of your funds. That is better than nothing, but it does not explain risk.

Consumer Reports uses a different approach that is interesting. They indicate risk by measuring the fund's performance relative to the return on Treasury bills. That is reasonable because Treasury bills are arguably the lowest-risk investment one can make in financial markets. If a fund sometimes does worse than Treasury bills, that would be the very essence of risk. You don't have to agree with them, but the approach is worthy of consideration. Using this approach, you would pick a standard, whatever standard you think is useful for your decision making, and measure the performance of the fund relative to that standard over a period of years.

So the lessons in this are that risk is measured differently by different folks, and there is no single best way to pin it down. You cannot expect to find a clear and simple measurement of the risk levels of different funds. You can find a lot of words and the beta number dancing around the subject of risk. There is also a very real and legitimate question about whether beta has any validity in guiding investors to avoid risk, but at any rate it comes closer than any other measurement to being accepted in the investment community.

5. Fees

Fees are stated in the prospectus, and they are thoroughly discussed and compared in most of the publications we use. If you can't understand the fees description in the prospectus, don't buy the fund. It is not always appropriate to buy the funds with the lowest fees, but it is a mistake to buy a fund if you don't know about the fees. Refer to chapter 9 for more explanation of fees.

6. Earnings Reports

Read the earnings reports. You should at least see what kinds of assets the fund currently owns and what has changed in the past six months. I am very much influenced by the clarity and the presentation of the reports. I think they reflect the intelligence and the priorities of the management. One nuisance factor in funds' reports is the timing of the information. Some funds have up to a six-month delay between the end of a fiscal year and publication of their annual report. When you read a report, check to see if it contains up-to-date information.

7. Past Performance

This is the easiest data to find. Many newspapers and magazines and most of the funds broadcast huge volumes of data about past performance. They always say that "past performance is not a guarantee of future results," but we know what the real message is—they are actually trying to sell us past performance. But what is the value of past performance data? It clearly says something about the management during that time period. But is that the current management?

You should look at past performance data carefully. Examine the values for one year, five years, or ten to see if this fund is consistently among the leaders of its peer group. It would be asking too much to require that a fund consistently stay first or second in its peer group, but you could reasonably say you want a fund that was first or second last year, and in the upper half for the past three years. Appraise the fund's performance against that of its peer group. If you can't identify the peer group, spend some time studying the newspapers and magazines; especially study the Morningstar reports in your library, which will show peer group analysis. If your fund is a small-cap growth stock fund, it is in a relatively high-risk area and should give pretty good returns. If it doesn't, the risk may be higher than you want to accept for those possible rewards. Don't compare that stock against a municipal bond fund that is in a far lower risk group and carries tax advantages, too.

And even though past performance is no guarantee of anything, there is some reason to expect that the fund that was strong last year should do well this year, although it is helpful if you can separate the degree of success due to good management from the success due to simply being in a strong bull market. For example, there have been some years when just about any fund that specialized in computer technology did very well. If the entire sector was strong in 2001, that may not mean that the one fund you are looking at was especially good.

A Past Performance Is Past Performance

To illustrate that point, suppose the Fast Buggy Fund earned 16 percent total return in a year. Its peers are the auto industry funds. On average those funds earned 13 percent during that year and the auto industry stocks alone averaged 12 percent total return (price gain plus dividends). Then Fast Buggy looks pretty good. If the same manager was going to stay on this year, and if I wanted to have money invested in that sector, I would want to own Fast Buggy. Here's another example. Maybe the Slick Silicon Fund made 18 percent last year, but its peer group (high-tech and computer parts funds) averaged 24 percent return and its stock sector averaged 22 percent total return. That makes us think that the management of Slick Silicon may have dragged down profits instead of boosting them. A relative analysis of total return indicates that we should hold on to Fast Buggy, but we would be better off with a different high-tech fund instead of Slick Silicon. For both of them it is clear that in large part their results are due to being in the right sector. If you don't have faith in their respective market sectors doing well again, maybe you don't want either fund this year.

8. Tax Considerations

Depending on your current income level and your overall investment strategy, it might be important to consider tax advantages of different types of funds. If this is important to you, or if you are unsure about tax considerations, talk to a tax advisor or financial planner. Some funds produce little or no current income for the shareholders. If the funds take in profits, the funds' management have to disperse the profits to shareholders, but the funds' management can often manage so that they have little income or capital gains to report from year to year. If the fund holds stocks that are growth oriented, they will probably produce relatively little income from dividends. You can buy various funds that would give income exempt from federal, state, or local taxes, or sometimes all three. For example, if a fund only deals with municipal bonds from your (tax-reporting) state and it does not generate any capital gains, the income would be exempt from both federal and state taxes.

Even if you do not receive any income from the fund, you may have taxes to pay. If the fund generates taxable income and you have it all turned around and reinvested in fund shares, there is still a tax claim on that income.

If you are buying funds through your 401(k) or IRA or other tax-sheltered retirement plan, it does not make sense to buy tax-sheltered investments. Within your tax-exempt IRA or 401(k), the tax advantage of a fund gives no added value to you. Tax-sheltered funds produce lower relative returns just because they are tax-sheltered; other investors pay more to receive tax-sheltered income. If you want to use income-producing funds within your IRA or 401(k), go for the higher yield, not a redundant tax shelter.

For example, suppose two funds called AAAAX and BBBBX both have current net asset value per share of $10. Let's say that Tom could buy 1,000 shares of each fund for his IRA or for a separate income-producing taxable account. Tom has the 39 percent marginal tax rate. The AAAAX fund gives 7.5 percent taxable total return, and the BBBBX pays 5.2 percent tax-free total return. We can look at the net profit from each fund either in the IRA or not in the IRA:

Investment	Return	Tax	Net return
AAAAX in the IRA	$750	0	$750 subject to later taxes
BBBBX in the IRA	$520	0	$520
AAAAX in the taxable account	$750	$292.50	$457.50
BBBBX in the taxable account	$520	0	$520

So in the IRA, AAAAX is better, but out of the IRA, BBBBX is better.

9. Income Needs

Some people need to get current income from their investments and some do not. You decide for yourself which is more important to you. If you do get current income, it may be taxable, but you have some control over that. Some funds are designed to produce current income, others no current income, and others a mix of current income and other capital growth.

If you want tax-exempt current income, you probably want to use municipal bond funds. If you use U.S. Treasury bond funds, they will be only partially tax-exempt. Junk-bond funds may be ideal for generating high current income, but the chances for capital appreciation would be unpredictable.

Each fund is going to give a balance of profits from capital gains and profits from yield paid out by the fund. You have to pick and choose to make that balance suit your needs. Here are some generalizations of how the balance might go for various types of funds ("+" means more strength in this area, and "−" means less; a blank means no generalization can be easily made):

Type of fund	Capital gain	Yield
Small-cap fund	+	−
Large-cap fund	+	
Municipal bonds fund		+
Junk-bond fund	+/−	+
Growth and income fund	+	+
Income fund	−	+
International fund	+	

There are large variations within classes. If you want to own a fund to help produce income, don't just look at the classification; also look at the record of dividends paid over the past year or two. For example, utilities funds can be managed with an emphasis on producing current yield or an emphasis on producing asset value growth.

Even if you are primarily interested in current income, look at the other measurements of the fund's performance. It is possible for a manager to generate higher current yield by, in effect, robbing the fund's assets. In that case the current yield might be followed by a nasty surprise in the value of the investment if you need to sell it one day, or the yield might be unsustainable.

10. Current Holdings

In Morningstar reports, *The Value Line Mutual Funds Survey,* or the funds' own self-generated reports, you can find a list of the funds' largest holdings. That list, wherever you get it from, will probably be current as of several months before you read it. Listings of the ten largest holdings of funds are readily available through many of the Internet sites listed in this book. Look those over to get a feel for what the fund really does with your money.

11. Diversification

There is a reasonable assumption that a mutual fund will give you better diversification than you would find on your own. If for no other reason then simply because they buy a lot more securities than you would alone. That is a useful idea, but there are extreme ranges of how much diversification you get with different funds. A junk-bond fund (often called high-yield fund) may hold 100 different bonds and be diversified within the class of high-yield bonds. That is better than the one or two bonds you might buy on your own, but does not come close to providing the overall diversification you need for your total portfolio. On the other hand, an asset allocation fund will specifically strive for very broad diversification by choosing and regularly modifying a mixture of different types of stocks and bonds. There are many choices of funds that give you a component of diversification or funds that try to provide total diversification.

You could take advantage of the opportunities in several ways:

1. Suppose you just want to keep everything as simple as possible. Then find one or two asset allocation funds with good track records and low values of beta, and put all your money into them.

2. Suppose you want to get a well-rounded and broadly diversified mix of funds that each specialize in one area of the market. Try three bond funds: one for long-term–high quality bonds, one for low-duration bonds, and one for high-yield bonds; and then for your stock market money, buy three stock funds: one for international equities, one for large-cap stocks, and one for small- or mid-cap stocks.

3. Suppose you want to select and buy some individual stocks on your own and want to use mutual funds to round out the portfolio for good diversification. You might buy four to ten individual stocks that you have selected, buy two or three bond funds, and buy two or three stock funds that hit different sectors than your individual picks.

There are a million ways to use the diversification qualities of mutual funds to get a good mix for your portfolio.

Stars

If you are going to do anything with mutual funds, you will hear about stars—one star to five stars, the stuff that builds advertising campaigns.

The *Morningstar Mutual Fund Reports* include a rating of one star (worst) to five stars (best) for each fund. The star ratings are assigned relative to one-year, three-year, and five-year risk-adjusted returns. If you read their publication, you can find a good explanation of how they do it. For our purposes, it is sufficient to note that when you see stars it is not a good time to turn out the lights and snooze. The stars are very widely advertised and there is some danger that investors might think of them as a final and complete grade of the fund's value. Even the editors at Morningstar take some pains to warn their readers that it is not that easy. By all means look at the star ratings, but do not quit there. Stars should tell you something, but they will not do your thinking for you.

Evaluation Form

The first few times that you try to evaluate a mutual fund, it might be helpful to use a copy of the form provided on page 268. It might help to ensure that you don't forget some important points. You have my permission to make as many copies as you like of the form. Indeed, you have my blessing to modify the form if you have some other good ideas—and please, send me those modifications for the next edition of this book.

Recommended Further Reading

The Hirsch book, now out of print, has some debatable conclusions that may not be useful to all investors, but the ideas are instructive.

Hirsch, Michael. *Multifund Investing.* Homewood, Ill.: Dow Jones Irwin, 1987 (out of print).

Laderman, Jeffrey. *Business Week's Guide to Mutual Funds.* New York: McGraw-Hill, updated annually.

Barron's Mutual Funds Quarterly

Forbes Annual Survey of Mutual Funds

U.S. News & World Report Annual Investor's Guide

Morningstar Mutual Fund Report

Morningstar Closed-End Funds Report

The Value Line Mutual Funds Survey

Websites for funds research—there are a lot more, but these are among the best:

	substantial good free content	good mutual funds screening tools
www.morningstar.com	✓	✓
cbs.marketwatch.com	✓	
www.smartmoney.com	✓	✓
www400.fidelity.com	✓	✓
www.quicken.com/investments	✓	✓

	substantial good free content	good mutual funds screening tools
www.ici.org	✓	
screen.yahoo.com/funds/	✓	✓
www.forbes.com/finance/screener	✓	✓
www.usatoday.com (follow links to the Money page)	✓	✓
www.fundz.com	✓	
www.businessweek.com (follow links to the Investing page and the Mutual Funds page)	✓	

MUTUAL FUND EVALUATION FORM

Name of the Fund: _____

Name of the Investment Company: _____

Their toll-free customer number: _____

Objective:
- Is this consistent with their current top ten holdings? ❑ yes ❑ no
- Does this fit my diversification needs? ❑ yes ❑ no

Manager's Name:
- How long has he or she been there? _____
- Does the performance over that time frame look good? ❑ yes ❑ no

Size: Dollar value of total assets = _____

Risk:
- What do I see as the risks in their investment style _____
- Does it fit my needs? ❑ yes ❑ no
- What is their beta? ß = _____

Fees:
- Front load = _____   • Redemption fee = _____
- 12-b1 fee = _____   • Ongoing expense level = _____
- Did I understand the fees presented in the prospectus? ❑ yes ❑ no

Reports:
- I have read the prospectus ❑ yes ❑ no
- And the latest annual report ❑ yes ❑ no
- I understood them ❑ yes ❑ no

Past performance:
- Total return for past year = _____
- For past five years = _____
- Is that okay relative to the market in general? ❑ yes ❑ no
- Or relative to their peer group? ❑ yes ❑ no

Taxes: Will this fund generate taxable income? ❑ yes ❑ no

Income: Will this fund generate any current income? ❑ yes ❑ no

Current holdings: I have looked at them ❑ yes ❑ no

Investing or Gambling— What's the Difference?

Experienced people who take a long view of the markets offer similar advice. As mentioned earlier, Charles Dow said it best: The people who try to get rich quick usually lose badly, and the people who try to earn a consistent reasonable return on their money sometimes end up by getting rich.

Investing, Trading, or Gambling?

Those who are following Dow's advice, trying to make a reasonable steady return on their money over a long time frame, are *investors*. Others, people who commonly buy into financial positions expecting to turn the deal around within weeks or months, are called *traders*. And those who not only work within the short time frame, but also expect to make big profits within that short time, are *gamblers*.

Investors buy stocks expecting that over the long run prices will go up, and that if the company is well managed, their profits will mount.

Investor

Traders

Gamblers

They hope to buy stock with gradually rising prices and dividends that will pay back more each year, or they may buy a AAA- or AA-rated bond and plan to hold it to maturity.

When I was cautiously and nervously getting started at actively managing our money, one of my first decisions was to start with safe and sound investments to hold for a long time. My personal investment strategy led me to use stocks and mutual funds. Many mutual funds make their current holdings available online. Also, some investment advisors who write or lecture will talk about their current investments. So from these sources I was able to get a pretty strong consensus opinion on buying electric utilities, as well as samples of the current holdings of a few successful prominent money managers. I started out with Potomac Electric, Allegheny Power Systems, Carolina Power and Light, and Bell-South. They all fit into specific areas of my investment strategy, including investment prejudice in favor of good dividends, companies that operate in the southeastern United States, large-capitalization companies, and companies with strong histories. In the first year, each of those companies gave us over 10 percent total return with very low apparent risk. Just as with every other investment, over the years the reward and the risk

The Small Investor Is Not Too Sure about This

have been due partly to their business operations and management and partly to market psychology. The favorable factors were a generally rising stock market, dramatically falling interest rates, and something of a flight-to-safety mentality in the stock markets at various times during those years. All of those factors have helped my utility stocks investments. All of them will change from time to time. But at any rate, when I bought them those four stocks represented a long-term investor's hopes and good luck.

The investor is like the driver who knows where she is going, plans accordingly, and works the plan. She does not expect to make the trip faster than everyone else. The trader, on the other hand, is more like a taxi driver who is never locked into a long-term trip but expects to turn a profit on a bunch of short trips.

Traders look for quick results and will often buy stocks to keep for only a few months, or less. They have to do their research and analysis, but they are hoping to find something that others have missed. If a trader thinks that she can buy a stock today at $25 and sell it within six months at $40 or more, she must see something that the rest of the analysts don't see. If everyone saw the same prospects, the price would have been bid up closer to $40 already. She may see some evidence that the company will be bought out at a premium over market price. It may be that the trader thinks that she (or her sources) knows more than others do about new product development within the company. The trader's nightmare is that there may be a good reason why no one else is buying the stock that she has just jumped into. The strategy of the trader is apparently workable for some, but it carries great risk and requires specialized knowledge and experience that most of us don't have.

During the worst of the bull market mania of 1995–2000, many people tried short-term trading of technology or telecommunications or Internet business stocks. Most of those stocks were highly speculative because they:

- had short-term records and inadequate revenue,
- paid no dividends,
- were in businesses that invited quick and easy competition, and
- were in businesses with rapidly changing markets and technology.

In other words, those stock investments were not serving anyone's PIG, unless they could foresee strong growth. Growth was the theme song of the day. The prices of many stocks went up just because more bulls kept buying in. They had little relationship to business fundamentals. However, the market psychology implications were enormous. It was difficult for people to ignore the supposed opportunities when they heard or read about every programmer and salesman who could spell "B2B" making millions overnight. (B2B is sharp-talk for business-to-business.) This grew into a market mania if there ever was one. In 2000 and 2001, it all fell apart. Many small investors suffered terrible losses. Many of them will never recover.

If you ever think that you can make dramatic short-term profits on a stock, then you must be finding unusual conditions and opportunities that 50,000 professionals have overlooked. What are the chances of that? Slim!

I generally recommend long-term investing, but I have tried a bit of trading as part of my diversification scheme. I mix not only investments, but also methods. Two of the trading ideas that appear reasonable to me, when followed in moderation, are momentum driven and advisor driven.

The momentum idea is based on the old Wall Street truism that a trend will continue until it changes. Stock technical analysts like to look at "volume momentum," in the belief that increased volume lends momentum, and hence credibility, to trends in prices. That idea got me into Westinghouse (symbol WX) at $16.75 and out two months later at $19.38. That result looks good percentage-wise; the actual dollar amount was small because I considered it a bit of a gamble. Short-time holding is not always bad; every investor will have reason to rethink a position occasionally. But it shouldn't be a way of life.

In the summer and fall of 1991, I had been watching Westinghouse go through an unhappy slide in both stock price and profits. The stock finally got down to around $15 a share with 1991 earnings at $1.60 and the dividend paying $1.40 per year. It looked very interesting for a genuine blue chip. A cut in the dividend was widely forecast, but one day in late December the price started bouncing around and moving upward—was this the beginning of a trend? I thought the worst was over and the risk was minimal—the price then was about 1½ times book value, and they had been pounded by bad news for a year. The stock had sold in the high 30s just a year and a half earlier. Revenues per share were still 90 percent of their all-time high, and they were making money. That was not too bad in December 1991. I bought WX at $16.75 on December 27.

Over the next few weeks, the stock went up to near $21, and I was feeling pretty clever. However, in the meantime, as is the case with all of my investments, I was tracking news about Westinghouse. The news was all bad. Early in March the price dropped below $20, and I was spending too much energy worrying about it, so I sold at $19.38 on March 11. A decent profit, after commissions, of 9 percent in ten weeks. Does that make me a trader? Or a gambler? I think that makes me a conservative small investor with a three- to five-year horizon who watches the store and dumps something if it becomes uncomfortable.

Some days I also get wrapped up in thinking I'm smarter than I am. I had been watching a lot of technology stocks during the great technology mania of 1995–2000 and thought they looked interesting. But I never made up my mind to pull the trigger and jump in. Finally, around the spring of 2000, Cisco had fallen to $70 from a previous high near $80. I thought the company was great and the stock was just over-sold, so I bought at $66.88—big mistake. I at least had the discipline to sell out at $58.44 three weeks later, so my loss was just about 13 per-cent. The people who stayed with it are looking at a 70 percent loss, depending on whether they ever sold.

> If you just have to take a speculative fling on a stock some day, then you had better keep an eye on it and be willing to cut your losses pretty quick if it becomes obvious that you were wrong. That is very difficult. You'll be tempted to wait until it comes back up a little. Forget it. It won't come back up. Sell it! Salvage what you can.

Treat your investing like a military or business project. You have to have a well-thought-out objective. Be willing to take the necessary risks to achieve the objective. However, if the situation changes or you get important new information, you should be ready to change your plans. That's the reasonable course of action for small investors. Plan in relation to your horizon. Plan to profit from dividends and long-term company growth. At the same time, keep an eye on your investments and be prepared to sell if you are no longer comfortable with a particular investment.

The advisor-driven part of my "trading" action is based on another aspect of my diversification scheme. I diversify in areas in which I find good advice and information on how to make decisions. I can do some good analysis and have confidence in my own judgment, but I always feel that there are other respectable opinions. There are other sources in which I have confidence. This is not based just on results, but rather on the fact that what they say and publish appears to have solid reasoning and research behind it. Two candidates for good advisors are the Value Line and Zacks. They both offer fundamental facts and figures, but their buy/sell recommendations are primarily short-term oriented. They are also not shy about changing a recommendation on short notice. Their opinions were factors in my decisions to buy four stocks, National Presto (NPK), FAB Industries (FIT), Bassett Furniture (BSET), and Schering-Plough. Good news, bad news. OK? All good companies,

The Small Investor Keeps an Eye Out

no doubt about that. The question is whether their stock was good for this small trader. So here's how that worked.

Presto was on a tear when I got it. Up from $40 to $60 in the past year. Balance sheet, sales, earnings, everything looked very strong, so I bought in at an all-time high of $60. What a thrill! It zoomed up to $65, $70, $75, $80, $82, $83, then dropped to $82, $80. At the time I was carefully practicing my personal rule of never giving back all of a good gain. Even though I thought that the company was great, I set a stop loss at $72 to protect my gains. What a stroke of genius! Presto slumped from $80 to $76, $72, $66, $60, $55. So I was out at $72, with a very good gain over about five months. This is a trader's dream, everything coming up roses. It's like golf, you see; if you ever do something right, you may be hooked. But it only works right if you have your sell discipline well in place.

Schering-Plough. Right! Good old Plough! Unquestionably a great and strong company, but is it a good investment for me or you? Same picture as Presto going in. Almost the same analysis. I bought in at $65, at an all-time high, in fact even on the same day that I bought National Presto. I made two mistakes: First, I did not set a protective stop sell limit; and second, I watched it nose-dive for six months because I was in love with it. Can you see it? $65, $60, $55, $52, $49, and I was still holding it! Well, we got lucky, it climbed back up to $50, $51, $52, and I bought more. I bought enough more to bring my average cost to $60 per share. Lots of fun: $52, $55, $58, $60, and I'm even! But this time I set a stop sell limit order at $55 for protection. Bang, three days later it hit the limit and I was out at $55. Net loss, with brokerage fees, about 10 percent in ten months. Now, I still believe that Plough is a good, solid building block for many long-term small investors, but I handled it like a chump trader, so you can see how that works.

FAB and Bassett? I bought both of them after strong runs, FAB at an all-time high. I bought FAB in April of 1992 at $30.63, sold in December 1993 at $34.50, and collected a little in dividends. I bought Bassett in July of 1992 at $40.75 and sold it in February of 1994 at $31.50. But there was a split, so I had 25 percent more shares than I bought. That was a small gain in share values, and they produced some small dividend payments.

Anyone who expects to try being a trader had better have their sell discipline very carefully worked out. Look where I would have been if I had sold Plough at $60 on the way down and bought it again at $52:

What actually happened	What might have been
bought 60 shares at $65	bought 60 at $65
	sold 60 at $60
bought 40 shares at $52	bought 100 at $52
sold 100 shares at $55	sold 100 at $55
brokerage fees total $165	brokerage fees $220
net loss $645	net loss $220

And, in the might-have-been case, I would have felt safer holding it for another year, which would have been a better move.

If you can't resist the urge to try a little trading, please consider the flip side of your hopes: if you think the market is missing some positive factor that you can see, it is possible that the others are seeing some risk that you have missed. In other words, you may outsmart the crowd on occasion, but you will not outsmart them consistently. Can anybody make a profit that way? Yes.

Apparently there are a few guys and girls out there who can manage that kind of action. The basic theory is that they may have to take a lot of little losses in trying different stocks, but they win by hitting a few big gains. If you have to speculate, you can try that: every time you buy a speculative stock, set a stop loss limit order 10 percent below the purchase price. Then, counting brokerage fees, you would never lose more than maybe 13 percent or 14 percent on any stock. Look at two ways that might work out.

First, if you just had $10,000 to speculate with, you might buy one stock and take a 12 percent loss; buy another and take a 13 percent loss; buy another, hit your winner, and take a 50 percent gain. If that entire cycle took one year, the net for the year would be a gain of $1,484. That's 15 percent on a year. That's good work. But did you have the stomach to stick it out? After the first trade you were down $1,200; after the second you were down almost $2,300. After those losses, did you have the nerve to put your remaining money into yet another speculative stock? And did you enjoy the headaches of working that kind of business when you could have bought a nice, safe utility or mutual fund and had a fair chance at a 10 percent return?

There's another way to look at the trader's action. Instead of buying just one stock at a time, you might have $30,000 to use equally in three stocks: three $10,000 purchases. Say they give the same kind of (percentage) results as shown above, so the gains/losses are −$1,200, −$1,300, and +$5,000. This is a net gain of $2,500, or 8 percent on your $30,000. Is it worth the headache and risk? That depends on how you react to the thrill of the action.

What all the pros and gurus say is that it's best to cut your losses and let your winners run. They are telling us to get out if a stock has been behaving badly, but stick with it if it is behaving well. Ha! Easy for them to say; tough to do in practice. If you did your homework and had good reasons to buy a stock at $21, it's difficult to reverse your judgment and sell it when it drops to $18. On the other hand, if it went up to $30 during the subsequent three months, you would feel that you earned your profits, and you might want to grab them. That is the really tough call: when you are looking at a 40 percent profit, do you cut and run, or let it have some more time to work? Remember Rule #7.

I've heard advice advocating both approaches. Some respected managers have advised people to take a fast 20 percent gain anytime they have a chance, because you can never know what's going to happen tomorrow. But if you want stocks that double, you'll never have them if you always bail out after 20 percent. This is a place for planning and discipline.

When you buy the stock, and periodically thereafter, look at the company, the stock price, and the market, and make the tough decisions: Do you hope to get 25 percent out of this stock, or do you hope to get a price of $37? Will you sell at $32, or keep a stop loss limit price set 15 percent below the stock?

In 1992 I bought IBM at $85.25 and watched the price go up to $100 pretty fast. I wanted to hold it, but I didn't want to give up all the gain, so I set a stop loss order at $92. Pretty quick, it fell right through $92, on the way down to $40. I got out with an 8 percent gain in a few months. If I hadn't set the limit price, I might have held it all the way down.

That was a tough decision. I know IBM and I know their business. I was confident that the stock was a good long-term holding (but at what price?). See Rules #5 and 7. If you don't want to practice selling and protective discipline, you had better not even consider trading for short-term gains. My experience has been that my protective sell-limit prices have saved me a good bit of money, even though every time I use them I worry about selling too soon and I feel bad about abandoning a position. I have made my mistakes in buying and I have made my mistakes in holding, but, usually, when I have sold a stock it turned out to be the right move. Who knows how long that record will last? But I think I am learning something.

Some people make money in the fast-action trading mode, but this requires a different set of skills and a different kind of work. A trader may typically buy stocks based on technical analysis of turning points in the market or in the price of a particular stock. A trader may also sell stocks or switch mutual funds because of a sense of market momentum swinging from one sector to another. The basic hope of the trader is that good profits can be made on short-term trends. That's true, if you can measure and forecast the short-term trends. That's probably

The Small Investor Bails Out of IBM

where we small investors drop out. It requires ready access to changing information and steady, experienced evaluation of the information. It's too much work and too much analysis for the average small investor. It's better left to professionals. You may read and hear widely differing opinions among professionals about whether anyone can do this for consistent profits, but it's certainly no business for amateurs.

One last, forlorn group is the gamblers. The gamblers may rely on luck, hot tips, advice from someone who has no investment at risk, or analysis from someone who has no credentials to do the analysis. The gamblers may be people who think they can beat the crowd all of the time, or who think they can find huge gains that almost everyone else is overlooking. The gamblers I have known seldom look twice at an investment unless they are thinking about a 50 percent run-up within a few months, so they tend to ignore the steady eroding effects of repeated 2 or 3 percent costs in brokerage fees.

I have two friends who are to some extent gamblers. One is a forty-five-year-old married man who uses a large brokerage firm. I also know his broker, who is an honest, capable man, but the two of them made some mistakes. When my pal (let's call him Frank) got started playing the stock market, the broker was hot into biotechnology stocks, just like a lot of people were. Frank had reasoned that he deserved to, and could, make 30 to 40 percent a year on his investments. He and his broker overloaded on drug and biotechnology companies. Each time I talked to Frank about it, he said he was convinced that something or other was going to come back to where he bought it and he could get out even. Frank is now holding a bunch of losers. Incidentally, Frank has another account where he doesn't use a broker's advice. He does better and works much more cautiously in that one. In that way, he is smart. He keeps the gambling account separated from the other investments where he has particular long-term needs in mind.

The other friend, Jack, is more analytical. A twenty-seven-year-old bachelor with a very good job and a solid career, he wants to have some fun and excitement in the markets. He looks to double his money in a few months, or he won't touch a stock. He studies his plunges, but he plunges! Penny stocks, very small capitalization companies, biotechnology firms that are five years away from ever having a product: that is his terrain. Who should criticize? Jack knows what he is doing. He is using venture capital that he can afford to lose. He will probably lose most of it. If he loses every penny of it, he will still have a good job and great career prospects. When he is forty, he'll probably change because he's a smart guy, but right now he is a very aggressive gambler.

When Am I Investing and When Am I Gambling?

So how do you know when it is investing and when it is gambling? After all, the market risks and the great unknown are always out there. The way you can know is to consult your PIG. If you are looking at a new stock purchase, always ask yourself:

1. Do I see any Protection here? The protection might appear as:
   - a good, safe dividend yield;
   - a low P/E ratio, perhaps lower than its immediate competitors;
   - a low ratio of corporate debt to assets;
   - a couple of years' history of the company reducing its debt load;
   - a safe and secure market segment, perhaps grocery stores, since people have to eat;
   - a long-term history of profitable operations;
   - a unique and profitable product line;
   - a great brand name;
   - and so on.

None of these things guarantee protection, but the right combination of them may point to protection.

2. Do I see any Income here? For a stock investment, that means a dividend yield at least as good as the market average and supported by growing earnings that easily more than cover the dividend payout.

3. Do I see any Growth here? Growth might be indicated if:
   - earnings have increased for several years in a row;

- the company's market share is increasing; the company has new and clearly superior products to bring to market; or
- the company is acquiring other companies without incurring outrageous debt loads in the process.

It is unlikely that you will ever find positive, encouraging answers to all of these questions regarding one company, but if you don't find encouraging answers to some of them, then your PIG says you should keep your money at home.

Your PIG can also help you with bond purchases.

1. Do I see Protection here?

   - What are the Standard and Poor's, or Moody's, or Fitch Investment Services ratings on both the company and the bond?
   - Do I know anything about the markets and competition of the company?
   - For noncorporate bonds, do I know anything about the history and ratings of the issuing agency?
   - Do I know anything about the special contractual conditions of the bond, such as convertibility or call provisions?
   - How far away from maturity is the bond?

2. Do I see Income here?

   - What is the yield?
   - How does the yield compare to that of other available bonds?
   - How much of that yield will be taken away in taxes?
   - For how long is that yield safe and secure?

3. Do I see growth here?
   - Say what? Growth for a bond?

Yeah. The market value of the bond can appreciate depending on prevailing market rates, the bond's rating changes, and the condition of the company or agency that issued it. Bonds can produce growth of principal. Many mutual funds invest in bonds with very specific goals in growth of principal.

Options and Futures: If You Had to Ask

Futures Contract

A *futures contract* is a contract to buy or sell something in the future at an agreed-upon price.

Examples of futures contracts:

> Farmer Jones has planted corn in March and expects to harvest 12,000 bushels in August. He is nervous about price fluctuations. Kellogg Company wants a steady supply of corn for producing cereal. It is worthwhile for both Farmer Jones and Kellogg to agree in March on the sale and delivery of corn in August. Jones and Kellogg agree to a contract that on August 31 he will deliver 12,000 bushels of corn priced at $2.07 and they will accept it. That agreement is a futures contract. Both parties are obligated to fulfill the contract.

> General Motors may need to convert dollars to Euros. Trader Jim is a currency speculator. Jim and GM may agree that next March 31 GM will deliver $100 million to Jim and he will pay them 111 million Euros. Jim makes this deal because he thinks that, in the meantime, he will be able to buy the 111 million Euros for less that $100 million, and that he will take a profit on the resale. Their agreement is a futures contract.

Option

An *option* is a contract that gives one party a future choice of buying, selling, or not buying or selling, a security at a given price. The one who gets the choice will pay the other, who is said to write the contract.

Example of an option:

Call Option

> Susan holds 100 shares of Procter and Gamble, priced at $75, which she wants to keep. In order to make a little extra money, she writes a contract that says she will agree to sell the shares to Jack, if he chooses, on next January 4, for $80 per share. Jack pays her $200 up front for the agreement. That agreement is the option for sale of stock, called a *call option*. Susan gets the $200 and might get to keep her stock. Jack gets a chance to buy the stock on January 4. If the price of P&G stays below $80, Jack will simply decline to exercise the option. If the price of P&G goes above $80, Jack will buy the stock at $80 per share, which is better than he could do in the open market. Susan has her $200, and Jack has his chance to buy the stock at below market rates.

If Jack had initiated the agreement, he might have written a contract allowing Susan to sell him the stock or decline to do so, in the future. Susan would pay Jack for that agreement, which is called a *put option.*

Put Option

The futures and options traders are very important in maintaining market sanity and liquidity. They help us all by putting up big money on movements in prices of many stocks or commodities or indices. They are also ready to step in and close positions after relatively small price moves. The effect is that markets, stocks, and commodities become more liquid than they might be otherwise. They also provide a kind of insurance policy for people who already own the stocks or commodities. That insurance goes under the term *hedging.*

Hedging

Hedging is a legitimate and important financial practice—for the professionals who have large positions at risk. Hedging is a form of insurance for people or companies who have very large investments in a single asset. Remember one of the advantages you have over the manager of a large mutual fund—you can dump all of your stocks or invest all of your cash in a controlled, predictable way within a few minutes. He cannot. He has a legitimate need for hedging. He has the experience and research tools to use it profitably. We do not.

In November 1984 a young man named Chris Christensen went to work for the brokerage firm Prudential Bache. It was his first experience in the securities industry. Within two years he had earned a half million dollars in commissions and won the Pru-Bache Rookie of the Year Award. Chris was either very good at working the stock market, or he managed to convince someone that he was. That half million in commissions may represent something close to $50 million in customer orders. During the same two years he lost all of it in the options markets. Over the next four years he went from Prudential Bache to E. F. Hutton to Dean Witter and back to Bache, picking up substantial bonuses and new commissions each time he moved. By the middle of 1990 he had collected well over $1 million in commissions and signing bonuses—and lost all of it in the options markets.

It's not just the derelict and naïve who get burned. Chris Christensen had been trained by one of the premier brokerage firms in the country. He was considered a prize recruit by two other large firms. He had access to Wall Street's best market analysis. He had the edge of seeing what was happening to his own customers. If it can happen to people like him, and it does, every day, it can happen to any of us.

The options markets are zero-sum markets, almost. That means for every dime won, a dime is lost. It is gambling no matter how you describe it. If a small investor was as good as average among options and futures traders, the long-run result would be to break even in those markets, with steady, small losses in brokerage fees. But the small investor is not as good as average among those people. Among small-time speculators who make one to twenty trades in commodities futures, fewer than one-third come out ahead. The success rate goes up among those with more trading activity, but it never exceeds 50 percent. Futures trading is dominated by professionals who have time and experience and research on their side. They get hourly updates on their information and are ready to open or close a position on a moment's notice. The small investor, meanwhile, is at his regular job or on vacation and may lose a lot of money before he even knows what's going on.

There is also a reasonable suspicion that the game is occasionally rigged by inside information or big-money players manipulating prices. The same kind of stuff that went on in New York in 1928, 1929, and 1930. Stories about that kind of thing still show up in the press once in a while. Both the U.S. Attorney's office and the Commodity Futures Trading Commission have brought charges and gotten guilty admissions from traders, including even a former vice chairman of one of the commodities markets.

There are good reasons why the stock or bond markets are fairer and easier than options or futures. One of the best reasons is that if you buy a stock or bond it's possible for everybody to win. The person you bought from may have made a profit, and there are thousands of employees and managers of the firm working as hard as they can to make the firm successful. Part of their productivity will come to you in the form of either cash dividends or increased value of the firm. There is a reasonable chance that you will gain while you hold the stock, that you will sell it at a profit, and that the next person may gain in the same way. This is the process of profiting from the fruits of labor and capitalism. That's a respectable way for anyone to use their money. But in options and futures trading, there must always be a winner and a loser on every deal.

Among all the folks in the country who would like to be rich, there must be millions who have considered the lure of trying to make big money in a quick profit on Wall Street. Out of those millions, there appear to be a few dozen or maybe even a few hundred who can make a consistent good living at it. Go figure—what are *your* odds of success at that game?

Recommended Further Reading

The markets are not discriminatory, except on one count—you do have to bring money. But anybody with money is welcome into the fray. It should not be surprising then that the participants come in many shapes, sizes, and psyches. By all means, read *The Mind of the Market*. It will help you to recognize some of the other types of participants and know how to deal with them. More than that, in this business, as in all others, it pays to know yourself. Smith's book will make you think about how your personal approach to investing will be different from other people's. Rothchild's book is the only title that I have felt compelled to mention more than once in the end-of-chapter reading lists. It will probably put you as close to real trouble as you can get just by reading about it.

Rothchild, John. *A Fool and His Money: The Odyssey of an Average Investor.* New York: Viking Penguin, 1989.

Smith, Charles W. *The Mind of the Market: A Study of Stock Market Philosophies, Their Uses, and Their Implications.* Lanham, Md.: Rowman & Littlefield, 1981.

Train, John. *The Midas Touch: The Strategies That Have Made Warren Buffett "America's Pre-eminent Investor."* New York: HarperCollins, 1988.

Train, John. *The New Money Masters.* New York: Harper Business, 1994

Glossary

The terms are defined here in the sense that they are used in this book. This means that astute readers will note some occasional differences from more common usage.

12b-1 expense: A mutual fund's expense charge that is intended to compensate the investment company for their sales expenses.

401(k): Name given to a type of investment or savings account wherein workers may save part of their pay and invest it without current taxes on the pay or investment returns.

advisor: A person who helps with financial planning, usually a broker, investment advisor, financial planner, or insurance advisor; usually a professional in that field.

allocation: The process or results of dividing investment assets among different available choices such as stocks, bonds, mutual funds, or bank deposits.

American Stock Exchange: The second largest stock exchange in the United States.

AMEX: American Stock Exchange.

analysis: The process of gathering information, studying it through various tools and points of view, and drawing appropriate conclusions.

analyst: A financial professional who is employed to evaluate the potential risk, gains, or losses from financial investments.

annual rate of return of an investment: a rate of return, stated for one year, that would give the investment's results if applied each year of the investment's life (or each part of a year).

arbitration: The process of allowing a neutral party to settle a dispute, usually instead of using the courts.

asset: Something of financial value.

average: In mathematics, the sum of a set of numbers divided by the number of values included. In the financial markets, it usually refers to a weighted average of stock or bond prices used as an indicator of overall market performance as in, for example, the Dow Jones Industrial Average.

back load: A mutual fund expense charge that is imposed at the time of redemption of shares as a percentage of the value redeemed.

Barron's: A weekly financial newspaper published by Dow Jones & Company.

bear market: Any financial market during a period that prices are generally falling.

bears: Investors or analysts who predict falling prices for one or more types of assets and/or sell some of their investments.

beta (ß): A number that is used to reflect the level of volatility of an investment; it is almost always determined and used relative to the volatility of some appropriate market index. $ß=1$ for investments that fluctuate up or down as much as the relevant market index values; $ß>1$ means the investment is more volatile; and $ß<1$ means it is less volatile. Some investors or analysts use ß as a measurement of the historic risk level in the investment.

bills: Treasury bonds that are issued with a term no longer than one year.

blue chip: A stock that is issued by a large and secure company, or a group of investments that concentrate in such stocks.

bond: An investment in the form of a loan, or the security (promise to repay) that represents the investment.

book value: (1) The value of a business asset as it is carried on the company's financial records; (2) one view of the value of a company seen as the total assets minus the liabilities of the firm; frequently divided by the number of shares of stock and referenced as the book value per share.

bourse: A stock exchange.

broker: A person who acts as a paid agent between buyers and sellers for securities sales and is registered to conduct such business.

brokerage: A business that provides a service of completing securities transactions, usually charging a fee for the service.

bull market: Any financial market during a period that prices are generally rising.

bulls: Investors or analysts who predict rising prices for one or more types of assets and/or buy investments.

buy-and-hold: The investment practice of buying stocks, bonds, or funds with the intention of holding them for a long time.

call provision: A provision in a bond that allows the bond issuer to pay off the bond before its maturity date.

capitalization: The total value of money committed to something. See also market capitalization.

CD: Certificate of deposit.

certificate of deposit: An investment with a bank that promises to pay a fixed rate of return over a fixed time period; a bond purchased from a bank.

churning: The practice wherein a broker produces a large number of trades for a customer's account with the intention of collecting excessive commissions.

closed-end fund: A mutual fund that does not promise to issue or redeem new shares at any time. The investment company sells a number of shares to begin business and then those shares are traded like stock. The price of a closed-end fund's share is determined by whatever willing buyers and sellers agree to in the markets.

CNBC: A cable news channel primarily dedicated to financial news.

commission: The sales fee paid to a person, usually a broker, who manages a trade for a customer.

common stock: The shares of ownership of a publicly traded company.

compound gains: The results of growth and profit over several periods of returns when each period's profit is reinvested to gain additional profits in the next period. Also called compound growth.

compound growth: See compound gains.

compound annual rate of return: The annual rate of return that would provide the same final earnings as reinvesting all earnings and dividends during the life of an investment. For example, if an investment earned 2 percent in the first year and 0 in the second year, then the compound annual rate of return would be 1 percent.

contrarian: An investor who invests differently than most other investors.

conversion: Exchanging a bond or preferred stock for common stock according to the conversion rules written into the bond or preferred stock when it was issued.

convertible: A provision in a bond or preferred stock that allows it to be converted to another security form, usually common stock, after some specified date or circumstances.

corporate bond: A bond issued by a private business.

correction: A short-term change in the trend of a market. So, a correction in a bull market would be a short-term decline.

coupon yield: The original interest payment rate written into a bond when it is created.

crash: A sudden large fall in values in a financial market.

Curb: A historical term for the American Stock Exchange, still commonly used in casual reference.

current yield: The percentage annual rate of return from an investment calculated by using the current actual returns as the basis for computing a full year's return. The current yield of a bond is the annual interest divided by its current price.

debenture: A loan that is not secured by any assets of the borrower, meaning that repayment depends on the ability and the integrity of the borrower.

decisiveness: The ability to make decisions and carry through to completion whatever actions may be indicated by the decision.

default: Failure to pay the interest or principal due on a bond.

discount broker: A broker, or brokerage firm, that usually charges relatively lower commission fees and provides less customer service to the investor.

diversification: The process, or the results, of allocating investment capital among different investments that might be expected to behave differently in various economic situations.

dividend: Money paid to the owners of common stock out of the profits of a publicly traded company.

dollar-cost averaging: A practice, or discipline, of investing a regular, fixed, predetermined amount in some security or mutual fund on a periodic basis.

Dow: The Dow Jones Industrial Average. See average.

duration: A number that can be calculated for a bond, which indicates how volatile the bond would be in reacting to market interest rate changes; lower duration means less volatility and presumably greater safety for the bond.

earnings: The profits earned by a company after taxes, interest on debt, depreciation, and dividends to preferred shareholders. The amount that represents profits to the common stock shareholders.

earnings per share: Total earnings of a corporation divided by the number of outstanding shares of common stock.

EPS: Earnings per share

equity: A share of ownership in a company, usually represented by the stock.

face value: The original principal amount for a bond when it is created.

family of funds: A group of funds that are managed by a single investment company.

financial data: The information that describes all the assets and liabilities, revenues and expenses, and the changes in those as shown in the public reports of a company. Every publicly traded stock company is required to issue public reports of its financial data.

fixed-income investing: A reference to investing in bonds or the bond markets. It only produces truly fixed income (constant and predictable) if the investor is buying and holding bonds to maturity. Bond mutual funds are referred to as fixed-income investing, but they do not actually produce fixed-income results.

flexibility: An investor's ability to buy and sell different kinds of investments and to move money among different kinds of investments.

front load: A mutual fund charge that is imposed at the time of purchase of shares, as a percentage of the value invested.

full-service broker: A brokerage firm that offers research, advising, and other financial services in addition to buying and selling in the financial markets.

futures contract: A contract whereby a party promises to deliver for sale a specific amount of a particular good at a specified price on a future date.

Greater Fool: An investor who buys stock when it has already been overpriced in the markets.

growth company: A company with increasing sales and profits—and probably increasing stock value.

growth fund: A mutual fund that generally concentrates its assets in stocks of growth companies.

growth stock: The stock of a company that is considered to be a growth company.

growth theory: A theory of stock selection that focuses on estimated future earnings and growth to forecast the future value of stocks.

guru: One who claims to know more than the rest of us.

hedge fund: A joint investment fund that works very much like a mutual fund, except that it is less regulated, has greater flexibility in investing, and generally may be expected to have higher fees.

hedging: Investing in certain securities, options, or futures, with a view to balancing the risks in other investments.

index: A calculated number that represents the price levels and price changes for a group of securities, for example, the Dow Jones Industrial Average, the Dow Jones Utilities Average, the S&P 500 Average; each index is usually a weighted average, but the weighting methods differ between indices.

Individual Retirement Account: A retirement savings account that has special tax avoidance advantages.

interest: The annual return that is paid for a loan as a price for the use of the loaned money.

intermediate term: Time period for bond holdings of two to six years, or for stock holdings of three months to a year; this is subject to widely varying interpretations by different investors or advisors.

invest: To use one's money to (hopefully) earn more money by lending it or buying securities that may produce future income or growth in market value. Essentially, to give money to another party in hopes of getting it back later with a profit.

investment club: A group of private investors who agree to pool their investment capital and share the work and risk of investing through group analysis and discussion.

investment company: A company that owns and operates a mutual fund.

investment grade: Describes a bond or group of bonds that are rated BBB or Baa or higher by the ratings agencies.

investor: A person who puts money at risk in financial markets in hopes of making profits.

IRA: Individual Retirement Account.

junk bonds: Bonds that are rated below BBB or Baa by the major investment ratings companies; these are considered to be less safe than investment-grade bonds for expected repayment of yield and principal.

liability: A claim against the assets of a firm; for example, a bond sold by a firm represents a claim against the assets for both interest payments and final repayment, and this is a liability of the firm.

limit order: An order to a broker to buy or sell a security at the best price they can get above (for a sale) or below (for a purchase) some price specified by the investor.

Lipper Analytical Services: A company that collects and analyzes information about investments and sells their results to other financial reporting companies.

liquidity: The ability to recover the cash value from an investment or other asset.

load: A fee charged to mutual fund shareholders as a percentage of their shares' value, either at the time of purchase or redemption of the shares.

mania: A period of great excitement or public rush to buy stocks that causes prices to rise rapidly.

market capitalization: The total market value of all the stock of a company. This changes as the stock price changes.

market order: An order to a broker to buy or sell a security at the best price they can get in current market conditions.

market price: The price that is currently being accepted by both buyer and seller in the open markets; for a stock or bond this is recognized as the sale price for the last sale of the security.

market rate: The coupon yield of a bond divided by the current market price.

market sector: A group of companies that have some common characteristics in their businesses or stocks, such as the auto sector or the small-capitalization companies.

market value: Market price.

markets: Organizations, places, or groups that are established for the purpose of buying and selling financial instruments.

maturity: The time at which a bond matures and must be repaid.

momentum: Refers to trends in stock prices or volume of sales of the stock.

money market fund: A mutual fund that specializes in short-term bonds or very short-term loans among financial institutions.

Morningstar: A firm that does extensive research on mutual funds, publishes their own periodical review of funds, and sells their research to other firms.

municipal bond: A bond issued by a state or local government or agency backed by a state or local government.

mutual fund: A fund collected from the investing public by an investment company, for the purpose of investing in stocks, bonds, other funds, or anything else that the investment company declares in the fund's prospectus.

NASD: National Association of Securities Dealers.

NASDAQ: The NASD automated quotation system, a computer network that provides brokers with information management services for trading stocks of over 2,000 companies.

National Association of Securities Dealers: A self-regulating professional association of securities dealers.

NAV: Net asset value.

net asset value: The value per share of a mutual fund that is computed as the total of assets owned by the fund minus the total liabilities of the fund, divided by the number of shares outstanding.

New York Stock Exchange: A stock exchange in New York City that provides registration and trading services for stocks of most of the largest American companies.

niche fund: A mutual fund that invests in only a small sector of assets—perhaps Brazilian bonds or European automobile companies.

no-load: Used to describe a mutual fund that does not charge an initial sales commission.

notes: Treasury bonds that have original term to maturity of two to ten years.

NYSE: New York Stock Exchange.

objective: The description (in the prospectus) of the things that a mutual fund may invest in.

option: A contract that promises that the originator of the contract will buy (or sell) a specified number of a security at a specified price within some time frame. The second party to the contract has an option, but not an obligation, to take the other side of the future transaction, as well as to let the contract expire with no action taken.

original issue discount: Term used to describe a bond that is originally sold at a price below its face value.

OTC: Over the counter.

over the counter: Term used to describe either markets away from regulated stock exchanges or the stocks that are traded in those markets.

panic: A period during which investors rush to sell all of their financial assets and cause a rapid fall in prices.

par value: The value of a bond equaling the face value.

P/E: Price/earnings ratio.

personal investment strategy: An individual investor's plan to allocate and manage investments to suit his or her personal needs and risk acceptance.

POP: The public offering price of a mutual fund.

portfolio: The collection of investments owned by an investor or a mutual fund or other organization.

preferred stock: A class of stock that has provisions for a specified dividend rate and seniority over a company's common stock in case of a distribution of the company's assets. The preferred stock may commonly have various other provisions attached that distinguish its value from the common stock, such as voting rights or convertibility.

prevailing rates: The interest rates that the markets impose on a bond or group of bonds to determine their current prices.

price/earnings ratio: The ratio obtained by dividing the price of a stock share by its associated earnings per share. This is useful only if the earnings per share are positive, i.e., the company has some profits to distribute.

principal: The dollar value of an investment.

prospectus: A description of a mutual fund that is provided to prospective shareholders.

public offering price: The price per share of a mutual fund when an investor buys it; it is equal to the net asset value for no-load funds and slightly higher for front-load funds.

publicly traded: A stock that is registered and approved by the SEC or a state securities agency for sale to the public through financial markets.

rate of return: Usually refers to the annual rate of return.

redemption: Selling mutual fund shares back to the investment company.

registered investment advisor: A person who has passed an examination on investment law and ethics, and has registered with the SEC or the state where he or she practices.

research: Analysis or study that is carried to a higher level by repetition, sophisticated methods, dedication, or the professionalism of the worker.

risk: The possibility of losing money in an investment or, more broadly, any danger or obstacle that an investor may face.

risk-free investment: A lie, a bad joke, a figment; there is no risk-free investment.

risk-oriented investment: Investment practice that recognizes and analyzes opportunities and risks to suit one's personal investment strategy.

Roth IRA: An IRA account that accepts contributions that have previously had the taxes paid, and then exempts the earnings from future taxes.

Russell 2000: A group of stocks, or their associated price index, that includes 2000 small-capitalization stocks; this is a representative index for the behavior of stock values for all small-cap stocks.

sales load: Commission on sale of mutual fund shares, also called front load.

S & P: Standard & Poor.

S & P 500: A group of stocks, or their associated price index, that includes 500 large-capitalization stocks; this is a representative index for the behavior of stock values for all large-cap stocks.

savings bond: U.S. Treasury bond identified as series E, EE, or HH, with a ten-year term and certain tax advantages.

screens: Methods used to find stocks or bonds that satisfy specific conditions, frequently used with computers and databases to select a few qualifying securities from among a large group.

SEC: The United States Securities and Exchange Commission.

secondary market: The market that deals with buying and selling bonds, or any securities, after their original issue.

sector: Market sector.

Securities and Exchange Commission: The U.S. federal agency that regulates the registration and sale of securities.

security: Principally a stock or bond, but sometimes other types of financial instruments; anything that indicates ownership, or right to benefits of ownership or rights to payment.

seniority: Provision attached to a bond that its interest and principal will be paid before some other obligations of the company.

share: A part of the ownership of a company, represented by the common stock; sometimes share, stock share, and stock are used synonymously.

socially responsible funds: A class of mutual funds that write their objectives to be in some way in the public interest.

split: The practice, or results of the practice, where a company issues new shares to its current shareholders in a fixed ration of old to new. They also reduce the price per share so that the total capitalization is unchanged. If you held 200 shares, priced at $20, of a company that gave a 2 for 1 split, then they would issues 200 new shares to you, and reduce the price to $10 per share. The total value of your holding would remain at $4000.

spread: The difference between the offered and asked prices for a stock or bond.

Standard & Poor: A securities analysis and research firm that publishes important reports and opinions on the value of stocks and bonds.

stock exchange: A business or association that is established to help people buy and sell stocks.

stock market: Usually refers to all of the organizations, people, securities, and activity that support public buying and selling of stock.

stop order: An order to a broker to sell a stock at market value if the price ever drops to some value specified by the investor; a stop order becomes a market order after the trigger price is realized in the market.

strategy: An investment plan to allocate funds among diverse investments over a period of time.

subordinate: Provision attached to a bond, or other obligation of a company, that its interest and principal payments will occur after some other debt is paid.

technical analysis: The practice of predicting prospective price changes of a security, or group of securities, by analyzing prior price changes and looking for patterns and relationships in graphs of price history.

term: The time to repayment of a bond from its original issue.

trade: The act of buying or selling a security; sometimes used to denote a short-term investment.

trader: One who buys and sells securities, sometimes used to connote an emphasis on short-term investing.

trading: (1) Buying and selling financial instruments or securities; (2) frequent or short-term buying and selling.

transaction: Any purchase or sale of securities.

Treasury bond: Bond issued by the U.S. Treasury Department.

Value Line: A financial analysis and research firm that publishes reports and opinions on the value of stocks and mutual funds, including one titled *Value Line*, which includes analyses of companies and their stocks and securities along with recommendations for what stocks to buy or sell.

value theory: A theory of stock selection that focuses on current earnings, products, management, and financial reports to determine the value of a company and its stock.

volatility: The tendency of prices to increase or decrease in some specified time period; usually measured through the calculation of a quantity called beta (ß) relative to some specified market index.

volume: The number of shares traded within some specified time period.

Wall Street Journal: A daily newspaper published by Dow Jones & Company, and specializing in business news.

Wilshire 5000: A group of companies, or their associated price index, that represents the majority of all firms traded in regulated American public stock markets.

WSJ: *Wall Street Journal.*

yield: The rate of interest payments on a bond, which may refer to either current yield, yield to maturity, or coupon yield.

yield ratio: The ratio of the annual dividend paid for a stock to its price.

yield to maturity: The compounded interest rate that would produce the current value of a bond considering both interest payments and final repayment of principal.

zero coupon bonds: Bonds that, instead of paying interest at regular intervals, save up everything and pay it all at once at the maturity.

Index